DATE DUE

BRODART, CO.

D1261572

WINNING AT INNOVATION

*To my daughter Blanca, because during
her childhood she taught me the crucial
points of imagination and disruptive thinking.*

Fernando Trías de Bes

*To my two brothers, Milton and Neil Kotler,
for the innovative work that you've done in
the public sector and the world of museums.*

Philip Kotler

Winning at Innovation

The A-to-F Model

Fernando Trías de Bes

Associate Professor of Marketing
Management, ESADE Business School

&

Philip Kotler

S.C. Johnson & Son Distinguished Professor of International
Marketing, Kellogg School of Management, Northwestern University

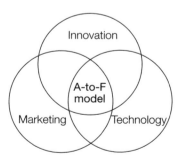

palgrave
macmillan

First published 2011 by
PALGRAVE MACMILLAN

Palgrave Macmillan in the UK is an imprint of Macmillan Publishers Limited, registered in England, company number 785998, of Houndmills, Basingstoke, Hampshire RG21 6XS

Palgrave Macmillan in the US is a division of St Martin's Press LLC, 175 Fifth Avenue, New York, NY 10010.

Palgrave Macmillan is the global academic imprint of the above companies and has companies and representatives throughout the world.

Palgrave® and Macmillan® are registered trademarks in the United States, the United Kingdom, Europe and other countries.

ISBN–13: 978–0–230–34343–6

This book is printed on paper suitable for recycling and made from fully managed and sustained forest sources. Logging, pulping and manufacturing processes are expected to conform to the environmental regulations of the country of origin.

A catalogue record for this book is available from the British Library.

A catalog record for this book is available from the Library of Congress.

10 9 8 7 6 5 4 3 2 1
20 19 18 17 16 15 14 13 12 11

Printed and bound in Great Britain by
CPI Antony Rowe, Chippenham and Eastbourne

Contents

List of Figures, Tables and Boxes

Figures

Tables

Boxes

Acknowledgments

We'd like to give a special acknowledgment to the companies and innovation professionals who have facilitated putting some of the theories and thoughts described here into practice. Especially to Nestlé, Pepsico, Novartis, 3M, and Google. Also, we want to thank Alfons Cornella (the founder of Infonomia), who provided us with valuable information about the innovation practices of important companies throughout the world. This information was vital in our documentation process and served to validate our A-to-F model. And, finally, to all the innovation professionals, authors and researchers and those who, through the Internet, promote the debate and sharing of ideas on the topic of innovation. Their thoughts, contributions, and research have been an infinite source of inspiration.

The authors and publishers would like to thank Stage Gate International for the use of Figures 11.1, 12.1 and 12.2 and Harvard Business Publishing for the use of their material in Figures 5.1 and 5.2.

FERNANDO TRÍAS DE BES AND PHILIP KOTLER

Introduction

To whom is this book addressed?

This book is addressed to the people who want to learn how to transform an organization into an innovative one.

This will be of interest to CEOs, general managers, R&D people, marketing professionals and new products or innovation managers – and also to all line managers who want more creativity and innovation from their people. The book is equally valid to business administration or management students in general.

The main objective of this book is to set down the principal elements that form effective and creative innovation management. We will try to accomplish this through the A-to-F model, which allows the reader to rank logically into a conceptual structure most of the key ideas on innovation published in recent years. This book provides a quick and insightful guide on innovation; a handbook that covers the most important theories, techniques and recent findings in this area.

How this book has been organized

To transform an organization into an innovative organization it is necessary to work in four areas. These four areas are like the four legs of a chair. If one is missing, the chair will be unstable and may even fall.

If managers want innovation to occur inside their company, they must manage the four areas simultaneously. The good news is that the four areas feed each other, reinforcing them mutually. This is what we have called the Total Innovation System.

The first area is the strategic planning for innovation, where priorities and objectives are defined and coherence with the general strategy, mission and objectives is ensured. Innovative strategic planning will generate innovation projects. The projects will be put through innovation processes. The innovation process is the fundamental tool for transforming an idea into an innovation. We will dedicate a large part of the book to the innovation process. There are different and varied designs and types of innovation processes. The most well known is the Stage-Gate system. In this book we propose a new and different scheme for innovation processes that will allow companies to design their own innovation processes in a flexible way. We have named this scheme

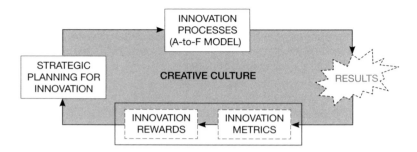

Figure 0.1   **Total Innovation System**

the A-to-F model and it is valid for any type of company, industry and innovation. Innovation projects – whether new products, services, processes, business models – when finally implemented produce results, which can be positive or negative. Obtained results can and must be measured. As T. Davila says: "we cannot manage things that we cannot measure."[1] Innovation results measurements are called innovation metrics and can be used, at the same time, to establish a rewards system to incentivize the managers in charge of innovation. That's the third area: metrics and rewards. The three areas (strategic planning for innovation, processes, metrics/rewards take place against a background or atmosphere that is called creative culture (the fourth area), something that is essential if we want innovation to happen at every company level and avoid ghettos of innovation.

The book is organized according to this Total Innovation System. But we will not follow the sequence of the cycle. We will start with the processes, developing and explaining our A-to-F model, the most unique contribution of these pages. We also want to explain processes first because they are the key element of the innovation engine. It is easier to grasp the function of strategic planning for innovation, culture and metrics/rewards when the innovation process is fully understood and one knows how it can be designed.

In Part One, Chapter 1 will cover the main barriers to innovation and creativity that we find inside companies. Chapter 2 will introduce an overall picture of the A-to-F model. Chapters 3 to 8 will cover, one by one, the six roles of the A-to-F model: activators, browsers, creators, developers, executors and facilitators. Chapter 9 will present the A-to-F model advantages, the new collaborative tasks that emerge from the model and how to use it in order to design innovation processes in any type of business or innovation.

Part Two (Chapters 10 to 13) will cover the other three areas of the Total Innovation System: Chapter 10 will be dedicated to the elements that define the innovation strategy. Chapter 11 will review the different metrics used to measure the innovation results of a company. Chapter 12 will explain how to implant a creative culture in a company. Chapter 13, finally, will review the mechanisms for rewarding people who innovate.

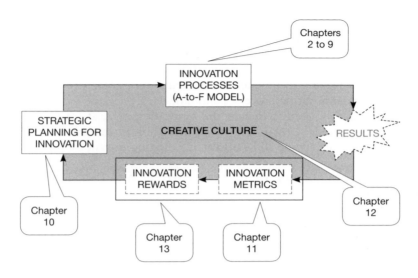

Figure 0.2   **Total Innovation System and chapters**

How to read the book

There are several ways of reading this book, depending on the reader's knowledge and experience in innovation.

If you are new to this topic, we recommend reading the book in the written sequence, from beginning to end.

If you are a manager who has already implemented any kind of innovation process in your company, but have not worked or developed the other areas of the Total Innovation System, you may find it more useful to start reading Part Two and then, if you are interested in a different way of organizing the company's innovation processes, read Part One, starting with Chapter 9 and then moving on to Chapters 3 to 8.

If you are already an expert in innovation and want to focus only on the novelties that this book brings to the innovation field, then we recommend going directly to Chapter 9 and, afterwards, reading the concrete elements of Chapters 3 to 8 that are of interest to you. The content of Chapters 3 to 8 can be found in the templates of Chapter 9 and, of course, in the index of the book.

Finally, we want to highlight that this book is a quite exhaustive compendium of what has been published and written in the current literature on innovation. Many of the other books on innovation take one or another specialized approach: our book, we believe, provides the most comprehensive blueprint view of the whole innovation process. If you are in a company that has come to recognize that companies die without innovation, and that your company needs to erect a new structure for creating successful innovations, this is the right book for you.

The main contribution of this text is not in each one of the elements and techniques described, but in the way in which we have organized them. The A-to-F model contains techniques that already exist, some are recent and others have been with us for many years. The value of the model comes from how all those existing techniques can be structured, organized and used to design flexible innovation processes and models.

We, the authors, think that in the innovation area, at least regarding processes and models, there is a strong need for an integrative model, a methodology which could allow organizing existing and future theories and techniques.

This has been our aim. We have conceived the A-to-F model under this premise. It had to serve as a system to guide your innovation thinking, much as the 4 P's helped marketing professionals organize their activities and theories. We hope that the A-to-F model of innovation provides the needed framework for building a successful practice in the exciting management area called *innovation*.

1 Entrepreneurial Barriers to Innovation

The gap between the need and the capacity to innovate

In the business world today, innovation, as a discipline, has not reached the stage of development where it can satisfy the pressing need to innovate. We find that, where innovation is concerned, in many companies need exceeds capacity. A revealing statistic: although 96 percent of executives see creativity as integral to their businesses, surprisingly, only 23 percent have succeeded in making it an integral part of their businesses.[1] And without creativity, there is no innovation. And that's not the only statistic. A number of surveys on how companies innovate show that there is a broad consensus on the need to innovate, but also widespread dissatisfaction with how innovation is carried out. Executives are well aware of this gap:

> Innovation is a messy process – hard to measure and hard to manage. Most people recognize it only when it generates a surge in growth. When revenues and earnings decline during a recession, executives often conclude that their innovation efforts just aren't worth it. Maybe innovation isn't so important after all, they think.[2]

> Executives say innovation is very important, but their companies' approach to it is often informal, and leaders lack confidence in their innovation decisions.[3]

Something similar happened a few decades ago with marketing. When the superiority of marketing as a management tool was first demonstrated, there were few marketing professionals with sufficient experience, since business schools were just starting to add marketing to their curriculums and it would be some time before the fresh crop of graduates would join the labor market. Likewise, there were few specialized agencies or consultancies, aside from the fact that companies did not feel entirely comfortable with outsourcing such an important function. Moreover, marketing departments were created out of what were then called sales departments, which also implied internal restructuring, with all the conflicts that such change entails.

Similarly, innovation has been synonymous with technological innovation, thus it was mainly the R&D department, and primarily engineers, who were responsible for innovation.

Today we know that this is a too limited a view of the sources of innovation. Figure 1.1 shows a diverse set of sources of innovative ideas.[4]

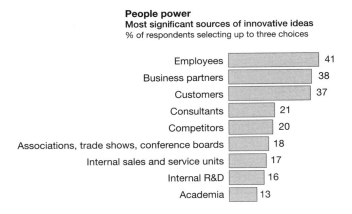

Figure 1.1   **Sources of innovative ideas**

Source: IBM, The Global CEO Study 2006 (based on interviews with 765 CEOs and business leaders)

Moreover, as we shall see in dimension A of the A-to-F model presented here, there are many other types of innovation (business model innovation, process innovation, market innovation, target customer innovation, and so on). In many cases, these types of innovation require no new technology, but rather new ways to exploit existing technologies. A clear user of this philosophy is 3M, where, based on just 38 core technologies, the company managed to place 50,000 products and 2,000 brands on the market.[5] ExxonMobil, to take another example, developed its successful Speedpass system, which lets drivers pay automatically at the pump, based on observing customers and using technologies that were already being applied to other products and services.

Another clear example of this philosophy is the fact that in ranking the world's most innovative companies, the Boston Consulting Group (BCG) gives the highest ratings to business ingenuity in terms of products, customer experience, business models and processes. Whether or not technology forms part of innovation is irrelevant.[6]

When a company limits its approach to the technological aspect or to its R&D department, it misses out on the creative potential of professionals working in other departments. Don't get us wrong: we are not saying that R&D shouldn't innovate or be involved in the innovation process. What we are saying is that, in addition to R&D and technology, there are lots of other departments and ways to generate innovation in the company. Part of the gap between the need to innovate and the limited capacity to do so has to do with narrow-minded policies that restrict innovation policy and strategy exclusively to technical departments.

The consequence of such a limited vision is that managements in many companies don't have much to show for their investments in innovation. Some succeed, but many others lose money and even put their business in jeopardy. Technological innovation, if not coupled with value creation and capture, will not meet customers' wants and thus will fail.

> Increasingly, companies have been claiming that they have been making their innovation process more market-focused and customer driven. Yet failure rates for new products remain unacceptably high, with estimates ranging from 50% to 90%.[7]

The underdevelopment of innovation, as a branch of business management, is not the only problem. There are other barriers and constraints that one must recognize.

Problem one: what innovation really means

When a company launches a breakthrough or radical innovation, like Apple with its iPhone or Google's phenomenal success on the Internet, it makes headlines and is held up as an example in the press and at business meetings. "That's real innovation," experts and journalists exclaim in awe. Over time these sorts of headlines and product launches have the effect of creating a distorted picture in our minds of what innovation really means. We have come to believe that innovation is a new product, service or application that dazzles the world and completely redefines the rules of the market.

It is true that radical innovations outshine everything else, but that's not what all innovation is about. Indeed, it could even be dangerous or counterproductive for a company to be continuously launching radical innovations: they entail a lot of investment, they take time to turn a profit and, moreover, inevitably they are a big gamble.[8]

This myth of radical innovation as the only, or at least the most visible or recognized way to go, causes a lot of problems for business management professionals. When a senior executive demands more creativity or innovation, employees automatically assume, erroneously, that they are being asked to come up with some dazzling new product or service. The consequences are disastrous, because the pressure on employees utterly paralyzes them. Proposing a radical innovation means sticking your neck way out and, rather than jeopardize their careers, people often prefer to keep their ideas to themselves.

In fact, innovation doesn't always entail giant leaps forward. Gradual, step-by-step innovation is innovation too – and it is just as or more necessary than the radical version. This is what really makes a business sustainable. Innovation should also be understood as developing an innovative culture within the company, which is what will enable it to produce and bring out onto the market a steady stream of smaller, incremental innovations.

That's when, as paradoxical as it might seem, radical innovation eventually appears. It is very hard, if not impossible, for a business to make a successful launch of a groundbreaking innovation without first launching a good number of smaller innovations. In the absence of this initial process, it is unlikely that a company can develop its culture of innovation to the point where it can pull off such a groundbreaking feat. A company that hasn't developed the innovative habit can hardly expect to perform well when it comes to extraordinary innovations.

The fact that gradual or continuous incremental innovation over time eventually leads to radical innovation is easy to demonstrate. Take for example the automotive industry. Over the past decades, the aim of engineers was not to come up with a completely new car. Almost all the innovation has been gradual, targeting specific components and aspects of performance: better brakes, lower fuel consumption, more horsepower, quicker acceleration, and so on. As a result, based on small modifications, if we compare a car of today with one made 50 years ago, the difference is huge. And we arrived at this difference step by step, not in one fell swoop.

The solution therefore is not to think of creating a radical innovation today but rather to think of innovation as occurring in a set of small innovative steps over time, hopefully culminating eventually in a major innovation.

Problem two: fuzzy responsibility assignment

Who in the company is in charge of innovation? In the late 20th century, innovation was the responsibility of the R&D department, since everybody pretty much assumed innovation meant technological advances. Whenever a company needed some sort of non-technological innovation, the immediate reaction was to hand the responsibility to the marketing department. But the marketing departments were too busy with their day-to-day business. They had to demonstrate their efficiency in product and brand management, but that did not necessarily mean they were ready to innovate. Moreover, innovation marketing is radically different from continuity marketing, which is where marketing departments' real potential lies. But we saw a conflict between the R&D and marketing departments, where the former felt that marketers didn't know how to capture value and the latter felt that engineers weren't creative enough.

> We contend that Product Development (i.e. R&D) and Marketing must become intimate partners if a company hopes to optimize its innovation performance. Unfortunately, too often the Development and Marketing relationship is ill defined and challenging.[9]

In certain companies, innovation, was split between R&D and marketing but left without any strategic management. There was a short circuit between those who were supposed to be coming up with innovations and the top management needed to bring them to fruition.

In consequence, as the *McKinsey Quarterly* has pointed out,[10] many executives opt to get ideas and innovation from external, informal sources, rather than from their own business units and the in-house teams that they themselves have directed to work on innovation. Usually, when a company outsources all its innovation, it later run into real problems when it comes to implementing the innovations proposed by external consultants. As in the case of the company that never innovates and, suddenly, launches a radical innovation, when you force professionals to implement changes that they themselves have neither devised nor approved, you are bound to run into breakdowns and counterproductive side effects.

But, given that it is so integral to the survival of a business, why this persistent absence of responsibility in the realm of innovation? One aspect that differentiates innovation from other forms of management is that while the different departments of a company are assigned clearly defined functions, innovation, as we understand it today, happens on different levels without belonging to any one department in particular. Of course, the marketing department needs to innovate. But so do human resources and finance. And these departments must innovate not only within their own domain, but also with an eye on the market and capturing value. As shown in the book *Marketing Moves*,[11] marketing today means holistic marketing, and it needs to be spread throughout the organization. The same is true with innovation. Someone in the finance department might discover an investment tool, for example, that translates into lower costs that translate into price innovation and – why not? – perhaps eventually a new product line for the company. Innovation is not a matter for a chosen few. It is the responsibility of the entire organization. But we know that when everyone is responsible for something, no one takes responsibility, and responsibility gets watered down.

The result is that innovation, beyond technological innovation, becomes the company waif, lost and wandering blindly from one department to another without quite knowing where to turn. According to the *McKinsey Global Survey*,[12] only 24 percent of business leaders fix innovation budgets and only 50 percent decide who will work on innovation projects.

In companies with low levels of innovation, the levels of responsibility are unclear. On the other hand, companies that perform better in terms of innovation do not have this problem; the role of innovation is well defined and there is someone in charge who, moreover, does not depend on the marketing or the R&D department. Innovation is actively managed from the top down, eventually including various parts of the company. For example, at Starbucks, Howard Schultz, the company founder and president, is the person at the helm in strategic innovation management and business expansion.

Another option – one that is also very effective, as we shall see – is to name someone head of innovation and give them a 360-degree view of all the innovation going on throughout the company; according to a previously approved plan, of course.

In truly innovative companies, innovation is not located any one place in particular, rather it happens at the same time at various levels of the organization. It's not a question of which department, but of who; particular people who might be located anywhere, even outside the organization. We will further clarify this point later on, when we talk about the Open Innovation model.

The fact that innovation is spread around the organization does not mean there is confusion or chaos. At Google, everyone innovates and the processes are perfectly ordered and defined. When a company innovates at all levels, there are also responsibilities at all levels and in each stage of the innovation process.

Some companies even go a step further, bringing in outside monitors. We have gone from closed innovation (limited to the laboratory or R&D department) to collaborative innovation (where all members of the organization are encouraged to come up with ideas), to open innovation (with people from outside the organization involved in the innovation processes).[13]

Problem three: confusing innovation with creativity

The third element hindering the development of business innovation is the widespread confusion regarding applied innovation and creativity. There are times when an idea with potential spends years bouncing around the organization and never quite materializes because there's no one to take responsibility for managing it.

The contrary is also possible: great ideas, left to their own devices, can be harmful to a business. Theodore Levitt, in an article in the *Harvard Business Review*,[14] explains how creativity that is not coupled with proper innovation management can spell death for a business or enterprise. The message is clear: creativity, ideas and new technologies alone won't get the job done. The innovation process must have people to manage it; new skills, more related to business management, are needed to guarantee success in bringing the idea to market.

Many managers complain that their companies lack creative talent. The problem with these organizations is not so much a shortage of people with enough creativity, but rather a shortage of functional idea management. They don't have enough innovation or innovation management because they confuse creativity with innovation. There is no shortage of creative people; what business needs more of are innovation managers. Which is something that 3M is completely aware of and, to avoid this problem, it has a system it calls "dual ladder," which lets employees choose freely between a technical track and a career in management within the company. Whichever path a person chooses, promotion and level of responsibility within the company are the same. 3M does not try to turn research scientists into managers, rather each plays his own role, since both are essential to making innovation work. At IBM, for example, some of the company's top talent, at the height of their careers, are not assigned to safeguarding mature businesses, but to turning new ideas into profits, that is, into new lines of business.

A clear demonstration of the widespread confusion between creativity and innovation is how companies invest heavily in creativity at the expense of innovation: lots more resources go to training in creative techniques than to developing innovative functions. Companies assume that if people act or work in a more creative way, if they promote creativity, sooner or later, it will translate into greater innovation. And this is not necessarily so.

It is true that creativity – that most human of gifts – when applied to business, leads to innovation. But an organization filled with creative people is not necessarily an innovative organization. As Theodore Levitt points out in the above-mentioned article, this may even be counterproductive.

In fact, companies that look exclusively to the creativity of their personnel for innovation are shirking their responsibilities. They prefer to have the organization propose the ideas and then have management decide whether to accept or reject them. But success is a not question of luck. Innovation requires creative people, but it also means setting clear goals for innovation, defining strategies, establishing what your resources and risks are, allocating responsibilities and, most importantly, clearly delimiting and defining your innovation processes, with someone in charge in each respective area.

Companies that confuse creativity with innovation, and many do, eventually find that the habit is not only a brake on productivity but can even be counterproductive. People propose ideas and, due to the lack of any clear rules about what to do with them, the ideas wither away before they can go anyplace. As a result, people get demotivated and stop proposing new ideas. Encouraging them to do so again will be much harder the second time around.

Problem four: lack of a framework

There are a number of aspects to innovation that make it completely different from any other area of business management. Companies must function efficiently on a daily basis in order to stay profitable and generate cash flow. Meanwhile, in anticipation of an uncertain future, they must innovate in order to keep ahead of change and preserve their lead in their sector. These needs can be somewhat contradictory. Change is at odds with efficiency. It is very difficult to think about how to do things differently while you are actually doing them. As John Lennon once said: "Life is what happens to you while you're busy making other plans." It is not easy to change the way you work while you are working. Indeed, it is almost impossible. We need to stop, think about what we've done and then change it. In management, effectiveness and efficiency rule. In business, your job is not to change what you do, but to do it right.

Second, innovation often means changing something that, for the time being at least, works. If a company launches an innovation to replace an existing product or service that is still performing well, it sacrifices the chance to continue exploiting the investment it originally made in that product or service. On the other hand, if, for the sake of maximizing profit on its current portfolio, the company doesn't innovate, the competition may slip ahead and then it might be too late. The people who should be making changes in what works are busy keeping the business running as usual and nobody knows when the time is right to change rules that, for now, are getting good returns.

When it comes to innovation, companies cannot look to any generally accepted management or operating framework. This is not the case with other disciplines, which are divided into clearly defined departments and personnel with their own special well-developed methodologies and tools. Thus, all managers know that in marketing you need market segmentation, you have to define your brand positioning and market your products according to the famous 4 P's. In finance, any manager knows the main tools of the financial department: operating account, balance sheet, cash flow analysis. But what about innovation? According to *Marketing Week*,[15] 44 percent of business leaders admit they don't know what essential tools they need to make creativity and innovation happen in their organizations.

A lot of research and publishing is being done on innovation, but, despite some progress in this direction, we do not yet have a comprehensive, unified and universally accepted theory on the subject. There are books with helpful ideas on creative techniques, on innovation processes, on how this or that company does it, on how to develop an innovation culture and so forth. And all this literature is filled with interesting facts, worth taking into account. But for the manager in search of a single, clear work scheme, no one book or article can provide all the answers. Innovation is in its infancy as a field of management and, although we are learning more and more about it, there is still no broad consensus on what processes and tools to use, or on a general framework to build on.

In the first part of this book we present the A-to-F model for innovation. It is a complete model that can be applied to any past or future developments in business and market innovation. We don't know whether it will be the model used by managers in the future, but we have tried to make it comprehensive, just as the 4 P's of marketing were in their day.

Problem five: lack of control

Logically, this problem is a direct result of what we were talking about in the previous section. If the function of innovation is not well defined, if you don't have consensus on your management framework and if responsibility for innovation is not ingrained and properly allocated, you are bound to lose control of your innovation processes.

In the above-mentioned McKinseystudy,[16] most companies lacked consistent, centralized management to ensure the monitoring of innovation in their business units. For example, only 34 percent of top managers – and only 22 percent of other managers – say that innovation is part of their work agenda.

This situation won't change until innovation is considered an area of business management. As soon as that happens, the control problem will disappear. Once responsibilities for innovation are assigned, control becomes possible.

People think of innovation as a creative and nonlinear concept. But that does not mean that it is not manageable. In an interview, A.G. Laffley, CEO of Procter & Gamble 2000–2008, said that the company can manage innovation because "we have a clear definition of innovation."[17]

In our chapter on the metrics of innovation, we offer a range of useful ideas on how to measure and monitor your company's innovation efforts. Similarly, our A-to-F model is about how to gain complete control of a business's innovation processes, from idea generation to execution to feedback and to control.

Problem six: lack of coordination

Lack of coordination between departments is considered one of the main barriers to innovation.[18] But collaboration means more than tearing down partitions and walls between insular departments. It means creating information flows and physical spaces for collaboration. Innovative companies create cultures of innovation. There are two types of problems: horizontal and vertical.

Lack of horizontal coordination

By horizontal coordination we mean coordination between departments, between equals on a similar level in the chain of command. We do not mean just the classic lack of coordination or conflict of interests between R&D and marketing that we talked about above, but between all the departments in a company in general. According to Professor Robert Shaw, author of the report "Return on Ideas",[19] creativity is overly limited to the marketing department, and thus he calls for enhanced interdepartmental cooperation: "If everybody has a stake in how marketing ideas are used financially and operationally, creative thoughts become larger than ideas; they become strategies," he says.

The problem may well not be a lack of coordination but rather a failure to involve from the outset in the ideation processes the departments that will be involved in them later. There is a clear tendency to isolate certain departments from innovation projects, even where companies are aware of the negative impacts of this practice.

Lack of vertical coordination

On the other hand, no less important is vertical coordination, that is, coordination between top management, general management and the rest of the organization. This malfunction usually occurs between general business policies and innovation policies. Companies' strategic objectives or acceptable target risk often are out of step with the innovations coming out of both the R&D and marketing departments. We frequently find that someone proposes launching a new product that management is unwilling to finance or that involves more risk than it is willing to assume. In other cases, management accepts an innovation but only to give it a try. But since management commitment is low, the innovation does not get enough support and the execution turns out to be a disaster. An imbalance between company goals and the goals of innovation is an endless source of problems in the implementation of innovations.

Problem seven: lack of customer focus

What's the difference between an idea and an innovation? Answer: an innovation offers increased value for the customer.

This is a key point. Today it is impossible to innovate if you don't keep one eye on the end customer. Real innovation, sooner or later, must be accepted by an end customer, who has to make the effort to switch from one service or product to a new one. This switch entails an effort that the customer will only make if he gets a clear and superior benefit from it.

Many recent innovations have come as a result of observing the customer. And we don't mean traditional market research, but modern methods, where, based on interaction with customers or observing behavior, companies have been inspired by ideas that customers themselves would never have been able to put into words. This is what we call an ethnographic study, the aim of which is to get a perspective or consumer insight. 3M got the idea for its Post-it Picture Paper by observing how digital Post-its' users were switching their laptops, cell phones or BlackBerrys for sending digital photos.[20]

Brainstorming as a technique for generating ideas is giving way to ethnographic techniques, which are much more inspiring and closer to market realities. Innovation that starts with an understanding of the current behavior of end customers is far more likely to be successful.

Note that we're not talking about that marketing mantra "meeting customers' needs." It's deeper than that. It's a matter of enhancing customers' circumstances by observing their present behaviors and imagining ways to enrich their lives. We will deal with generating new ideas, that is, creativity, in a later section of this book.

PART ONE

2 Overall Picture of the A-to-F Model

In this part of the book we introduce our A-to-F model. This model is the outcome of our analysis of a large number of companies that we consider to be innovative or that get good results from time and from resources devoted to innovation: Apple, Google, Netflix, 3M, Procter & Gamble, General Electric, BMW, Frito-Lay, IBM, Toyota, Southwest Airlines, Starbucks, Microsoft, Tesco, Royal Dutch Shell, Walmart, Exxon, IKEA, Ericsson, Nokia and Corning have been the main ones.

The A-to-F model is intended to overcome the barriers to innovation identified in Chapter 1. We have tried to make it flexible, applicable to any business and comprehensive enough to adapt to any past or future practice involving innovation.

Why do organizations need processes?

We should remember that people are by nature averse to change. Change is usually seen as meaning extra effort and added risk in our jobs. People working in an organization, who have enough to do with performing their daily duties adequately, wonder: Why the extra effort? Why the added risk? Human beings see change as something to be avoided, something which will bring no good, at least in the short term. As a result, in organizations, and in the world at large, inertia and the desire to preserve the status quo obstruct innovation and improvement.

For the company, the implications are clear. If no one has the job of activating, of launching the processes of change and innovation, the people in charge of day-to-day business will remain focused on their routine. This is an important factor in the business world and it explains why innovative companies are a minority. In organizations, efficiency matters above all else. Companies are out to make money and, to this end, they design processes and market products and services that sell readily. Companies focus on what works. Virtually all tasks, from those performed by an assembly line worker to those of a salesperson, are governed by a certain set of rules. The person is instructed in how, where and when to do what. The more one operates within the rules, within the work system that the company has designed, the greater the efficiency. In the short term, therefore, a company does not thrive on change; on the contrary, it thrives on its rules, its routines, on the processes that work well and, day in day out, generate profit.

Strategos, Gary Hamel's consulting firm, released a survey with senior executives in 2004 on the key barriers to effective innovation. The main factor, with 63 percent of mentions, was "Short term focus and focus on day-to-day operations".[1]

However, as everyone knows, stability and certainty do not exist. Everything is constantly changing and that change is coming faster and faster. Global competition is also becoming more and more intense. The environment is changing with incredible speed, largely due to technological advances and capital flows. The result is that what is efficient today will soon cease to be so and thus companies face the challenge of reconciling daily efficiency and maintenance of existing rules and work systems with processes of change, improvement and innovation.

We are facing an absolute paradox. The company makes money if it is efficient, if it applies rules in line with its plans, avoiding as far as possible anything that is unaccounted for. However, as time passes, the company will sustain its profits only if it has the ability to adapt to change and to lead innovation in its sector and market.

The challenge of innovation, and the key to making it happen, lies in the capacity to reconcile these two apparently contradictory tasks.

The innovation process as a solution

The reason that innovation must be achieved through processes and independent projects is the natural consequence of this contradictory dual objective: to remain efficient at the same time as we're thinking about changing what works today. For someone to change the way they work today, they must stop doing what they are doing, step back, think, rethink assumptions, compare and look into how other organizations work, think of new possibilities, assess them, design them, refine them and test them, and finally to extend them to the rest of the organization as a task that then can and must be adopted as a standard and accepted as a new routine.

It is better to leave one person to follow the efficient routine and set up another to figure out a more efficient routine. In the best practices of the world's most innovative companies, the people assigned to perform a particular innovation-related task are removed, in whole or part, from day-to-day operations. We repeat: it is impossible and even counterproductive to have someone trying to change the way a task is done while demanding that they perform that task efficiently.

Innovation projects will change the company's routines and rules, whether you call that routine a product, a service, a sales method, a logistics system or a production method.

Continuous innovation as a sum of projects

Innovation projects have a start and end date, they are allocated specific resources, manned by their own teams, have defined goals and someone responsible for their results. But innovative activity must be continuous and constant in companies. Thus, we say that a company is innovative when it is capable of combining independent innovation processes, as well as starting and carrying them through on a regular basis.

Let's say that innovation is a continuous activity composed of discontinuous tasks, that is, processes. Innovation processes are designed to achieve projects. They are specific tasks to be completed within a specific period of time. An innovation process that goes on indefinitely can only generate costs and can never become a source of income. Innovation processes must have a deadline. When that deadline rolls around, the process must be terminated and others launched. Innovative companies keep several innovation processes going simultaneously; continually implementing new ones and winding up those that have met or not met their goals. Likewise, their innovation processes occur at all levels, with goals ranging from the introduction of minor upgrades to the launch of a groundbreaking product or service. This is the system used by most organizations, whatever their nature, to innovate.

The innovation process: roles versus stages

The fact that innovation projects are achieved through processes has forced the experts to investigate what such processes should look like. Just about every week a new book comes out explaining a new innovation process, and all of them have their strengths and their weaknesses.

A process is a set of sequenced tasks over time. This has led to the conclusion that in order to innovate we need a project to move through a number of stages. Writers vary in the number of stages they prescribe. Many of the innovation processes in such books are illustrated with the type of diagram shown in Figure 2.1.

Traditional stages or steps of the innovation process

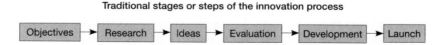

Figure 2.1 **Innovation process steps**

It is even common to find drawings that look like production lines, conveyor belt included, meant to communicate visually the idea that the innovation process is like a sausage-making machine. Proceeding step by step, if we introduce ideas at one end, out of the other end will eventually come useful products and services. In this regard, some authors approach the innovation processes as if they were writing a cookbook or instruction manual.

Most likely the fact that it doesn't work that way is the reason why inevitably each week a new method, a new innovation process, appears.

Our view is that, in reality, the stages or phases of an innovation process must be the result of the interaction of those involved in the innovation processes. Certainly, each innovation, depending on the goals and nature of the project, will require its own ad hoc process and sequence. The stages to follow to upgrade a motor are completely different from the stages to follow to improve the quality of a fabric, for instance.

The main idea behind our book is this: the phases or stages of an innovation process cannot be predetermined, but must emerge as a result of the interaction of a set of functions or roles performed by certain individuals.

As a result, instead of having a process that certain people should follow, we have a group of people who, out of their spontaneous interaction and needs throughout the project, design a process. In other words, in the traditional innovation processes the stages or phases determine the people we are going to need. In the approach we propose here, the roles come first and the innovation process is a result of interaction among these roles.

We believe this approach is more appropriate because, as we have explained, innovation processes can barely be parameterized. Creativity requires analogical, not sequential thinking, and so does innovation, which is nothing but creativity applied to a particular discipline. Innovation requires a lot of "coming and going," returning to the same idea, dismissing it, taking it up again, revising it, looking for more information, designing, realizing that that design is not optimal and that we need to go back to the drawing board. Innovation is not a linear process, rather it is a process that advances, but with much backtracking and detouring.

Thus, the A-to-F model we introduce here is not an innovation process, but the list of the key roles we have found to exist in the companies that have shown the best innovation practices in recent years. Our proposal is that if a company wants to innovate, it must define and assign these roles to specific individuals and then, having established goals, resources and deadline, let them interact freely to create their own process.

The roles we identified are:

(A) ACTIVATORS: These are the people who will initiate the innovation process, without worrying about stages or phases. Eventually, but not necessarily, they may influence the components of the innovation team (who is going to take on what roles). Essentially, their mission is to **initiate** the process.

(B) BROWSERS: These are the experts in searching for information. Their task is not to produce anything new, but to supply the group with information. Their mission is to **investigate** throughout the process and to find the information relevant both to the start of the process and to the application of new ideas.

(C) CREATORS: The people who produce ideas for the rest of the group. Their function is to **ideate** new concepts and possibilities, and search for new solutions at any point in the process.

(D) DEVELOPERS: People specialized in turning ideas into products and services; they are the ones who "tangibilize" ideas, who give form to concepts and develop a rough marketing plan. Creators come up with ideas; developers invent things. Their function is to take ideas and turn them into solutions. In short, to **invent.**

(E) EXECUTORS: The people who take care of everything to do with implementation and execution. Their function is to **implement,** that is, bring the innovation under development to the organization and to the market.

(F) FACILITATORS: Those who approve the new spending items and investment needed as the innovation process moves forward. They also manage the process to prevent it getting stuck. Their mission is the **instrumentation** of the innovation process.

To each of these roles we will devote an entire chapter, addressing not only the sort of profile and skills they require but also the best and latest tools available to aid them in performing their functions.

Dynamics

As we have explained, the innovation process will take shape based on the interaction among all these roles. Let's look at two examples of entirely different innovation processes designed for the six functions above:

Example 1

  A–B–C–A–F–D–B–D–F–E–C–E

Description: The activators request information from the browsers, who deliver the results of their research to the creators. The latter go back to the activators to examine new ideas that were not taken into consideration at the start of the process. The activators approve them and ask the facilitators for their appraisal and for additional resources. From here, the developers start working on how to translate the idea into value, and realize that they need additional market information, so they ask the browsers for a relevant market study. The browsers pass the information they find back to the developers, who present a prototype to the facilitators, who approve the budget to start production. The executors start working on the launch and marketing. They realize that the new product requires new marketing ideas, and again enlist the help of the creators in coming up with alternative ways of selling the new product. The creators propose a set of marketing ideas, out of which the executors select the best before proceeding to the definitive launch.

Example 2

A–D–E

Description: Another company may not need the help of the browsers or creators, since they have identified a product abroad that they are going to market in their own country. The new product just needs a bit of adapting. In this case, the activators hand the project to the developers, who adapt the product to the local market and pass it on to the executors for launch without the need for approval of additional resources and, thus, without any need to go to the facilitators.

Figure 2.2 shows the six roles A-to-F and their interactions. Figure 2.3 shows the corresponding six I's of innovation.

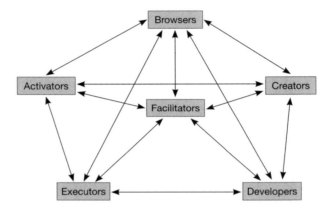

Figure 2.2   **A-to-F model**

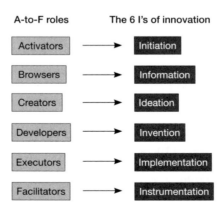

Figure 2.3   **The 6 I's of innovation**

Now, we can examine the Total Innovation System including our A-to-F model in Figure 2.4.

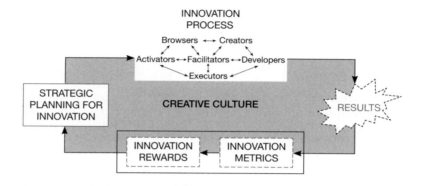

Figure 2.4   **Total Innovation System and A-to-F model**

In the remaining chapters in this part of the book (Chapters 3 to 8) we will take a closer look at the six roles that make up this model.

3 Activators

Let's start with the first role of our model: activators. Their role is strongly linked to innovation planning and strategy. Therefore, we will also introduce in this chapter some elements that will be fully developed in Chapter 10.

What an activator is, and why there's a need for this role

An activator is the person(s) or mechanism(s) that launch innovation processes within an organization.

In analyzing the innovation processes of the most innovative companies, we consistently found the presence of an innovation activator. The innovation activator is the engine whose function it is to lift the company out of its routine, its systematic mode, get it to step back from the day-to-day and change what works today, even when there is no imminent need for such change.

When the objective is efficiency, people need to be overseen. When the objective is innovation, people need to be "provoked." Here's an unavoidable truth: innovation processes will not happen in an organization if there isn't someone (or something) to start them up.

All companies must define their innovation activators, not only to ensure that a particular innovation process gets going, but also to ensure that the innovative activity is sustained over time.

Prerequisites for activators

Before describing the types of activators that a company should look for, we identify three prerequisites that are critical to the effectiveness of the process: the *innovation framework*, the *innovation guidelines* and the *innovation checklist*. These three prerequisites must come from top management and be passed on to the activators, who must incorporate them in the process and communicate them to all involved.

These prerequisites are somewhat similar to an innovation brief and are generated within the innovation planning process (see Chapter 10). The innovation framework, the innovation guidelines and the innovation checklist are a mirror of the innovation strategy and their function is to ensure that activators start innovation processes that are relevant to the organization. There must be a high coordination between the A-to-F model (or any other type of innovation process) and the innovation strategy (see Figure 3.1).

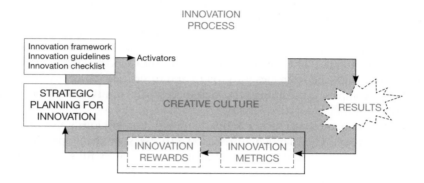

Figure 3.1   **Coordination between activators and strategic planning for innovation**

Innovation framework

The activator of an innovation must work in alignment with the overall objectives and strategies of the company; otherwise sooner or later the process will hit a dead end, costing the company precious time and money.

There is a widespread misconception regarding innovation: the belief that any restriction on innovation will act as a brake on creativity. This leads many companies to designate innovation activators without any sort of limits. A policy of "anything goes" is adopted and innovation is allowed a virtually limitless field of action.

This is a serious mistake. Limiting the scope of creativity does not necessarily limit the ability to innovate – on the contrary. Creativity needs a framework of action. This is true in any discipline, including art, which is the paradigm of "free" creativity. A painter, before executing a work, decides whether to use oil, charcoal or watercolor and also chooses the theme or model. These are not limitations, but rather a framework. And they do not restrict or diminish the creativity of the painter. The same goes for the field of innovation. Nothing is more absurd, costly and frustrating than an innovation process that results in a novel concept the organization will never be able to exploit because it does not fit in with the its vision, scope or resources.

We will admit that if the scope is unlimited, you have a greater potential for generating new ideas. However, the probability that the ideas will be useless increases exponentially. In our experience, whatever you lose in creative potential by limiting the field of action is more than offset by the increased likelihood that the products, services or concepts derived from the innovation process will be feasible.

What we are advocating here goes against the commonly accepted rule that says that you first have to let creativity flow and, if necessary, impose limitations afterwards. But in reality the two things are not incompatible. Focusing creative effort does not undermine its potential. Creative capacity depends not so much on the breadth of its scope as on the methods and tools used to generate and develop relevant new ideas, and the profile of the people involved.

Today innovation is essential. But innovation should not determine strategy; rather it is strategy that should dictate what direction innovation processes are to take. The mission of a company, the objectives set by management, along with the strategies for growth and diversification of markets and products, comprise the framework that necessarily limits the scope of a company's overall innovative activity.

Many companies that lack a defined strategy unconsciously use innovation as a proxy. They launch innovation processes in the hope that the resulting new ideas and concepts will give rise to a successful strategy. This may happen in some cases, but when it does it's sheer luck. Most often the result will be an idea for a product or service so far from what the company is willing and/or able to produce that the initiative has to be discarded.

Top management is responsible for avoiding this common error, and should clearly indicate to activators which markets the company is not interested in and the types of products and services that it doesn't want to produce or sell. This may seem obvious, but it is one of the fundamental requirements for an effective innovation process. In our chapter on strategic planning for innovation (Chapter 10) we delve further into the relationship between innovation and strategy.

So, how do you define this framework? How specific should the limits be? There are three levels of specificity in a framework for innovation processes. From lowest to highest, these are: limiting the scope of innovation; specifying the level at which you want to innovate; and the choice of a specific focus.

Limiting the scope of innovation

At the very least, an innovation framework should delineate the geographic markets and the types of products and services where innovation is wanted. An example would be an airline that decides to operate exclusively within its home country and focus its activities on air transportation services. Thus, international flights, any business other than transportation and any form of sea or overland transport are excluded. At first glance, that looks like an awful lot of restrictions for the people who will be collaborating in the innovation processes. But in fact this definition is quite broad: it leaves open the possibility of thinking about air transport services by helicopter, small plane, airliner, and – why not? – balloon, blimp or ultralight aircraft. Thus, we can easily see that a defined framework need not undermine creativity. Additionally, we avoid wasted effort in coming up with ideas for, let's say, marketing gift items at airports, because the framework clearly states that this is not a target business despite the many opportunities that it may offer or all the great ideas that it could generate.

This product/area definition is perhaps the broadest and most generic possible. Top management may decide not to further restrict the scope of activity for the innovation process, or it may prefer to impose further limits, in which case it will be necessary to define what we call innovation levels.

Defining innovation levels

There are essentially four innovation levels, ranging from the most strategic to the most tactical:

Level 1: Business model innovation
Level 2: Process innovation
Level 3: Market innovation
Level 4: Product and service innovation

Business model innovation is a type of innovation that entails profound change in how a company creates value and thus it requires either major restructuring of the company or the creation of a new business unit or division. An example of business model innovation would be a traditional bank that launches a new online bank providing services exclusively through the Internet. When Apple decided to share its programming code so that any software company or individual coder could develop iPhone apps, that was a change in business model. These are some examples of successful and innovative business models:

▷ Fedex
▷ Barnes and Noble
▷ Club Méditerranée
▷ Dell

▷ iTunes
▷ IKEA
▷ Online banking
▷ Amazon

Process innovation means changes in the company's current logistics, sales or production operations. An example would be if Apple were to switch from having one operator per country as the exclusive iPhone distributor to allowing any operator to sell their phones. Or when a manufacturer decides to outsource to China the production of some its components.

Market innovation means targeting a new buying public, meeting new needs or being present in new purchasing and consumption situations. For example, when a bank decides to allow customers to make payments via cell phone it is moving into a new situation in the use of banking services (mobility) that it didn't have before. Market innovation is largely related to the concept of lateral marketing,[1] which we recommend those interested in this kind of innovation to read up on. In Table 3.1 you will find a list of market innovations for the three dimensions: consumers, need and situation.

Table 3.1   Market innovations in the three dimensions

Target	Need	Situation
Gillette is a brand for men which, through Gillette Venus, was addressed to women	Wonderbra incorporates an aesthetic need to the functionality of a brand	Nesquik Night is a cocoa beverage for bedtime rather than breakfast
Kidiboo is a cheese brand which makes cheese ice cream desserts	Mobile phones for household alarm connections	Gas stations open 24 hours a day, including for the sale of bread
Baby Einstein is a video collection for children	Buying CDs as a way for voting in a TV contest	Home Cinema takes the cinema sound effects to homes

Source: Adapted from *Lateral Marketing*, Philip Kotler and Fernando Trías de Bes. John Wiley, 2003

Finally, product and service innovation consists of technological change, new models or expanding lines targeted at the same consumers, needs and situations. Each updated version of the iPhone, for example, represents a product innovation. The consumers, needs and situations remain unchanged vis-à-vis the previous version; the only change is better performance, capacity and processing speed, as well as some design improvements.

These levels can be even more specific and detailed. This is part of the innovation strategy and we will describe a further development of these levels in Chapter 10.

Each of these four levels entails completely different risks, investments and implications for innovation. Accordingly, each of these levels is associated with a specific level of responsibility. The responsibility for launching a new business model lies with the CEO; that of a new process, with the managing director; that of a new market, with the marketing director or, depending on how radical the innovation is, top management; a new product falls to the marketing director, while a new model or expansion of a line to the product manager or brand manager.

Many companies starting out on an innovation fail to match the kind of innovation with its corresponding level of responsibility. In such cases, total dysfunction is guaranteed, and things end up with product managers devising business models or general managers spending time on expanding lines – things they should not be dealing with, but they do so on the grounds that any innovation process must go through them.

Define the focus of innovation

Once you have defined the level at which you want to innovate, it is helpful, though not strictly necessary, to limit as far as possible the focus of innovation. The focus is the thing or set of things you want to change or upgrade.

We have enough studies on creative thinking to know that it is essentially inductive rather than deductive. Deductive thinking starts with broad rules or observations to draw specific conclusions. Inductive thinking, on the other hand, starts with the specific in order to reach a general rule.

Creative thinking is inductive because it is impossible to create something out of nothing. Creativity is the ability to discover new ways to connect up existing things or concepts. By specifying a focus we provide a much more precise framework for innovation teams. The scope of a focus can refer to a particular thing or parts of it. For example, you might launch an innovation process to improve a soft drink, the bottle it comes in or the cap of the bottle. These are three distinct focuses (soft drink, bottle, cap), but each is narrower than the preceding one.

Each of the four innovation levels we set out above allows for different focuses. Table 3.2 shows some examples of focus for each of the four levels.

Table 3.2 Example of focuses at the four innovation levels

Business model	Process	Market	Products and services
Type of agreements and suppliers	Warehouse systems	New customers according to social class	Product expiry date
Customers' selection	Quality controls	Point of sale Policies and merchandising	Packaging
Customers' pricing and payment schemes	Production plans Organization	New segments according to age of customer	Customers' waiting time to receive a service

Which is preferable: a broad or specific innovation framework?

Is it necessary to specify the focus? Is it enough to define the level at which we want to innovate or do we only need to narrow down the area or product we want? The answer relates to three factors:

▷ how open or closed a business wants its innovation processes to be
▷ the degree of control over them
▷ the number of processes carried out simultaneously

Where companies choose very open, loosely defined processes, they will operate with few guidelines or restrictions: they probably will not even indicate the level at which they want their staff to respond during the weekly think session. By contrast, in companies where the processes are very narrowly defined in terms of assigning people, resources and deadlines, a greater degree of specificity is required.

On the other hand, there are companies where innovation processes are very tightly controlled and actively monitored. Monitoring consists of verifying the achievement of goals, so these cases call for a higher degree of specificity in the innovation framework.

Finally, there tends to be a correlation between the number of ongoing innovation projects (see Chapter 10 on strategic planning) and their level of specification. When a company has several innovative projects going on at once, it needs to divide up the duties involved so that no two teams are working on the same front. The way to coordinate them is to be as specific as possible in terms of what the focus of their efforts should be.

Our view, however, is that it is advisable to narrow the framework as much as possible, especially in times of crisis or when economic conditions are adverse. It is true that if you assign a team to innovate on something as specific as a bottle cap, for example, their creative scope will be narrower than if they are given the job of changing everything from the drink to the label. If you limit the focus, however, the results of the innovation process will be fully aligned with the detail of the company's strategic objectives and available resources.

Perhaps an effective solution would be a good mix of both levels of focus. That is, designate some teams to innovate in a very specific area and others to think more openly, with the aim of using the results of their work in areas of change not initially foreseen, and which would be simply a set of thought-provoking or off-the-radar suggestions for management to assess. We call this *exploratory innovation* and will describe it further in Chapter 10. Even in this latter case, however, we recommend that you at least specify the area/ product scope, as explained in the previous section.

In any event, as soon as we know the level of innovation that an activator is considering (whether it involves a product, process, market or business) as well as what managers the proposed change will affect, this information must be communicated to the organization right away, so that a decision can be made as to whether or not to continue the process.

This is the second contact point between activators and innovation strategy before the process is definitively formalized. Activators' proposals must be approved by the responsible head of innovation, giving a definitive green light to the process with the subsequent budget allocation and rest of B-to-F roles' assignments (see Figure 3.2).

There are countless companies that fail to take this point into account and keep a team working on an innovation whose eventual overseer would have rejected it outright long before, had he or she been informed previously. In this sense, the function of the innovation planning and strategy overseers is critical: not only must they give the green light for an innovation process, they must also involve the higher management levels that will be affected by such an innovation, should it continue.

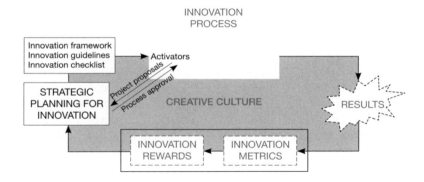

Figure 3.2 **Formal approval of processes that emerge from activators**

Innovation guidelines

Some companies reinforce the innovation framework with innovation guide-lines in order to communicate further what types of innovations are actually going to be taken into consideration. For example, a large company might specify that it will invest only in innovations whose projected sales exceed a certain amount of money; another might say that an innovation must break even within three years; a third option would be to determine the expected return on investment (ROI); another possibility is to limit the amount of resources (investment) available for each innovation; and, finally, another option would be to require that the proposed innovation make use of, for example, two of the company's competitive advantages.

These guidelines are not mutually exclusive; more than one might be specified at the same time. For example, sales achieving a certain level and timeframe for doing so. Guidelines provide very useful criteria for the teams that are going to be engaged in innovation.

The function of innovation guidelines is to reduce the number of proposals submitted for consideration and approval. At the same time, they are a means of ensuring that a given, accepted level of risk is not exceeded. Finally, they indirectly define the extent to which innovation is to be incre-mental and low risk or radical and high risk.

In Table 3.3 we show some examples of innovation guidelines used by well-known leading companies.

Table 3.3 Example of guidelines in an innovation process

A launch must generate minimum sales of one million dollars
Profits must be obtained within three years of launch date
Launches must use existing brands of the company
Innovation processes cannot last more than 18 months

Innovation checklist

The last factor we recommend for activators before embarking on the innovation process is the innovation checklist. This is similar to the checklist that airline pilots go over before take-off. One by one, they must check a number of components and functions of the aircraft in order to ensure that they are all working properly and that everything is ready for a safe, comfortable flight.

Similarly, in the field of innovation, it is very useful to develop a series of key questions whose answer must be yes before we can move ahead. Table 3.4 gives some examples of the sorts of questions usually found in such a checklist.[2]

Table 3.4 Checklist example for an innovation process

• Is the project truly necessary?
• What benefits the project, when complete, will bring to customers?
• Is the project going to help employees or the company at large in any way?
• Is it necessary to undertake the project now or will there be any adverse repercussions if we postpone it?
• Will the project work impede business operations and affect business goals?
• What are the end objectives of the project and how practical are they?
• What is the overall timeframe and how to measure progress?
• Is the project cost-effective and what are the cost-benefit advantages?

The questions must be answered at any point in the process, whether it's just about to begin, during development or testing of prototypes, or when it's time to put our idea into practice. We recommend such frequent checking because the unpredictability of innovation processes accentuates the likelihood of deviation from the points on the checklist.

Having set out the criteria that the activators should have before starting an innovation process, we move on to the subject of who in the company can be activators, what types of activation they can undertake and what their optimal profile is.

Types of activators

There are four types of activators:

1   *Management or top management:* In this case, it is the top management of the company that activates the innovation process through a specific request.
2   *Workers:* In this case, it is the members of the organization who activate the innovation processes. This may happen spontaneously – for example an employee makes a suggestion – or in a structured manner through the information channels designed for this purpose.

3   *Stakeholders:* These are agents who are external to but connected with
    the organization. The kinds of stakeholders most commonly chosen as
    innovation activators are suppliers, distributors and customers. Less
    common, but equally valid, are investors or shareholders.
4   *The scientific community and researchers:* In this case, the activators
    come from academic or research institutions, and may be inventors,
    engineers or any sort of scientist.

Types of resultant activation

By combining two dimensions – the person who activates the need and the
person designated to take the responsibility – we obtain the following types
of innovation activation:

▷ *up-bottom activation:* starts from top management and is directed at the
   company's employees.
▷ *in-out activation:* starts from top management and is directed at the
   stakeholders or the scientific community.
▷ *bottom-up activation:* starts from the company's employees and is directed
   at management.
▷ *out-in activation:* starts from the stakeholders or the scientific community and is directed at top management or functional area managers.

In the following, we describe in detail each type of activation using real cases.

Up-bottom activation

Up-bottom systems are those in which innovation is activated by an explicit
decision from top management, designating a dedicated team who give up
part or all of their duties to work on the innovation project.

This is one of the best known and most common types of activation,
found both in companies that do not have permanent resources devoted to
innovation and in businesses that, while innovative, prefer to work with a
system of teams and projects.

There are many examples of up-bottom activation. Shell, for example, in
the mid-1990s created the "GameChanger" panel, a small group of creatively
minded mid-level executives who could also draw on other technical resources
across the company. They were given the task of developing new ideas and a
$20 million budget to implement ideas that would break with existing rules
and conventional wisdom. The GameChanger panel, in turn, created several
more dedicated teams to perform some of the basic functions of the innovation process: an innovation lab, whose job was to refine and improve their
ideas; an action lab to explore ideas in a controlled environment; and a board
of entrepreneurs to assess and finance the best projects. The GameChanger

experiment started in one division: exploration and production. Now it has spread throughout the company and each division has its own GameChanger panel process. There is even a special GameChanger team dedicated to radical projects that fall outside the boundaries of Shell's existing businesses.

General Electric also uses up-bottom activation. In a system they call "Bubble Assignments," a manager is freed from his or her usual duties and assigned to a different project for a short period of time. Normally, the company mobilizes experts from different disciplines and promotes mobility between departments to foster internal relationships and connect up projects.

Dedicated innovation teams usually have an appointed team leader, someone who oversees the group. For example, at Corning, a global leader in the glass industry and pioneer in fiber optics, they are called "Champions". Each team has its Champion, the person designated to lead the group and ensure that the innovation process gets off the ground and, in the event, is shepherded through successfully.

These dedicated teams may be short-lived – when the team is only expected to get an innovation process started – or they may last several years – when the team is required to lead and oversee the entire process through to the end. For example, at BMW multidisciplinary teams shifted from their usual duties to innovate full time can last up to three years. In contrast, at Southwest Airlines this period is limited to a few months.

Up-bottom activation is also done at Starbucks, where CEO Howard Schultz doubles as head of strategic innovation management, and, working alongside other managers and a support team, activates innovation process whenever an opportunity is detected.

In-out activation

In-out activation happens when management enlists someone from outside the company to collaborate in the innovation process. This responsibility is not necessarily externalized due to a lack of capacity in the company. It may be simply because the type of innovation demands that it be done that way, as with innovation of business models or new technologies. This option may also be preferred to expedite the process or where internal resources are occupied elsewhere.

In this type of activation, a company usually contracts researchers, specialized consultancies or ad-hoc teams that may range from customers to suppliers. Another common system is partnerships with the academic world (university researchers) or with an organization that employs a large number of scientists and is looking to diversify its services (both NASA and Ferrari have provided such services).

An example of in-out activation is the Tesco supermarket chain, the UK's largest employer, with 250,000 workers, which in the 1990s enlisted the Cardiff Business School in Wales to study how Toyota's successful production principles might be adapted for the retailer's supply chain with the goal of saving time and energy. By the end of the process, in soft drinks, for example, the time from bottling to the customer leaving the store with the drink dropped from 20 days to five. The number of inventory stock points was cut from five to two and the supplier's distribution center for the items simply disappeared.

IBM also applies in-out activation to identify business areas that might hold opportunities. The company calls on customers, external observers and venture capitalists to propose areas of business where IBM does not have a presence and that have potential for the future (IBM calls them EBOs, emerging business opportunities). IBM doesn't look to its own R&D department for such proposals because the latter is focused on current areas of business and therefore lacks the outsider perspective to think about new business opportunities. IBM's strategy manager picks the most promising proposals out of the lot and then identifies company executives with long experience and, at the head of major divisions, with responsibility for a large team of people, but with little room for maneuver to invest in new, higher-risk projects within their own unit. They are then designated to build the future. At the height of their careers, they are called on to put their experience to work on an internal startup. Since launching this system in 2000, IBM has generated 25 EBOs, of which only three have failed. Four of them, Digital Media, Life Sciences, Linux and Persuasive Computing, obtained earnings of over one billion dollars each in 2003 and 2004.[3]

Here is an enlightening story from Procter & Gamble (P&G) on how external resources can quickly increase a company's ability to innovate:

> We knew that most of P&G's best innovations had come from connecting ideas across internal businesses. And after studying the performance of a small number of products we'd acquired beyond our own labs, we knew that external connections could produce highly profitable innovations, too. Betting that these connections were the key to future growth, Lafley made it our goal to acquire 50 percent of our innovations outside the company. The strategy wasn't to replace the capabilities of our 7,500 researchers and support staff, but to better leverage them. We estimated that for every P&G researcher there were 200 scientists or engineers elsewhere in the world who were just as good – a total of perhaps 1.5 million people whose talents we could potentially use. We needed to move the company's attitude from resistance to innovations "not invented here" to enthusiasm for those "proudly found elsewhere." And we needed to change how we defined, and perceived, our R&D organization – from 7,500 people inside to 7,500 plus 1.5 million outside, with a permeable boundary between them.[4]

Bottom-up activation

Bottom-up innovation activation systems are those where the activation of an innovation process comes not from the managerial level, but from staff members lower down the chain of command, whether or not they belong to departments directly linked to innovation.

The most common bottom-up activation systems are innovative projects that come out of R&D, the marketing or design department, or some combination thereof. For example, P&G, which managed to make the break from being profoundly conservative and tradition-bound to being one of the world's most innovative companies, applied, among other mechanisms, this sort of policy. At a time when the company was restructuring and radically downsizing management, it took an important decision: quadruple the number of design personnel, and put them to work directly with R&D to develop new projects. Out of the interaction of these designers and engineers came many ideas that later turned into new products.

3M also uses a bottom-up system for continuous activation of innovation processes. 3M employs more than 7,000 researchers at their innovation centers located around the world. These researchers can spend up to 15 percent of their time on projects of their choice. That does not mean they waste company time on ideas without potential, because a committee, acting like an F (facilitator), according to our A-to-F model, continuously evaluates the projects and ideas proposed by these engineers, rejecting those deemed to be unviable or lacking potential.

But the marketing, R&D and design departments are not the only places from which innovation activation can emerge. Some companies prefer to empower all members of the organization to generate good ideas. Google, considered one of the world's most innovative companies, activates its innovation processes through a bottom-up system that is open to everyone in the company. Each and every one of its employees spends part of their time on R&D (called "free day thinking" and fully compensated). Any Google employee can "post" an idea for new technologies or businesses on an electronic list of proposals. This list is continually checked and assessed by all staff, who critique proposals and vote for the best. This is a democratic system, typical of the Internet world. Like on a forum or a blog, the ideas that receive the most comments are eventually handed over to the engineers to develop. There is even a "miscellaneous" list, which includes items varying from suggestions for the staff restaurant to criticism of the organization. Another system is "Open Office" hours. Google executives are required to keep their doors open two or three times a week to meet and discuss the ideas of other employees. The time devoted to this task is usually divided up half for batting around new ideas and half to teaching new employees to go further in their proposals.

Out-in activation

Out-in activation systems are perhaps the newest and most surprising. This system is based on the development of a business model in which it makes sense for individuals or small businesses that are not part of our organization to innovate through our business platform. In contrast with in-out activation, it does not stem from a specific request. Out-in activation innovation occurs more or less spontaneously because the business model is designed such that other companies become partners or take advantage of our business to innovate independently.

This type of activation includes what is known as *open innovation*, although there are other systems. A clear example is Apple and iPhone applications. The company decided to share its programming code with any programmer who takes an interest, and thus thousands of applications have been invented for the iPhone.

But open innovation is not the only out-in activation system. We can include here any other networking system in which we attract and motivate external researchers to think for us without any specific commission or assignment. For example, in 1991 Walmart launched its WIN (Walmart Innovation Network) initiative in collaboration with the Innovation Institute and the College of Business Administration of Southwest Missouri State University. The idea was to connect the creative talents of independent inventors with Walmart's financial, managerial and product development resources, with the goal of turning projects into real products.

In the case of out-in activation of open innovation, we see that the framework need not be explicitly defined since it is already implicit in the business model and partnering system.

In the case of activation that comes from unsolicited proposals from universities or the scientific community, there is not necessarily any defining framework, as there is in the case of a partnership agreement or any stable, ongoing relationship. Rather, here we are simply talking about externally generated proposals without any kind of stipulations or commission.

Which type of activation is best?

First, we should point out that the four types of activation and activators described here are not mutually exclusive. In fact, the world's most innovative companies use them interchangeably and simultaneously. So long as there is someone in charge of the innovation (see Chapter 10) with a bird's eye view of all the processes being activated in an organization, for purposes of avoiding duplication, it's hardly a problem to have several of these activators working at the same time.

That said, it is true that the question of which of these mechanisms is most suitable depends on the desired type of innovation, resources, internal capacities and existing innovation culture. The chapter summary shows the relationship between the four types of activations and each of these factors.

Apart from this, it is important to bear in mind that when the activators come from within the organization, there is a greater tendency to develop a culture of innovation, which is accordingly also more likely to take on a life of its own. And this is even more so when the activators are drawn not just from management, but also from among the workers.

TOTAL INNOVATION SYSTEM – Summary Chapter 3

Main person/s in charge of each role

	A Activators	B Browsers	C Creators	D Developers	E Executors	F Facilitators
	Top management (GM or Chief Innovation Officer)					
	Employees					
	Suppliers					
	Distributors					
	Clients					
	Investors					
	Universities					
	Scientific community					
	Inventors					
	Engineering companies					

Up-bottom activation
In-out activation
Bottom-up activation
Out-in activation

Techniques employed by each role

A Activators	B Browsers	C Creators	D Developers	E Executors	F Facilitators
Scope of innovation					
Innovation levels					
Focus of innovation					
Innovation guidelines					
Innovation checklist					

INNOVATION
PROCESS

Innovation framework
Innovation guidelines
Innovation checklist

STRATEGIC
PLANNING FOR
INNOVATION

Browsers ←→ Creators
Activators ←→ Facilitators ←→ Developers
Executors

project proposals
process approval

CREATIVE CULTURE

INNOVATION
REWARDS

INNOVATION
METRICS

RESULTS

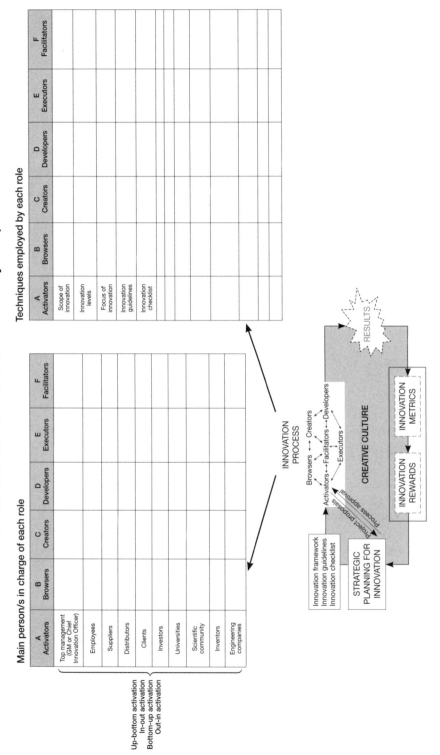

4 Browsers

After an innovation process has been activated, approved and budgeted, any of the other roles can set in. In this chapter we cover the browsers' role.

What a browser is, and why there's a need for this role

Browsers are people whose mission it is to gather information that assists, enlightens, inspires and resolves whether a new idea should continue further in the innovation process.

Traditionally, the search for information related to the field of business innovation has been associated with market research. Two instruments have caught the attention of specialists in innovation.

First, there will be browsing for descriptive information that quantifies the size and growth of markets and the different categories where the company intends to look for opportunities. Second, there will be exploratory research, using qualitative techniques to identify unresolved consumer needs and possible sources of innovation. In the case of technology-based innovation, information search has focused on in-depth study of the various patents and technological advances that might be included in the product or service marketed by a company.

In innovation processes, information searching is carried out in the early stages, generally as the stage that takes place immediately before the creation of specific ideas. In some cases, the information search is performed even before the objectives of an innovation are defined.

From our point of view, the role of the browsers must go further. First of all, information browsers should focus their efforts not only on the early stages of the innovation process, but must remain active and provide information to innovation teams throughout the whole process. For example, in the development of concepts, information providers' role is to facilitate the developers' task through the analysis of prototypes and products launched in any region or product category. Turning ideas into products is one of the most complex processes in innovation and traditionally the search for information that this requires has been entrusted almost exclusively to engineers or the R&D department. Today, a single technology may be transferrable to many products and services, so analysis of how it applies to other fields is of great use to an R&D or technical development department. Information browsers can save a lot of work, effort, resources and time for engineers who develop new products and services.

More important still is gathering information on the implementation and rollout phases of innovation. Again, this work has been left to the marketing departments assigned to launch the new product, trusting that their knowledge of the markets will be sufficient. Each innovation, especially a radical one, requires its own approach to distribution channels, pricing policies and communication strategies. A marketing manager is accustomed to a particular market, but faces many unknowns and information gaps when it comes to releasing an innovation on the market.

Finally, information browsers play a key role when assisting facilitators, who must continually assess and approve fresh expenditure items and investments. In doing so, facilitators base their decisions on the sales prospects for the proposed innovation. Unfortunately, in too many companies such forecasts are based on purely subjective criteria. Even companies that do otherwise, and use market research in making their forecasts, often turn to customer intelligence departments, who have been removed from the innovation process and who then run a standard market test. These tests are useful but must be accompanied by other, less direct methods and based more on monitoring of the products and services or technologies in which the innovation process has been inspired. It is essential that those who compile information about the sales potential of an innovation also participate in earlier stages.

Thus we see the browser as someone who integrates information or coordinates multiple roles that are normally delegated to different departments or people who have barely participated in the innovation process. That does not mean browsers themselves must gather the information required in each case. They may depend on any or all of the previous actors (technicians, market research specialists, external research institutes, and so on) as well as others we deal with in this chapter. But the key is that those who play the browsers' role must have a comprehensive view of all the sources and snippets of information that form part of the process.

This is because research must provide more than just information, it must, above all, inspire the innovation teams. Inspire means to shed light, it means to "steer" thinking towards fertile territories and viable actions. We are talking about active information; that is, linked to the innovation process. It is not information that describes or identifies, but rather that points to innovation routes and paths that lead to greater probabilities of success.

In this chapter we address some of the key practices of companies that make information browsers essential to the innovation process. And we describe new research techniques beyond the standard qualitative exploratory research that has traditionally been used in the innovation process.

Given that information browsers are, in a certain respect, providers for the rest of the players (who can be described as internal clients), we have structured this chapter in four modules, one for each role with which they relate most actively: the information they supply to the creators (B to C), to the developers (B to D), and to the executors (B to E); while the fourth is the techniques and methods for gathering information. As an exception, we will deal with the facilitators (B to F) in a separate chapter, since the information they receive is intrinsically linked to their function.

B to C: innovation diagnostic

Before the creators propose ideas for products and services it is essential to have an innovation diagnostic. We suggest that this should include the following elements, which we will deal with in greater depth later:

▷ Innovation review
▷ Analysis of adjacent categories
▷ Internal consultations
▷ Social trends (B2C markets) (or business trends in B2B markets)
▷ Social classes (B2C markets)
▷ Market trends
▷ Buying process
▷ Innovation routes

Let's take a closer look at each.

Innovation review

This is a component of research which we consider essential and which, paradoxically, almost no company does. Before drawing up the year's marketing plan, brand managers are given the task of drawing up what is called the *brand review*, an assessment of what has happened with the brand in recent years, especially the past year. This is a comprehensive study that deals with the situation in the different distribution channels, the results of different promotions and communication campaigns, the changes in positioning or indicators of penetration levels, and trial and repeat recorded among customers or consumers.

It is ironic that while every year companies evaluate the status of their brands, they do not evaluate the status of innovation in their markets. An innovation review is an assessment, as comprehensive as possible, of the innovations that have occurred in the market or product or service category in which we trying to innovate. ExxonMobil is among the exceptions of companies that make this type of review. Before launching Speedpass, its innovative automatic pay-at-the-pump system, the company first reviewed the innovations launched in gas stations since the 1940s.

For example, if the innovation process is intended to launch a new product in the coffee market, an innovation review would consist of a list of all types of launches and innovations, from breakthroughs (for example Nespresso) to the most marginal, which would include a promotion or expanding a line (for example coffee in reusable packaging).

Our recommendation is to go back ten or more years, both in the country where the innovation is going to be launched and in countries where the relevant market is most developed. For example, in the case of coffee, it would be wise to examine what has been happening in countries like Italy, where there is a strong coffee tradition. Depending on the time and resources available, the wider the geographical scope the better.

In describing each innovation, whether it has already been withdrawn from or is still on the market, we recommend recording all the information on a form, as shown in Figure 4.1.

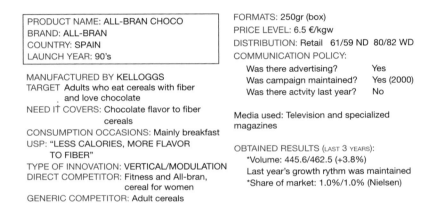

PRODUCT NAME: ALL-BRAN CHOCO
BRAND: ALL-BRAN
COUNTRY: SPAIN
LAUNCH YEAR: 90's

MANUFACTURED BY KELLOGGS
TARGET Adults who eat cereals with fiber
         and love chocolate
NEED IT COVERS: Chocolate flavor to fiber
                cereals
CONSUMPTION OCCASIONS: Mainly breakfast
USP: "LESS CALORIES, MORE FLAVOR
      TO FIBER"
TYPE OF INNOVATION: VERTICAL/MODULATION
DIRECT COMPETITOR: Fitness and All-bran,
                   cereal for women
GENERIC COMPETITOR: Adult cereals

FORMATS: 250gr (box)
PRICE LEVEL: 6.5 €/kgw
DISTRIBUTION: Retail 61/59 ND 80/82 WD
COMMUNICATION POLICY:
    Was there advertising?   Yes
    Was campaign maintained?   Yes (2000)
    Was there actvity last year?   No

Media used: Television and specialized
magazines

OBTAINED RESULTS (LAST 3 YEARS):
    *Volume: 445.6/462.5 (+3.8%)
    Last year's growth rythm was maintained
    *Share of market: 1.0%/1.0% (Nielsen)

Figure 4.1   **Example of past innovation summary**

The usefulness of this information is manifold. First of all, it is helpful simply to have an inventory of all the innovations in the market, something that few companies keep in a systematic and organized manner.

Second, having a record of new products from the past provides us with a picture of the innovation strategies and trends in each market. When you perform this exercise, it is very interesting to find how different companies are clustered around a few specific innovation routes. In Figure 4.2 we give an example of innovation routes based on past innovations in a coffee market.

Figure 4.2   **Example of innovation routes for roasted and ground coffee category**

The identification and understanding of these routes is essential, since one of the big decisions that you have to make is whether or not you want to discard any of your current innovation paths. For example, in the case of coffee, the company may decide not to innovate in the route "coffee by origin" but is instead interested in the route "degrees of caffeine strength."

As we showed in the previous chapter, delimiting or eliminating one or more innovation routes does not diminish the innovativeness of an innovation team, but simply steers it in a certain direction.

The inventory of past innovations can be grouped in a manner complementary to the routes, categorizing the types of innovations. We recommend here what we argued in our previous book, *Lateral Marketing*,[1] classifying vertical innovations in six different types, and distinguishing them from disruptive (lateral) innovations. Classifying innovations by these categories is a very useful diagnostic of the direction innovation has taken in a business sector. Figure 4.3 shows an analysis of the coffee category based on this classification method.

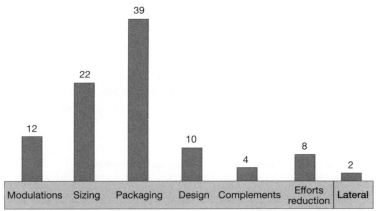

Note: the figure measures the number of innovatons appeared during the last 20 years in each one of the innovation types

Figure 4.3　**Example of diagnosis of types of innovation in the roasted and ground coffee category**

Finally, there is the possibility of relaunching innovations which failed in the past, but which, due to changes in tastes or because of new social trends, may now have a good chance of succeeding. For example, in 1993 the multinational perfumes and cosmetics company Puig Beauty & Fashion launched an oat-based shampoo, Avena Kinesia, which proved a tremendous success. They had launched a similar shampoo before, but it failed. The difference was that in 1993 in Europe there was a strong trend towards dermatological consumer products and general acceptance of cereals as an ingredient, a spillover from the food market.

Although we demonstrate our point here with coffee, the innovation review is not solely aimed at innovations in mass-market goods. Any kind of innovation, whether in services, in B2B markets, in industrial markets or even purely technological innovation, can be the object of a similar analysis, and its usefulness is just as relevant.

Analysis of adjacent categories

A historical analysis of adjacent categories, although more limited than the innovation review, is of tremendous value to creators in their brainstorming sessions. What do we mean by adjacent category? These are categories of products and services that are not our direct competitors or that are not operating in the market where we are thinking about innovating, but that nonetheless share with our products some of the dimensions that define a market: client, need and situation. In other words: they either target our customers even if they meet different needs; or they target different customers, but they cover similar needs; or they simply operate in situations similar to ours.

For example, for the coffee category, energy drinks are an adjacent category. They meet one of the needs that coffee satisfies (to keep you active or awake). Biscuits would also be an adjacent category because, although they cover a different need, like coffee, they are part of breakfast.

The analysis of adjacent categories should trace the routes innovation has taken in the past. Figure 4.4 shows an example of this sort of analysis for categories adjacent to coffee.

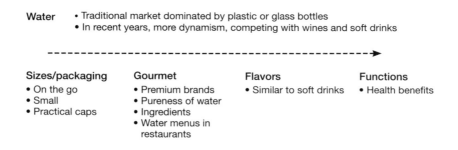

Figure 4.4   **Innovation routes example (water considered as adjacent category of coffee)**

The usefulness of this sort of analysis lies in the fact that, in identifying similarities with categories adjacent to the market where we seek to innovate, multiple opportunities for innovation emerge naturally and spontaneously. The idea is that this information will inspire creators to ask questions such as: does it make sense to innovate in coffee in the way it's been done in energy drinks? As we will see in the next chapter, adjacent categories are an endless source of ideas.

Internal consulting

When we undertake an innovation consultation for a company, the first thing we ask from the client is to be able to use internal information regarding:

▷ *Internal staff:* In any organization a lot of people have ideas and suggestions, but, in the case of relatively non-innovative firms or those lacking systems for channeling innovations, they have no one to explain them to. This latent intellectual capital within the organization is precisely the first source of inspiration for creators that information browsers should tap into. Naturally, it is impossible to interview or consult with all members of a large organization. What browsers should do is make a shortlist or send out a formal communication, department by department, explaining the objectives of the innovation project that the company is starting and the interest of the project team in knowing what things should be taken into account or what relevant ideas other members of the organization have. Sometimes it is even necessary to establish qualitative or quantitative techniques for collecting this information either by questionnaire or via the company's intranet. This should be accompanied by in-depth interviews with selected people who have particular qualities: a given minimum experience, strong commitment to the company, a positive attitude and a proven level of creativity.

▷ *Sales, R&D and marketing:* These three departments should be dealt with separately. Sales personnel, who have daily contact with customers and distributors, possess a useful level of knowledge about the market. We cannot expect them to solve the company's innovation problems, but their assessment of the company situation and the market is likely to be realistic and sensible. For marketing professionals, equally fundamental is their knowledge of consumers, of the barriers to consumption and purchase motivations, and the strengths and weaknesses of the current portfolio and the competition. Finally, R&D departments can advise us about the technical limitations of the products and services that we want to innovate. They can also offer a full description of our manufacturing processes, with the aim of getting not only a picture of the production constraints that we have as a company, but also a detailed diagram of a company's production processes, which is another very useful stimulus in brainstorming sessions.

▷ *Market research:* When companies start working on an innovation, they tend to have an almost pathological urge to go out and ask the customer. They ignore the fact that within the company there is a huge amount of stored information. Today we have more information than we can process. The first thing information browsers on an innovation team must do is to find all previous market research and data warehouse studies. With these in hand, they should then proceed to select the most relevant ones according to the objectives of the innovation project. Finally, they should study them and draw up a diagnostic with their main conclusions.

1 There are three key components to this analysis that any innovation diagnostic should include. The first is called *market sizing*. This means measuring, within the target geographical area, the evolution and current size of the market and each of its categories and subcategories, in terms of value, units (if applicable), customers (if applicable) and distributors (if applicable). The same goes for the average sales price, manufacturing costs and the margin structure of the sector, from the components of the product or service, to the business margins, to the distributors and the tax rate.

2 The second is a *list of insights* that act as mobilizers for our customers and distributors. Much has been written recently about insights and just about every author has his or her own definition. We understand insight as the motivation that drives individual consumers because it is innate to them.[2] Insights should be identified by means of qualitative market research. In the absence of the latter, although we do not recommend this method, they can be inferred through the sales and marketing department's knowledge of customers. Whatever the source, a list of insights on current products and services is an essential component of any innovation diagnostic.

3 The third is *visits to customers, distributors and suppliers.* Information providers and possibly other A-to-F roles (mainly creators and developers) need to take some time (between two days and one week may be sufficient) to "hit the street" and visit customers, suppliers, distributors and retail outlets. Starbucks chairman Howard Schultz visits between 30 and 40 Starbucks around the world on a weekly basis. It is very difficult to innovate in something you do not know firsthand. For example, at Tesco, many innovations arise from frequent visits to delicatessens, ethnic food shops and cooking schools.

Social trends

In recent years, we marketing and innovation experts have paid a great deal of attention to technology and design, while forgetting, to some extent, sociology. A good analysis of social trends (where customers are consumers – B2C market) or business trends (where companies are concerned – B2B market) has two major uses.

First, social trends are a tremendous source of inspiration for creators (C). Social trends help explain the behavior of our customers, regardless of what products and services our organization sells. The channeling of a social trend through innovation is in itself a creative technique that produces many good ideas.

Second, social trends are like a passport to acceptance of an innovation in the market. Lots of innovations – interesting, original innovations, even ones that were useful to consumers – have failed because they ignored social trends. They didn't take into account that their value proposition was not in tune with the social trends of the time. In such cases, it is rare for consumers to embrace the innovation. Consumers would have to swim against the tide of practices, customs and fashions that they themselves have adopted. Similarly, an innovation that strengthens or reaffirms consumers in a prevailing social trend will have a greater chance of success.

This applies mainly to what we call mainstream products, that is, those aimed at mass markets. Another case all together is that of products aimed expressly at starting a new trend or fashion. This is an area where many companies try and few succeed. The reason is that trendsetters (opinion leaders who start fashions for certain items within a particular social group) are the antithesis of big-brand imposed trends. They, and not the brands, are the ones who *decide* what is in vogue. Generally speaking, when your aim is to win over the trendsetters, you should watch their signs and movements.

In the sphere of social trends, however, what is assumed to be a long-term trend often turns out to be as fleeting as the life of a butterfly. All social groups adopt trends of varying duration. This applies equally to children, housewives, executives, sporting types and people who love to travel. Many companies innovate by latching on to a social trend without considering how long it is likely to last.

Usually, we talk about four timeframes for social trends: macrotrends, trends, fashions and fads. We can say that each feeds off the previous one. Many fashions began as fads that lasted maybe a few weeks, but that, due to different factors, gathered momentum and spread until they became fashions.

Social trends emerge from fashions that have survived longer than a season or a year, turning into something more stable and lasting. Finally, a macrotrend is a trend that has sustained its popularity for more than five years and that is one of the traits of a generation. Therefore we distinguish the following:

▷ *Macrotrends:* lasting a minimum of five years and up to ten years. They are unlikely to last more than ten, because every seven years there are substantial changes in a generation's life goals.

An example of a macrotrend is caring about the environment. Some years ago this was something that was restricted to green types and anti-establishment groups, but gradually it began to spread to the rest of the population to become a common feature among educated people.

▷ *Trends:* lasting at least one year and no more than five years.

An example of a trend is the gradual disappearance of the tie among executives and managers. The yuppie, typical of the 1980s and 90s, is being replaced by a new type of professional, more casual, less formal, more independent, something which is on its way to becoming a macrotrend.

Another example of a trend is downshifting. Currently on the wane due to the economic crisis, this was a trend that spread among many groups of professionals who, after reaching the age of 50, with a relatively high level of income, wealth and some savings, preferred to sacrifice part of their income and professional success in exchange for having more leisure time. As a trend, downshifting was popular in the period 2003–2007, but it is now disappearing.

▷ *Fashions:* lasting a season, a calendar season in the case of footwear, and at most one year in the case of other products and services.

An example is the colors that are popular in clothes for a season of the year. Other examples are the sorts of things collected by school kids within a city or region, or popularity of certain actors and characters generated by hit television shows or movies.

▷ *Fads:* lasting up to a month, sometimes just one or two weeks. These are often linked to sports, cultural, political or media events: for example, when the Pope's visit to a country leads to a brief boom in sales of images, badges or pins.

Table 4.1 gives examples of macrotrends, trends, fashions and fads.

Table 4.1   Macrotrends, trends, fashions and fads

Macrotrends

• Online purchasing

• Google and YouTube as content browsers

• Piercings and tattoos

• Downloading music on the Internet

• Smart phones

• Digital newspapers and magazines

• Men's concern with their physical appearance (metrosexuality)

• Environmental awareness

• Low-cost products

• "Light" foods and beverages

• Pre-cooked and pre-prepared foods

• Bungee-jumping, kite surfing

• The Beatles

Trends

• At-home produce gardening among urban apartment dwellers

• Factory outlets, as a place to purchase goods at the lowest price

• Online games, such as Farmville on Facebook

• The switch from minivans to SUVs

• 3D cinema

- Yellow cancer-awareness bracelets
- Ecological rationalization in purchasing
- Awareness of domestic energy and resource waste (water, electricity, gas, and so on)
- eBooks and, for example, iPads and other electronic tablets
- Social networking
- Networking
- Electric vehicles
- Rubik's cube

Fashions

- Rubber bracelets
- Hit songs of the season
- Movies of the year (for example *Avatar*)
- Balconing (jumping from hotel balconies into swimming pools)
- Bestseller books and records

Fads

- Political and social movements and protests for a short period
- News in the gossip press
- World days in favor of causes (Aids, hunger, and so on)
- Certain festivals and public gatherings
- Limited-edition designer collections at mass-market outlets
- Sales seasons
- Public appearances by high-profile politician, actors, and so on
- High-impact news stories with global reach (for example the miners trapped underground in Chile)

Critics of trend analysis often argue that by the time a trend becomes visible, it is usually too late. They forget that the intention is to identify how this trend can manifest itself in the market. For example, if a trend such as downshifting has not been exploited in the automotive market, a car company might decide to look into the feasibility of a vehicle targeted at people who follow that trend.

Actually, the key is to have the tools to identify trends quickly. And thus it is useful for companies to have outside observers to identify and track emerging trends, fashions and fads.

For example, the advertising agency DDB offers a service called SignBank in which it has developed an impressive network of trend "sign-spotters" spread across the globe. These people are not necessarily employees of its network of advertising agencies, rather they also include people who join the network out of a desire to take part in the trend spotting.

Many observers are watching for signs of trends in the towns and cities where they live: on the streets, in the stores, everywhere. Any novelty they detect, any social change, fashion, taste or trend is added to SignBank. If, for example, a sign-spotter in Tokyo discovers that among certain people it has become fashionable to wear mismatched socks, combining different colors and patterns, he or she will add this information to the data bank that, through the Internet, all the sign-spotters participate in.

The remark "a different sock on each foot" will be attributed a series of "tags", a classification that enables the information to be easily found or to come up when someone searches for something related to the trend.

For example, "a different sock on each foot" would be tagged with the categories fashion, textiles, footwear, foot, color, pattern. Thus, if a creative director in San Francisco is looking for inspiring ideas or trends, he or she searches SignBank for "textile" and "a different sock on each foot" will come up as a result, among many others signs similarly tagged.

This is just one example of how to exploit the new technologies. Blogs and social networks are a tremendous source of potential external partners when gathering information or tracking trends. In the rest of this chapter we will delve further into these sources of information and how they can be used.

Social classes

Complementing the above information, something that is often overlooked and that is essential to the success of a company's commercial innovations, is the description, composition and evolution of social classes in the target region or country of an innovation.

It used to be that social classes evolved rather slowly, but today large movements of capital in global financial markets, changing bank lending policies, expansions and restrictions of central banks' monetary policies, as well as the continual formation and bursting of economic bubbles, mean rapid changes in the composition of social classes.

In the West, the consolidation of the middle classes, the disappearance of upper classes and the greater weight of the poor classes have had a tremendous impact on the structure of demand. The years of economic growth in the US and Europe resulted in the emergence of a wealthy class which consumed a lot thanks to credit and the revaluation of their real estate holdings. At the same time the gap grew between them and the population without access to credit, which, with the crisis, has seen its disposable income shrink significantly. The result is that demand has polarized at the extremes of those seeking price and those seeking quality. Increasingly, groups decide what to buy based on price or quality.

This is a simple example of how social class analysis affects innovation strategies. Such information is vital for facilitators (F) when it comes to choosing the most promising ideas for development.

Market trends

Straddling social trends and past innovation paths are market trends. These consist of a list of topical aspects of general trends, as well as pricing, distribution and communication policies in the target market for our innovation.

For example, if we are going to innovate in coffee, it is important to identify current trends in food and beverages, as well as the trade policies that are having the greatest impact. Table 4.2 shows the result of this example.

Table 4.2   Trends in the food and beverage market

General
• Concern with obesity
• Concern with child nutrition
• Mediterranean diet fashion
• Rise of distribution brand names
• Fashion of extending seasonal lines

Sales
• Preponderance of vending machines
• Internet buying and consumption
• Direct distribution of fresh products, from producer to consumer
• Diversion of investment from television to the Internet
• Low-cost packed goods
• Growth of locally produced and consumed foods

A grasp of these trends can be a source of inspiration for creators. We should ask ourselves, examining each of these market trends, if any of them are relevant to our category.

For instance, continuing with the coffee example, the creators may consider these questions: Does it make sense for coffee producers, as is done with fresh produce, to deliver coffee directly to consumers? Can we launch seasonal coffees?

Searching for information can be a creative task in itself. That is why browsers do not inform but inspire. We advocate an active role for information, data and insights that go beyond mere description and that, in a certain manner, are part of the creative process.

Buying process

The buying process is one of the first things marketing students learn and one of the first they forget when they enter the professional world. The buying process is defined as the set of chronological steps which a customer takes until he or she acquires and uses a given product or service. Figure 4.5 describes the most common stages of a buying process.

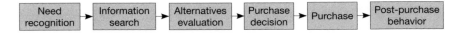

Figure 4.5 **Purchase process steps**

The customer's buying process is of vital importance in innovation processes. All too often innovation is considered as a physical modification of the product for sale or the introduction of new technology. We forget that the competitive advantages also arise in the buying process. The buying process is actually a series of efforts that customers make. These efforts refer not only to money disbursed, but also to the time spent getting information about the best choices, going out to make the purchase, the risk of error, after-sales warranties, and so on.

Any lessening of the effort that you can offer the customer in any one of these steps can be considered an innovation, without any need to modify the product or service being marketed. ExxonMobil continually updates and analyzes the various steps that its customers take when they go to the company's gas stations. Innovations continually arise from using detailed descriptions of the buying process as a stimulus for creativity.

Innovation routes

The result of the foregoing should be a list of possible innovation routes to follow. An innovation route is defined as a path creators can follow in generating ideas.

Continuing with our coffee example, innovation routes could be:

▷ Senior target marketing
▷ Direct sales by producers
▷ Packaging in cans
▷ Seasonal products

These routes are not innovations in themselves, rather they indicate the areas in which you want the creators to come up with ideas. Creativity techniques must be developed with these routes in mind.

As discussed in the previous chapter, "steering" creativity does not undermine its potential, but rather increases the likelihood that its outputs will be relevant.

It is therefore essential that the facilitators (F) and activators (A) of the innovation process decide what possible innovation routes to follow. If a company has no interest in developing direct channels between consumers and producers, it is best to take steps beforehand to avoid having creators waste their efforts on looking for solutions or ideas in this line of innovation.

By contrast, creators must be informed of the routes of greatest strategic interest to or agreement with the overall objectives of the company, so that they can focus their efforts on generating ideas relevant to them.

From B to D: technological and design solutions

Developers (D) are the people who will have to transform concepts and ideas into actual, that is, marketable, products and services. Obviously, much of the information in the previous section is useful when it comes to turning a concept into a product. Aspects such as market trends, social trends and especially adjacent categories are useful for engineers or technicians who develop products.

In general, developers require information of a highly technical nature, that is, related to technology, development and design. So their sources of information are usually in the R&D department, external suppliers or international fairs, where they can find or acquire the necessary technology.

However, there is information, not specifically technical, which can be very useful. We refer to technological solutions and design.

Technological solutions

One of the main difficulties faced by technical departments is not so much the availability of technology but rather its practical application to a given product or development. For example, when developing an online insurance sales service, the programming department may have the programming language, software, programmers, and so on, but not know what form the site with which customers will interact should take. For their part, R&D departments that incorporate new technologies into existing products need to know how the technology has been applied to other products. Let's suppose that a toy company is thinking about incorporating GPS technology in wristwatches; then it would be useful to understand how the manufacturers of sea or land navigation devices have made such products user-friendly.

The information browsers, in their relationship with developers, do not provide technology, but rather ways of using technology: the way a particular technology has been adopted – successfully – in other categories of products and services.

This sort of analysis is similar to that of adjacent categories, but of a different nature. Rather than tracing the history or evolution of a category close to ours, here we examine, for a given technology or incipient development of a prototype, how the manufacturer of a product, whether or not it is related to our market, has decided the customer should use that technology.

For example, when ExxonMobil launched Speedpass, a group of researchers examined how radio technology had been applied to other products and services so that they could explore the possibilities of an automatic payment service, using the same technology, at gas stations.

Another example is the growing trend, following Apple's lead, towards digital devices with one-button controls, very simple and intuitive menus and without any need for a user's manual. Take cars, for instance, where the menus for digital instruments, from GPS to the stereo system to the setup of the car, are inspired in the menus of the latest cell phones.

There are two aspects of technology: that which goes inside the product or service, and that which goes on the outside, which determines usability and plasticity. The form of the technology refers to the latter. And it has more to do with social trends in the use of technology than with technical aspects.

Design

To a large extent, the same thing goes for design. When it comes to turning ideas into products and, eventually, producing prototypes, developers need as much information as possible about what's happening right now in other categories of products and services in terms of materials, colors, shapes, sizes and designs.

Information browsers are not designers, but a brief report on trends in design is essential to ensure that a new product is ahead of the game and that it will be embraced by early adopters and trendsetters.

Table 4.3 is an example of the sort of information that browsers can provide developers with for the development a new memory stick (USB).

Table 4.3 Example of design points for a memory stick

Fashionable shapes: rounded
Proportions: more symmetrical than elongated
Sizes: small
Colors: white, light
Materials: lightweight
Finishes: smooth, matte
Complements: minimize; only ring or buckle, no string

From B to E: marketing formulas

For the execution or implementation of an innovation, that is, its market launch, browsers should provide the executors (E) with three pieces of information that will help define the best marketing approach:

▷ recent successful marketing strategies
▷ recent successful marketing tactics
▷ learning from errors

Recent successful marketing strategies

This is a report on the marketing strategies followed in recently launched products and services and that:

▷ were based on the same technological innovation
▷ or targeted the same customers, irrespective of product or service, category or technology
▷ or had nothing to do with our customers or technology, but that represented innovative, winning strategies.

Recent successful marketing tactics

In this case, the method is to propose, for each of the three Ps of marketing strategy (price, place and promotion), possible analogies between the prototype to be launched on the market and recent successful launches.

The technique is similar to the one we described in the section on possible routes of adjacent categories (can we innovate coffee along the same lines as innovation of energy drinks?), but taken to the tactical level of the marketing mix. You make an inventory of interesting and innovative tactics regarding prices, channels and communication, and then you examine how they might be applied in designing the launch of a product that has already been developed.

For example, let's imagine that the new product is a line of coffee-based beverages with seasonal flavors: coffee and mint, coffee and chocolate, coffee and cinnamon, coffee and caramel. Browsers could provide interesting information on the sorts of tactics used with other products as a source of inspiration in the development of the marketing mix of a similar product that launched flavors.

Learning from errors

There is a natural tendency to analyze marketing successes, yet very few publications or studies seek to document why certain products and services fail. However, the lessons to be learned from the mistakes of others are always helpful. In order to assist the executors, browsers should produce a report examining the pitfalls and mistakes of other manufacturers in similar innovations.

At the end of 2010, CNN published the list of the biggest technology failures of the year.[3] It is revealing to note that some of the companies on the list are also the most innovative. This proves that innovating is associated with a certain level of risk and failure:

1   iPhone 4 "Antennagate"
2   3-D TV
3   Microsoft Kin

 4 Nexus One
 5 Facebook Privacy
 6 Google Buzz
 7 Gawker Media Hackers
 8 Content Farms
 9 Digg Relaunch
10 iTunes Ping

Techniques and methods for gathering information

In addition to what we have discussed in previous sections, here we introduce three relatively recent main search areas (Internet monitoring; ethnographic studies; and geolocation) that are gradually outstripping the more
qualitative techniques used until now (in-depth interviews and focus groups),
which we won't bother to go into here because our readers should be familiar
with them.

Network monitoring

Just a few years ago, it was believed that the community of Internet users was
not representative of offline consumers. Internet use was not yet very widespread and any conclusions based on its users would be biased or relevant
only to certain segments of society. This is no longer the case. The Internet
has grown and its use spread so far that in many countries its representativeness is now accepted. Many of the traditional segments targeted by companies and brands communicate on the Net.

This offers the possibility to exploit blogs, forums and social networks as
sources of information in the innovation process. It is not even necessary to
develop new tools or search engines. Current tools used by webmasters to
find out what people are saying about their products and services in blogs,
forums and social networks enable us to listen in and get a grasp of how
brands can give customers what they really want.

The advantage of blogs and opinion forums is that Internet users express
better – and more openly! – their sentiments and thoughts about the products and services they consume. Bloggers and other contributors to online
content are, in themselves, avid about the things that drive them to write. So
when we read a blog we are, in general, reading expert consumers, deeply
involved, emotional and sincere. Writing is a form of expression that brings
out underlying attitudes and sentiments, so that blogs, forums and social
networks are a source of particular interest for detecting insights.

For example, in early May 2009, StubHub, an online ticket agency, used
the tool Scout Labs to identify a surge in negative sentiment posted on
blogs after a rain-delay in a Yankees–Red Sox game and hundreds of ticket-
holders were told it was cancelled. Initially StubHub refused to give refunds,

but after detecting the barrage of criticism on the Internet, the company offered disgruntled fans discounts and credits and is now rethinking its bad weather policy.

We take it for granted that our readers know the difference between a blog, a forum and information sharing on the personal pages of members of social networks. But: how can we sift through and analyze this vast amount of information floating around the Internet?

Today there are many ways to listen in on the Internet: a set of netnographic tools to keep up to date on changes in opinions within social networks, their effects on the image and positioning of brands, and the evolution of ongoing conversations. These include:

▷ **Google Trends**: tracks the relative frequency with which users have entered a literal query. It is a simple, quick and inexpensive way to quantify people's interests and how they evolve over time. Indispensable in, for example, monitoring fads, fashions, trends and macrotrends.

▷ **Technorati**: a blog search engine, in a sense the Google of the blogosphere. It enables researchers to find blogs that deal with specific issues (for example dieting), determine how relevant and/or authoritative a blog is and, finally, to track conversations within a blog.

▷ **Alerts** (on, for example, Google and Yahoo): a system for programming automatic message sending to an email address each time someone posts something on the Internet that contains a series of predetermined words or phrases. For example, if you want to monitor downshifting, you can set Google Alerts to send you an email whenever new information appears on the Internet, whether it's in publications, forums or blogs, containing the word "downshifting". It can also be managed through a news feed. Alerts give us the capacity to know who is saying what in real time.

▷ **StepRep** reputation monitor: a tool for tracking what is said on the Internet about specific individuals, companies or brands. It enables you to create a company or brand profile and share things with other companies and brands as well as to monitor relevant opinions posted on different networks, classified by the sign for the sentiments generated (very negative to very positive).

▷ **Social Mention**: searches the entire Internet for signs of the strength of a brand (percentage of times it is mentioned), the sentiments it arouses (number of favorable opinions per negative opinion), the influence of those who speak about the brand on the network and the likelihood that those who talk about your brand will do so again. Its usefulness in the innovation process is obvious: to mine for insights about brands and products and, once an innovation has been launched, to actively track how it's performing on the market in the face of rapid changes and whether changes are needed in communication.

▷ **Scout Labs**: enables you to monitor blogs, social networks, articles, websites, and so on for positive or negative views with an advanced system for assessment of what is said on the Internet. Many companies already use it to "listen to" and "talk with" their customers, strengthen their relationship with them and, ultimately, to innovate and give their products and services greater value.

Other new, increasingly sophisticated operational tools appear every day, for example:

▷ www.wefeelfine.org: website showing more than 2,000 sentiments being expressed around the world at the moment the consultation is made, segmented by gender, age, country, date and weather.
▷ www.wordle.net: generates "word clouds" from text you enter on the Internet. The clouds give greater importance to words that appear more frequently in the source text.
▷ http://twittersentiment.appspot.com/: yields the positive and negative opinions posted on Twitter regarding a word entered in its browser.

Between the time of this book being written and its publication, new tools will have appeared. The message is that this trend is unstoppable. Mining the online world for information is growing and it will continue to cut into the share of offline information, with the two complementing each other. We can see evidence of this in the emergence of market research companies that rely exclusively on blogs and social networks. People are doing very in-depth studies into how to get value from social networks, and one way is to provide market researchers and marketing managers with the tools to perform small surveys of targeted users of Twitter, LinkedIn and Facebook, who give their opinions as quickly and readily as they comment on what they are doing. This is similar to online panels, but in a social network environment in real time.

Ethnographic studies

Here is a very good way to introduce this topic:

> We all know what customers want. We're confident that we understand the problem. We look at reams of marketing reports. We conduct the focus groups. We survey them. We have plenty of data. Guess what? It's not enough. Data can only indicate facts. If we fail to descend into the field and take the long walk in the customer's boots, if we don't bother to look over their shoulders while they struggle with their problem, and if we take the customer's word at face value, we can't legitimately call our design strategy "customer centric". Rarely do customers know what they need. So rarely can they tell you. So rarely does a great innovation come from arms-length market research. The solution? Learn to see. Live the customer's life.[4]

For the sociologist Anthony Giddens, ethnography is the direct study of people using participant observation and interviews to learn about social behavior. Ethnographic research aims to reveal the meanings of the individual's social reality through the direct involvement of the researcher, who takes an active role in the daily activities of the person being studied, observing what happens, recording what he or she does in real time and, if necessary, directly asking the subject for explanations and interpretations of his or her decisions, actions and behavior. The result is a comprehensive description of customs, beliefs, myths, genealogies, history and language.

The idea is to study the subject in his or her natural habitat: at home, shopping, workplace or place of leisure, according to the aims of the research. Thus, the researcher becomes a "naive visitor" in the subject's world who closely observes the consumer in his or her everyday life. Objectivity is not the aim, given that the emphasis is on the perspective of consumers themselves and the meanings of their behavior. The main ethnographic techniques are:

▷ *Direct, face-to-face observation*, also called *participant observation*. This can be done in the home of the consumer (in-home visits), in stores (shopper trips) or for an entire day accompanying a group of customers who make up a representative sample of a company's clientele (a day in my life). For example, Vaughn Beals, CEO of Harley Davidson, directed his senior management staff to attend biker rallies and join mass Harley rides. On one such field trip, Willie Davidson, grandson of the company's founder, saw the phenomenon of customizing motorcycles that inspired subsequent Harley Davidson designs.

▷ *Video recording and logs.* This can be done in two ways: (1) Filming customers while performing different tasks related to purchasing, consumption or use of products. For example, Whirlpool, aware that the users of their appliances may find it difficult to articulate their needs, holds usability sessions, where three different cameras capture what happens from different angles. In one of these videos they found users had problems finding and replacing the water filter on their refrigerators.[5] Designers used this footage in redesigning some parts of their refrigerators. In another example, to improve design and website navigability, webcams film Internet users in action to see how they navigate by following the movement of their eyes, at the same time recording where they go and what they click on at any given moment. This information, aggregated quantitatively, helps to visualize how users move around websites; just as in the 1960s and 70s, researchers learned to understand how customers moved around supermarkets. (2) The second possibility is to supply video cameras to customers or consumers whose lives and needs we want to understand, asking them to film aspects of their daily lives. For example, we the authors did a study for Nike in which the aim was to understand the evolving world of young people. We gave cameras to a sample of young people from different cities and the results were astounding. Not only did they film the places they frequented, but they also showed us their bedrooms, inside their closets, the posters on the walls ... intimate and private parts of the lives of a focus group that would have had difficulty verbalizing or describing such things and instead filmed and recorded them, achieving a sort of immersion in this target group, of profound usefulness for the manufacturer.

▷ *Audio recording and logs.* The new digital recorders, with their high storage capacity, compactness and easy handling, offer a new tool for ethnographic studies. The method is to give the customer or consumer a recorder and ask them to always carry it with them, and in specified situations, to record their thoughts and opinions, what they feel and see. For example, to identify the services most often requested through a telephone operator using GPRS (General Packet Radio Service) technology, we gave recorders to a total of 50 potential users. During their daily movements, they expressed their information needs, the degree of urgency in obtaining such information and how much they would be willing to pay for it at the time. In real time, in traffic jams, we found a very low level of price sensitivity in receiving information on alternative, traffic-free routes. Using traditional techniques, in focus groups, where no one was actually running late for a meeting while stuck in traffic, the prices people would have paid for the same services were much lower. By recording needs in real time, we got a much truer picture of price sensitivity for services. This telecom operator designed its new mobile content service based on this ethno-graphic method.

▷ *Consumer diaries.* Finally, another way in which the people in a study can record in real time what you want to know about them is in writing. Traditional U&A (usage and attitudes) studies record weekly or monthly shopping and consumption in a structured questionnaire, typical of quantitative research surveys. The bias that stems from recall of the amount, frequency and brands consumed, such as a soft drink, is enormous. On the other hand, in innovation it is increasingly impor-tant to understand how we can generate consumption opportunities from desire competitors and situation competitors. There may be more opportunity for a soft drink manufacturer in launching an innovation that "steals" volume of coffee than in launching an innovation that "steals" from competitive beverages. If it is hard to get information from someone about their consumption of a particular product, imagine if in the same survey we also want to know about the habits of other desire competitors. The bias inflates exponentially. This can be corrected to a large degree with ethnographic studies on paper. The method consists in having the subject keep a sort of diary of products consumed, purchased or services used according to a number of specific categories, making entries at the end of or at several points during the day. Not only is the information more reliable (it is easy to remember what you've done during the same day!), but it is also used to get additional information on that particular recent moment (situation, location, time, social context, reasons for choice of product, reasons for choice of brand, purchases or products consumed at the same time, and so on). This information is very difficult to get when using a declarative recall or memory technique. Consumer diaries, notepads or the like can also be used for any other purpose. The idea is that the customer has the opportunity to note in real time or at end of the day the information we need.

These techniques have multiple advantages:

▷ *First advantage:* They enable us to detect consumer insights and market imperfections that customers would be unlikely to express in a focus group or in-depth interview, since, in many cases, they are either ignorant or unaware of such information.

▷ *Second advantage:* The quality of information obtained from a videotape or direct observation (an image is worth a thousand words) is infinitely superior to that of a verbalized description of what we want to study or know.

▷ *Third advantage:* In order to know what is going through the mind of consumers or customers it is imperative to enable them to express themselves in real time, while they are having the thought or experiencing the sentiment. Traditional techniques rely on memory or verbalization of such information, such that the subject focuses only on the most obvious, habitual or memorable points, leaving out many situations that may constitute opportunities or highlight unsatisfied needs for innovators.

Nevertheless, ethnography has become very popular recently, but its use and application by companies is not yet widespread. The time, costs and essential skills of specialists who conduct this technique are high, and therefore, not many companies are applying it.

Geolocation

Nowadays, using the Internet, it is commonplace for people to locate on a map the exact geographical position of all sorts of content (text, photo, video or opinion). Google Earth came first and led the way and since then innovative applications and platforms have been emerging to further expand the possibilities of qualitative consumer research.

A good example of this trend is Foursquare, a mobile social network with over two million registered users who share their location and opinions thereof, know where their contacts are and read their comments. Foursquare offers real-time information about the places visited or frequented in a given city based on the geographical location of the user. The users themselves generate their own trusted network of friends. The members of a network receive each other's opinions when they visit a given place. This facilitates monitoring of consumer behavior, obtaining quantitative information on the number and frequency of visits and qualitative information (comments and recommendations). Currently, Foursquare is growing by 15,000 new users a day.

Geolocation as a marketing tool is still in its infancy, but its simplicity and power, the advent of low-cost phones (smart phones) and the relating of real and virtual worlds by creating experiences and emotional bonds with brands augur a bright future for it, including as an ethnographic tool.

TOTAL INNOVATION SYSTEM – Summary Chapter 4

Main person/s in charge of each role

A Activators	B Browsers	C Creators	D Developers	E Executors	F Facilitators
Top management (GM or Chief Innovation Officer)	Market research department				
Employees	Market research suppliers				
Suppliers	Sociologists				
Distributors	Marketing				
Clients	Sales				
Investors	Opinion leaders				
Universities	Watchers' panel				
Scientific community	R&D				
Inventors	Other internal departments				
Engineering companies	Other suppliers or third parties				

Up-bottom activation
In-out activation
Bottom-up activation
Out-in activation

Techniques employed by each role

A Activators	B Browsers	C Creators	D Developers	E Executors	F Facilitators
Scope of innovation	Innovation review				
Innovation levels	Analysis of adjacent categories				
Focus of innovation	Internal consulting				
Innovation guidelines	Social trend/ social classes				
Innovation checklist	Market trends				
	Buying process				
	Innovation routes				
	Technological solutions				
	Design referents				
	Successful strategies and tactics/learning from errors				
	Network monitoring				
	Ethnographic				
	Geolocation				

INNOVATION PROCESS

Browsers ↔ Creators
Activators↔Facilitators↔Developers
Executors

CREATIVE CULTURE

Project proposals
Process approval

INNOVATION REWARDS

INNOVATION METRICS

RESULTS

Innovation framework
Innovation guidelines
Innovation checklist

STRATEGIC PLANNING FOR INNOVATION

5 Creators

What is a creator?

A creator is the person responsible for coming up with ideas throughout the innovation process. His or her ideas are aimed at becoming innovations.

There is an interesting contradiction in the role of creators. On the one hand, creators are a cornerstone of the innovation process. Before they intervene, we have clear objectives, a process underway and relevant, valuable and continual information. But as yet, there is nothing to develop, nothing to give shape to. Nothing we can hand over to R&D or product development to turn into something real. On the other hand, the creators produce ideas.

Some say that the world is filled with ideas and that ideas, in themselves, are not of much value. What matters is the ability to make them fresh, valuable and relevant. Creators should not simply provide ideas, they should provide plausible ideas which can be implemented and which add value for the customer. And that's not so simple.

We cannot dissociate the ability to generate ideas from their quality. The role of the creators is not just to create ideas but to create *good* ideas. The techniques and working methods we propose here are have to do both with the generation of ideas and with their relevance.

Who the creators are

A common complaint among managers is that their organizations lack creative people. We do not agree entirely with this statement. Toyota is an example of how widespread creativity can be in an organization. Toyota claims that every year about 70 percent of its employees provide ideas and suggestions, many of which are implemented. In businesses there is much more latent creativity than is often assumed. Before we start hiring creative people or outsourcing creativity we must examine carefully whether our organization really is lacking in creative types or whether the problem is that we put too many brakes and barriers on their creativity.

In our later chapter on how to develop a creative culture, we deal with this issue in more detail, examining the myths surrounding creativity and innovation in organizations, and the main factors that inhibit the creativity of human resources (see Chapter 12).

But for now, let's suppose that the organization truly is short on creative people. In this case, we have three options:

▷ train internal staff in creative techniques
▷ recruit new people with a creative profile
▷ outsource creativity to other organizations

The first option, training people to be creative, is perfectly feasible. Creativity can be taught and developed. The Whirlpool Company wanted to become a more innovative company and chose 4,000 of their employees to receive creativity training. They were to do their regular jobs but with an eye to innovating. This was a good investment because Whirlpool discovered a number of new businesses in which it successfully invested.

It is true that, as in sports, art or any other discipline, there will be people who are more capable and who have more innate potential than others, but the minimum levels of creativity required for innovation can be found in a very high percentage of the population and in virtually all people with a higher education. What people need – in addition to an innovation process that clearly defines the scope and role of creativity – are the right tools and techniques for generating ideas. In the previous chapter, we recommended that browsers produce bits of information that can become a direct stimulus for creativity. Our experience shows that among the people who are assigned to produce ideas, you don't need a large number of creators, provided that the techniques and tools they have are effective. Good creativity techniques and idea generation tools make methodical people creative. In this chapter, we will list, describe and illustrate some of these tools and how to use them.

The second option is to bring into the organization people with a truly creative profile. Samsung has followed this by organizing a standing venture group in each of its major product areas. One group of creative researchers works continuously to improve its TV sets; another group works continuously to improve its cell phones.

And what is that creative profile? There is much debate on the nature of a creative person and many authors have analyzed the structure of the personality and psychology of the most creative minds in history. Some conclusions and consensus have been reached on this matter, which we will address in the following section.

The third option is outsourcing. There are many creativity suppliers and experts that one can bring into a creative process on a temporary basis. When you outsource creativity you must be very clear about what you want from the supplier: ideas or the preparation and leading of a creativity session? In the first case, you pay for specific ideas that can be turned into value. This happens when a company hires IDEO, the design firm that has won so many awards and helped Apple come out with some of its best products. In the second case, you pay to have someone prepare and lead creativity sessions involving people from your organization. The first case is obviously the highest-cost option and the supplier must commit to contributing ideas that can be introduced into your innovation project pipeline. In the second case, you hire someone to organize part of the company's creative activity, one of the phases of an innovation project. The costs are much lower and you cannot expect that good ideas will necessarily emerge.

Let's say that in the first case you pay for output and in the second you pay for time. In the first case, we recommend that, since the role of creators (C) will be played by a third party, the latter be engaged from the start in the innovation process, signing on as another member of the team. This is not an easy decision. Creativity is the engine of innovation and the decision to put one of the primary functions of business survival and growth in the hands of an outsider should not be taken lightly. Which company should you choose? What level of confidentiality should you demand? Do you want a simple outsourcing contract or should you be thinking about a long-term agreement? These are the kinds of questions we need to consider when outsourcing innovation consulting or creativity specialists.

Outsourcing can be done in a collaborative manner, establishing a network of external agents for ongoing generation of ideas.

> P&G has helped establish several outside networks of innovators it turns to for ideas the company can develop in-house. These networks include NineSigma, which links up companies with scientists at university, government, and private labs; YourEncore Inc., which connects retired scientists and engineers with businesses; and yet2.com Inc., an online marketplace for intellectual property.[1]

We do not include here co-creation as an outsourcing formula, because we prefer to view it as a tool of creativity and, thus, we will address it a little later in this chapter.

Profile of creative people

In the previous section we said that, when faced with the absence of creative people or the need to identify them within our organization, we need to know what sort of profile to look for. How can you tell when someone has the potential to be a creator in the innovation process? We shall examine the personal characteristics, qualities and most common resources of creators, and the sensations and feelings they experience when they create, and how you can recognize a creative person.

Personal characteristics

According to Gilda Waisburd,[2] the traits of creative people are as follows:

▷ Flexible (they go beyond the obvious)

▷ Fluid (they generate many ideas about a problem)
▷ Elaborative (they expand the task in detail)
▷ Tolerant of ambiguity (they stand up well to conflict)
▷ Able to see the whole (systemic approach)
▷ Inquiring (interest in many disciplines)
▷ Sensitive to the interests of others (they understand the needs of others)
▷ Curious (interested in "playing" with things)
▷ Independent (with ideas of their own)
▷ Reflective (they think about what they see and hear)
▷ Action-oriented (they go beyond thinking and the idea, act)
▷ Able to concentrate (they work in a consistent manner)
▷ Persistent (they don't give up easily)
▷ Committed (they get involved with things)
▷ Sense of humor (they are able to laugh, use humor to put things in perspective)

Personal qualities

Barron, Gardner, Taylor, Stemberg, Torrance and Weisberg are among the authors who argue that creative people have the following qualities:

▷ Verbal fluency
▷ High IQ
▷ Imagination
▷ Ability to influence others and one's environment
▷ Ability to take risks
▷ Interest in properly defining the problem to be solved

Common resources

▷ Use metaphors
▷ Use images
▷ Use logic
▷ Usually ask themselves the "why" in what they observe

Feeling

Creative people are passionate about what they do and are not easily discouraged when faced with difficulties. They exploit their own potential and energy, aware that their time is finite. For them, creativity is an experience in which they forget their past and future and immerse themselves in a timeless present that puts them into a state of self-realization.

Manifestation

We can say that a person is creative when he or she has the ability to come up with original combinations and syntheses. Creativity is manifested in the capacity to associate and combine ideas in new ways. There is also creativity in breaking down an area and seeing its components. Some people are good at making Cartesian distinctions. That is, they are good at analysis as well as synthesis.

We will see that the main techniques and tools of creativity are based on the common resources of creative people and some of their qualities.

How creativity works

Before going into the set of creative tools and techniques most commonly used in business and marketing innovation, we need to understand how creative thinking works, what its logic is.

There is a prevalent opinion that creative ideas come about magically and accidentally. Farah Ramzan Galant, CEO of Britain's largest advertising agency, AMV BBDO, said "I think creative communities are always going to be a little bit eccentric and a little bit out of the box because that's the way creative ideas come about. They don't come about because you follow a set of rules, and they don't come about because you logically solve a problem. You understand diagnostically what a problem is, you use the data and then you make a leap to create an idea."[3]

We agree that many ideas occur quite spontaneously on a walk, taking a shower, attending an art show. But creative thinking can be enhanced by following well-known, well-defined stages, which can be followed deliberately, even deciding how much time we wish to devote to each one. Specifically, creativity follows three stages:

1   Choice of focus
2   Displacement
3   Connection (an older scheme talks about incubation, illumination, and implementation, the 3 I's).

Choice of focus

Creativity is a type of inductive thinking. It starts with the specific in order to establish general rules. So the first step in creativity is to define a focus, something in particular that we are going to concentrate on. A focus can be anything as long as it is concrete and well defined. Focuses tend to be problems, objectives or physical things. Here are some examples:

Focus in the form of the definition of a problem
▷ Motivation among the sales force is low

▷ Consumers don't like the way our products are packaged
▷ It's hard for us to attract new customers
▷ We are seeing a drop in repeat purchase rates
▷ We aren't doing well in the north

Focus in the form of the definition of a goal

▷ We want a greater presence in the over-60 market
▷ We want to improve the quality of service without higher costs
▷ We want to be able to innovate without disrupting the production chain
▷ We want to increase our market share by 10 percent
▷ We want to reduce our product portfolio without losing sales

Focus on a tangible item

▷ We need a new, more modern cap and label
▷ We need to upgrade to a hydraulic braking system
▷ We need to innovate in the startup speed of our computers
▷ We need to offer higher-speed internet access in our hotels

Defining the focus is enormously important. Indeed, the activators (A) and browsers (B) have already been working on narrowing down the potential focuses on which to concentrate when it comes to producing new ideas. As we explained in our previous book, *Lateral Marketing*, the scheme of the marketing process is ideal for choosing a focus. The marketing process follows these steps:

Stages of the marketing process

1 Definition of market (by the three dimensions: Need – Customers – Situations)
2 Segmentation (criteria for segmenting our current and potential market)
3 Target (which of the segment(s) we are going to aim for)
4 Positioning (attributes that make up the differential competitive advantage)
5 Product
6 Core benefit
7 Physical product and its components
8 Extended product
9 Price
10 Distribution channels
11 Promotional and communications policy

By the nature of this scheme, if we focus on the first stages in the marketing process, the resulting change or innovation will tend to be more radical or disruptive than if we focus on the later ones. This is only logical: a change or modification in the dimensions that define our market will mean a greater impact than if we simply modify an advertising policy or pricing scheme.

Of course, this scheme for defining the focus during a creativity session is not valid if the innovation is purely technological. In this case, what we recommend is subdividing into parts or components the technology with which we want to innovate through schemes that go from the most general and basic to the most particular or accessory. In any case, we should subdivide into parts whatever we want to generate ideas on. The second stage of the creative process requires us to make displacements in the focus, so the more we break down what we want to change, the more possibilities we will have.

The choice of one focus does not necessarily rule out others. Focuses are not mutually exclusive. Obviously, you can work with diverse and multiple focuses during an innovation process, especially during creativity sessions. What is advisable is to focus on a specific aspect, spend some time making displacements and then move on to a new focus.

Displacement

The second stage consists of displacing (also called provoking or disrupting) the logic. This means taking the focus and coming up with something illogical in relation to it. It is here that different creativity techniques, also called disruptions in logical thinking, come into play. Displacement is also called provoking because, in reality, we are proposing an impossibility, a paradox. We deliberately provoke, with the idea of stimulating new connections, which is precisely the third stage of creative thinking.

Let's look at an example. Taking as our focus the price of the product, a provocation or displacement would be, say, to propose the opposite: "instead of us charging our customers, we pay our customers."

Obviously, this is an absurdity, a paradox, a provocation, an impossibility. This isn't an idea. It's simply a provocation. Here there is no creativity because we have not connected (third stage); we have not completed the process, which consists precisely in finding how the provocation inspires us in a change in pricing, which was the focus of our change.

So we should not worry while making displacements. We aren't looking for the solution yet, rather we're generating inputs so that our brains will get down to finding solutions that become new connections, which is where the real creativity comes in.

In the next section we're going to examine in detail the different creativity techniques applied to innovation and we'll see that, indeed, all of them are established, organized systems for making displacements on or provoking specific focuses. Alex Osborn was a leading author and researcher on creativity who concluded that virtually all the games and creative techniques to cause a displacement or provocation are based on seven operations.[4] We've narrowed them down to six, under the acronym SECRET:[5]

▷ Substitute parts of the focus
▷ Eliminate parts of focus
▷ Combine elements of the focus with any others
▷ Rearrange elements of the focus
▷ Exaggerate aspects or qualities of the focus
▷ Transpose elements of the focus

The above example, where we went from charging to paying our customers, is nothing more than a transposition of the focus: the price charged to customers. Any of these operations, applied to a specific focus, produces disruptions in logical thinking and, therefore, displacements or provocations. Interestingly, these six operations are rooted in mathematics. Eliminating parts of a whole is like subtraction; combining is like addition (the number of items grows); substituting is subtracting then adding; exaggerating is playing with powers (one number raised to another); transposing is the operation of one divided by another number (the inverse of exaggeration). And finally, rearranging is changing the order of the factors.

Connection

The final stage is to connect through movement. This means taking the displacement or paradox and trying to make sense of it, finding an explanation – which will require changes or movements in the provocation. This is important because there are people who think that connections are made by taking the provocation and simply finding a rationale for it: which rarely works, since in that case it would already be resolved and would not be impossible. We need an additional movement. That means introducing new ideas or possibilities so that the paradox makes some sort of sense. For example, if we try to solve the paradox of paying the price to our customers, a possible solution would be to extend a loan to purchase the product at the supermarket. As we see, the paradox has been partially solved, but it has also been modified. We have introduced the element of credit so that the approach makes sense. Thanks to this movement (consumer credit) we have made the connection.

This way of making connections is not all that complex. The human mind, designed to make connections, unable to remain inactive when faced with an absurdity, will search, even the dream state, for ways to connect up unconnected ideas. That's why creativity has more to do with the art of dealing with impossibilities than the ability to solve them, a universal ability in which it is precisely those minds considered less creative and more analytical that get the best results. That's why we said that creativity and innovation are possible even in organizations considered short on creativity and strong on systematic thinking. All it takes is to challenge your top technicians and engineers with impossibilities, provocations and paradoxes. But not with just any absurdity, rather those that come out of a proper narrowing of goals and appropriate choice of focuses based on relevant information.

We recommend working first on the connections on an individual basis, in isolation, and then have everyone share the solutions, either complete or partial, that they have come up with for connecting the displacement. Some techniques propose the opposite, to try making the connections as a group. These are eminently group-oriented creativity techniques. In any case, what is important is that here we have presented the three steps of creativity sequentially. And the most efficient way, as we will see immediately below through the tools we present, is to choose a focus, allocate a certain amount of time (without trying to make connections for the moment) to generate a good number of displacements and then take those displacements, one by one, and take time to resolve them.

In other words, creativity works like this:

One focus → One displacement → One connection

But its practical application works thus:

One focus → Many displacements without trying to connect → Possible connections

Another focus → Many displacements without trying to connect → Possible connections

Another focus → Many displacements without trying to connect → Possible connections

And so on.

We give these details about how creativity works for two reasons:

▷ First, so that anyone can design their own creative techniques, either individual or group. In the last section of this chapter we will detail a number of techniques that have been thoroughly tested and that are complete in themselves. All have been designed by creativity experts and based on the above foundations. The advantage is that we don't have to do anything: just put them into practice. The disadvantage is that they are designed for specific situations. We have argued that each of the six A-to-F roles must interact freely with the others. Creators are not there only to produce ideas for developers (D), although that is the bulk of their function, but also to produce ideas as needed by the executors (E) and even the browsers (B) in each of their functions. Throughout, and at any point during, the innovation process there is a constant need for new ideas. With a good grasp of how creativity works in its most essential components, you can design creative games or creativity sessions to solve any problem in relation to any of the other A-to-F roles.

▷ Second, because this book is more oriented toward business and commercial innovation than technical, technological or scientific. With what we explain here, it would be relatively simple to "invent" or design new tools for each discipline or type of innovation required.

Methods for generating ideas

There are many techniques and methods for generating ideas, both in the creative processes in general and in those directly related to the realm of innovation. Those we present here are considered to be the most effective, most proven and most focused on business innovation:[6]

▷ Synectics
▷ Blue Ocean strategy
▷ Morphological analysis
▷ Lateral marketing
▷ Attributes listing

▷ Scenario analysis
▷ Visits
▷ Co-creation
▷ Redefining customer value

For each method we deal with the following points: what it is; how to apply the technique; a complete example; for which situations it is more recommendable; case studies of innovations obtained with this technique or, alternatively, companies that have applied it; and, finally, a commentary on the creative formula behind the tool. After dealing with this series of techniques, we enumerate the info-searching methods used by the browsers from the previous chapter that are most useful for each creativity technique.

Synectics

What is it?

Synectics is a problem-solving method that stimulates thought processes of which the subject is not always fully aware. The method was developed by George M. Prince and William J. Gordon in the 1960s and since then has continued to be refined, developed and used. Synectics takes a process in the form of a metaphor to make the familiar strange and the strange familiar. Although it has many different applications, here we describe the essence of the method in terms of business innovation.

How is it applied?

(1) The basic idea is to define the problem or area in which we want to innovate, specifying some of its elements. Then we think of (2) analogous situations, devices, natural phenomena or anything else that relates to one or more elements of the problem. (3) Then we describe these phenomena and (4) we look for possible connections with the elements of our problem.

Let's look at an example: (1) We need to develop policies and actions so that the sales teams will become more proactive and propose ideas to boost sales. So we enumerate the different elements of the problem: (a) All salespeople must participate. (b) We must not force them, their contributions should be free and voluntary. (c) All the ideas from all salespeople are equal in value. (d) This activity should not take up too much of their time.

Then (2) we look for analogies for some of the elements that make up our problem. For example, (a) "All salespeople must participate," is associated with democracy. (3) Now we describe the analogous phenomenon. How does a democracy work? There are political parties and candidates and people vote by depositing ballots in a box. (4) Last, we look for ways to connect the two ideas: democracy and active participation of salespeople. For example, we could set up a kind of party system – that is, working groups assigned in teams who then present their ideas to the others, like candidates in elections. And finally, there could be a box where salespeople could put the ballots with the ideas they want to vote for.

For each element of the problem, various analogies can be formulated. All connections are listed at the end and the best picked with the aim of coming up with a single final design that provides a solution to the problem.

Where is it best applied?

Synectics works especially well for solving problems, upgrading processes and generating new inventions or designs.

Cases studies

Synectics has been used since the 1960s, and in many organizations, from private companies and corporations to public institutions. For example, Nokia uses a technique derived from Synectics in designing cell phones for countries like India and China. One of the characteristics of these countries is that there are lower-class users with less education than the average user cell phones are normally designed for. Nokia took things to the extreme and asked what a cell phone designed for an illiterate person should look like. The company listed the characteristics and limitations of an illiterate person and, from there, the ideas for such a cell phone began to emerge. The outcome? A menu of icons that allows completely illiterate people to navigate through the cell phone, understanding intuitively the different options and utilities.

A famous example: NASA wanted to design a space suit that became airtight. The participants weren't told this. They were told to think about "closing" something. Ideas came up like zippers, bird's nest, buttoning, gluing, and so on. As this progressed, more was revealed, such as this is about closing an article of clothing. Finally they had a lot of ideas about closing a space suit.

On what creative rationale is it based?

Clearly, it is a system based on addressing a problem by dividing it into parts through means of the formulation of analogies.

Blue Ocean strategy

What is it?

Blue Ocean is a strategy designed by W. Chan Kim and Renée Mauborgne which seeks to break with the belief that competition is about either differentiation or cost, to show that the two strategies are not incompatible if you think in terms of how to redefine the industry in which you are competing, thereby creating new oceans (new industries or markets), free of competition. Its aim is to move beyond the fragmented, hypercompetitive markets, saturated with competitors (called red oceans, in reference to the blood let in the fierce fighting among competitors) in order to create new spaces where competition is irrelevant: in sum, temporary monopolies.

How is it applied?

Blue Ocean strategy is described in an extensive book with a wealth of details about its implementation.[7] Here we focus on the essentials, at the risk entailed in any simplification.

The main technique for creating blue oceans is to develop a "strategy canvas" that includes the main factors of competition, investment and delivering value to customers in a given industry. Then each factor is analyzed; deciding how to act on it is based on one of the following actions (the four actions framework):

▷ reduce (which factors should be reduced well below the industry standard?)
▷ eliminate (which factors that the industry takes for granted should be eliminated?)
▷ raise (which factors should be raised well above the industry standard?)
▷ create (which factors should be created because the industry has never offered them?)

Based on these actions, you completely redefine your competitive strategy, the value delivered to the customer and costs, which can attract not only potential customers who previously were not involved in your industry, but also non-potential customers, defined as those who reject outright the products and services of your industry and those who had not even considered them.

The most famous example of Blue Ocean strategy is the Cirque du Soleil. The defining factors of the traditional circus industry were: ticket prices, star performers, animal shows, aisle concession sales, multiple show arenas, fun and humor, suspense and danger, and unique setting. The four actions on each of the factors are shown in Figure 5.1.[8]

Eliminate Stars Animals Sales on corridors Multiple stages	Increase One stage
Reduce Fun and humor Danger	Create One theme Sophisticated atmosphere Multiple shows Music and artistic dancers

Figure 5.1 **Blue Ocean strategy (actions)**
Source: Adapted from W. Chan Kim and Renée Mauborgne. *Blue Ocean Strategy: How to Create Uncontested Market Space and Make Competition Irrelevant.* Harvard Business Press (2005)

As a result, a new curve gave rise to a new circus industry, a blue ocean, as shown in Figure 5.2.

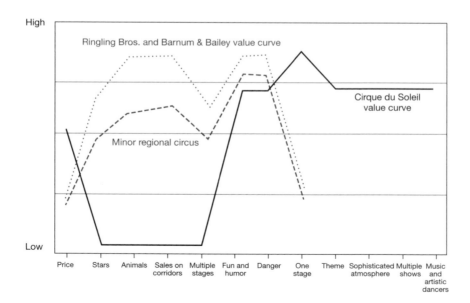

Figure 5.2 **Blue Ocean strategy (factors of competitor circus)**
Source: Adapted from W. Chan Kim and Renée Mauborgne. *Blue Ocean Strategy: How to Create Uncontested Market Space and Make Competition Irrelevant.* Harvard Business Press (2005)

Where is it best applied?

Blue Ocean strategy as a means of innovation is ideal for developing new markets (new customers, new needs or new situations) and business model innovation. It seeks to produce disruptive innovations rather than marginal or tactical ones.

Case studies

Kim and Mauborgne's book contains many cases in which either the technique is applied directly or, at least, the result of a strategy can be expressed in terms of the tool. The most striking example, apart from Cirque du Soleil, is that of Southwest Airlines in its emphasis, well above the industry standard, on friendly service, speed of aircraft and the frequency of point-to-point departures, as well as low fares. And all this at the expense of cutting well below the industry standard for on-board meals, waiting lounges, the range of classes and fares, and connections from hubs.

In her lectures, Reneé Mauborgne also presents the case of the Wii as an example of redefining the videogame industry by getting rid of all wires and also pioneering physical exercise, thus attracting a large number of older users.

On what creative rationale is it based?

Notice that, examined in our terms of how creativity works, Blue Ocean strategy focuses on the key factors that define an industry. As a result, the output will be eminently strategic. The innovation will be profound, resulting in a new market or a new business model, precisely because it is the key defining factors of a market that are displaced.

When displacing or provoking, we use four actions belonging to our group of six: eliminate, raise, reduce or incorporate new ones (which is nothing more than a way of combining).

The connection results from analyzing many different options and examining which might be most useful for the customer and profitable for the company, and can attract the greatest number of potential and non-potential customers.

Morphological analysis

What is it?

Morphological analysis is an analytical-combinatorial method created by Fritz Zwicky, an astronomer at the California Institute of Technology. Its aim is to solve problems by analyzing their component parts.[9]

How is it applied?

The steps are: (1) choose a problem to solve, and (2) analyze what attributes make it up (this should refer to physical parts, processes, functions or aesthetics). In deciding which attributes to include, we can ask ourselves whether or not a particular attribute is relevant. (3) Then we list the various options for each attribute. (4) Next, we make all possible combinations, in each case taking one alternative for each attribute (eliminating those that make no sense). Finally, we analyze all the combinations and test their creative possibilities. The process can be random or it may proceed in an orderly and systematic manner until we run out of possible combinations.

Let's look at an example. Suppose we want to make a better pencil. In step (1), we define an objective. Step (2), we analyze its component attributes: size, point, type of material, type of lead, color, accessories and price. Now (3) we list the options for each attribute (Figures 5.3a and b):

Size	Point	Material	Lead	Color	Accessories	Price
Large	Bold	Wood	Adjustable	Black	Eraser	High
Medium	Fine	Plastic	Non-adjustable	Colors	Spare lead	Mid
Small					Sharpener	Low

Figure 5.3a   **Example of morphological attributes**

Then (4) we start making combinations:

Size	Point	Material	Lead	Color	Accessories	Price
Large	Bold	Wood	Adjustable	Black	Eraser	High
Medium	Fine	Plastic	Non-adjustable	Colors	Spare lead	Mid
Small					Sharpener	Low

Figure 5.3b   **Example of morphological attributes**

Finally in step (5), we evaluate the above: how would a low-price, large, wood, fine-point, non-adjustable black-lead pencil with eraser and sharpener look?

And this is done systematically eliminating impossible choices (for example fine and thick at the same time). We take the different options, evaluate them, improve on them, think about where they take us and, from there, we keep the best until we see if they lead to some sort of innovation.

Where is it best applied?

Morphological analysis is an ideal technique for innovating a physical product or service design. It is also good for innovations in logistics, industrial processes and quality upgrades. It is suitable for marginal innovations, product line extensions, incremental improvements and finding niches within a given category. It leads, in general, to a more tactical than strategic innovation, although that depends on the problem we're dealing with. If we take, for instance, strategic elements of the business, the outcome would lead to more radical innovations. However, since its methodology is based on existing attributes and does not introduce new possibilities from outside the box, it tends to lead to less radical innovations.

Case studies

The changes in features that Olympus continually brings out in the digital camera market reflect a thorough analysis of the different combinations of features that define their product.[10]

On what creative rationale is it based?

We can see that the focus of this technique is on the definition of the problem, splitting the focus and then making combinations out of the different possibilities. It is basically a combinatorial method. The connection is made based on thinking about what possibilities each new combination leads to. It is a very comprehensive approach in the sense that it seeks to check and evaluate the maximum number of (if not all) possible combinations. That is, it generates from a single diagram a very high number of disconnections or provocations.

Lateral marketing at the market level (I): displacement

What is it?

This is a method developed by the authors of this book. It consists of displacing the product or service that you want to innovate to market dimensions (need, situation and customer) heretofore considered impossible.

How is it applied?

The way it's applied is very simple. (1) First you take the product or service you want to innovate. (2) You identify a number of adjacent categories with which you share any of the three dimensions (need, situation or customer). (3) You take the product or service from one of these adjacent categories and draw up an inventory of target customers and the needs it satisfies. (4) Next, you switch the adjacent product or service for the one you want to innovate. (5) When you assign to your product or service the dimensions of the adjacent product you produce numerous provocations, and try to resolve them (6) one by one. Figure 5.4 shows an example.

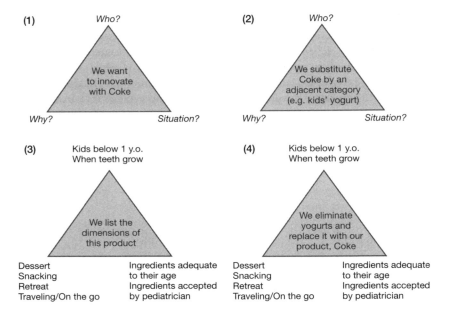

Figure 5.4   **Lateral marketing at the market level (I): displacement**

The fourth diagram in Figure 5.4 shows some interesting provocations Finally, we consider each provocation and try to look for solutions or new concepts. For example: a "Kids' Formula" soft drink with all ingredients accepted by pediatricians, so parents no longer feel bad about giving their kids soft drinks.

Where is it best applied?

Lateral marketing is a technique designed for disruptive innovations, for searching for opportunities beyond our markets, as a means of creating new categories and searching for incrementality, reducing the chances of cannibalization with our existing portfolio.

Case studies

This method has been used by Nestlé on several occasions. One of the innovations that came out of it was a powdered cocoa-based drink for kids, but for before bed rather than with breakfast, called Nesquik Night.

On what creative rationale is it based?

This technique is a simple but effective application of the substitution technique through the hidden analogies task. We substitute one product or service for another, thus causing provocations.

Lateral marketing at the market level (II): analogies

What is it?

As we explained in the chapter on browsers, innovation route analysis of adjacent categories is of tremendous utility as a creative technique. In this case, we will make analogies with the innovation routes of other products, asking ourselves whether it would be possible to follow these routes with the product or service that we sell.

How is it applied?

(1) We choose characteristics of our product. (2) We look for adjacent categories that match any of those characteristics. (3) We get the browsers to document their innovation routes in recent years. (4) We check whether these routes are transferrable to our category.

Nestlé has used this methodology. For innovating in coffee, Nestlé took a look at tea as an adjacent category. Among recent innovations in the tea category, health properties was found as a high-growth category. Next, some important functionalities of tea were browsed in the different types of coffee plants. Green coffee was selected as ideal, thanks to the anti-oxidants it contains, which are very healthy and delay the aging of cells. As a result, a new coffee was successfully launched: Nescafé Green.

Source: Nestlé Spain Coffee Division

Where is it best applied?

This technique is ideal for finding innovation routes with the aim of developing your portfolio and differentiating it from the competition. It can lead to both marginal and disruptive innovations.

Companies who apply it.

This is an easy technique for mass-market goods companies. Nestlé and Frito-Lay have used these techniques in the past.

On what creative rationale is it based?

This type of lateral marketing simply entails the use of analogies: a very efficient, simple and fast means of making relevant combinations.

Lateral marketing at the market level (III): comparisons

What is it?

Here, the idea is to make direct analogies with any element of other products and services that the browsers have picked as a paradigm or inspiration.

How is it applied?

We simply ask ourselves what features do other products or services have that our product does not. The answers we get are used as provocations, which we then try to connect.

Where is it best applied?

It is best used in roughly the same ways as for the displacement technique, but introducing possible solutions at the product level consisting in pure vertical or marginal innovations to extend the existing portfolio.

Case studies

Applying this technique, the pharmaceutical company Novartis asked itself what business conferences had that medical conferences lacked. They realized that business conferences often deal with issues that cut across all industries, such as innovation, human resources policies and strategies. They decided to change the medical conferences they sponsored and organized, moving from conferences for specialists to conferences that cut across all areas of expertise, including non-medical, of interest to the medical sector, such as the economic situation, staff management, how to get the patient more involved, how to generate new ideas, and so on. Novartis realized that the doctor is also a manager and as such has training needs that cut across all areas of expertise. They called this conference the Novartis Excellence Forum, and it was a tremendous hit with doctors, who are the main prescribers of their products.

On what creative rationale is it based?

This technique is based simply on the strength and power of comparisons.

Attributes listing

What is it?

This is a special type of morphological analysis that focuses solely on the attributes or traits of the product or service that you want to change.

How is it applied?

(1) You list the characteristics of your product and service. (2) Increase or decrease the number. (3) You check what the resulting product would be like and whether it might interest some of your potential customers or would boost the volume or rate of consumption among current ones.

For example, imagine we want to launch a new sort of a salad. After listing its qualities and characteristics, we play with the intensity of its properties: a very, very mild salad, easily digested and very easy to eat, very rich in protein but low in sodium, salts and phosphorus. We try out different possibilities until we hit on one or more with the potential to become a new concept.

Where is it best applied?

This technique is essentially designed with three objectives in mind: product redesign, product line extensions and repositioning.

Case studies

Almost all product and service line extensions have been done, directly or implicitly, using this technique: for example, sugar-free and caffeine-free soft drinks, vitamin-enriched products, and the like, which modify the characteristics of the product or service. It is also used to define positioning strategies in markets with relatively undifferentiated products.

On what creative rationale is it based?

The same as for morphological analysis, except that it focuses on upward or downward modification as displacement techniques.

Scenario analysis

What is it?

The scenario method, rather than attempting something as unlikely as knowing or predicting the future, is based on the opposite assumption: the acknowledgement that it is impossible to guess what is going to happen. Even without knowing what will happen, scenario analysis enables us to anticipate what the consequences might be in any given scenario and of each of the decisions we make.

How is it applied?[11]

(1) Decide on the question to be answered in the analysis: the more detailed the question, the better it is for shaping a scenario. Then, (2) list the influencing factors: describe as many factors as you can come up with that may

affect your business in your previously established place and time. These factors may be industrial, political, economic, technological, and so on. (3) Critical uncertainties: divide the influencing factors into two columns: one for major uncertainties and the other for the less important, predictable ones. This leaves us with a series of unpredictable driving forces. (4) Choice of uncertainties: out of the driving forces, choose two you consider most critical in creating your scenarios. (5) Identification of extremes: add these two factors to a simple XY diagram, indicating at its extremes how this uncertainty may vary. For example, economic situation: On one end (−∞) write "good, boom …" and at the other end (+∞) write "bad, bust …" (6) Define the scenarios: usually you construct two to four scenarios, but you can have more if the problem is complex and depends on a large number of critical influencing factors. In each quadrant, place the potential impacts arising from the situation. For example, if we are in the quadrant associated with a bad economic situation, our business will be focused on cheap products, unless we are targeting a class of wealthy customers. (7) Choose the most plausible scenario and define a strategy for that scenario.

Additionally, you can factor into the scenario analysis your probabilities of influencing or creating a favorable scenario. Also, future scenarios are usually classified into several sections.

Let's look at an example. (1) We are going decide our innovation policy for the coming years. (2) We choose the following influencing factors: expected level of innovation among the competition in the short term, changing economic conditions, expected sales increase in the category, probability of a technological breakthrough and the possibility of the entrance of competition from China. (3) and (4) Out of all of these, we consider the most critical: the evolution of the economy and the possibility of competition from China. (5) We develop a matrix of the possibilities that may occur and (6) we define the scenarios (Figure 5.5).

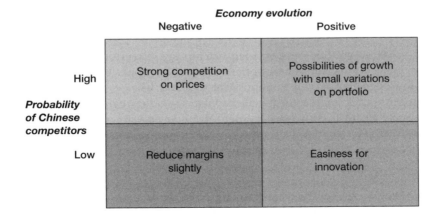

Figure 5.5   **Scenario analysis**

(7) Finally, we determine that we cannot influence these factors (evolution of the economy and the entrance of a competitor from China), so we move on to consider the most plausible scenario. The probability that the economy will not improve is high and we have evidence of Chinese companies moving into our industry. That puts us in a scenario of strong price competition. From there, we start designing our strategy, using, if necessary, other creative techniques.

Where is it best applied?

To focus on complex problems, identify focuses of innovation and to define business strategies and innovation.

Case studies

Scenario analysis is widely used in the military, political and economic realms. In business, it is used as a way to define business strategies. In innovation, it can be used to define what innovation strategies to follow based on the possible evolution (scenarios) of our market and our competitors' strategic movements.

On what creative rationale is it based?

It is based on the technique of continually asking yourself "what if?" – that is, it is based on questioning.

Visits and trips

What is it?

This method simply consists of visiting locations, related or not to our product or service, with the idea that what we see may serve us as inspiration and stimulate the generation of new provocations. In the case of locations related to our industry, visits are normally made to outlets or places where customers buy, consume or use products and services. In some cases, customers are interviewed, using a structured questionnaire, about the problems they encounter as users, their needs and aspirations and desires in regard to new products. This method is difficult and costly to implement, since you must find relevant customers and a good deal of preparation is required in order to get good results.

In locations not related to our industry, the method consists of visiting foreign countries to see how customers relate to our product category or to other, adjacent ones.

How is it applied?

In the case of customer visits, (1) you define a sample of customers or consumers. (2) You visit and observe them using or buying the product or service. (3) You take notes on what they do with special attention to improper use of or failure to take full advantage of a product's potential. (4) You interview them about their problems and needs. (5) All this information is examined later in an internal creativity session as a stimulus for generating ideas.

In the case of trips, (1) you define what you want to innovate or produce ideas about. (2) You think of places that might inspire you. (3) You choose the most promising ones. (4) You travel to them, recording the things you see and that particularly catch your attention. (5) All this information is used as provocations and shown to the group as a means of generating ideas.

Where is it best applied?

Given its random nature, this technique produces unpredictable results at all levels, from the most tactical to the most strategic. The impact of this technique on innovation depends more on the focus chosen to create provocations than on the technique itself.

Case studies

Starbucks Corp. uses this technique. Michelle Gass, Starbucks' senior vice-president for category management, took her team to Paris, Düsseldorf, and London to visit local Starbucks and other restaurants to get a better sense of local cultures, behaviors, and fashions. "You come back just full of different ideas and different ways to think about things than you would had you read about it in a magazine or e-mail," says Gass.[12]

On what creative rationale is it based?

It's a mix of randomness and combination of ideas.

Co-creation

What is it?

Co-creation is a very recent innovation technique that consists of bringing customers or consumers into the creative processes.

How is it applied?

This is usually done with the new technologies, particularly the Internet, creating spaces where people can propose, rank or improve on ideas, or the company can ask people to give their opinions and assessments of ideas that the organization is considering developing. Co-creation usually targets consumers and customers who are highly engaged with the brand or category, giving them the online (and offline) tools to express their ideas and help guide designers in developing prototypes. It can also be done using face-to-face work sessions, similar to directed group meetings, to which people from outside the organization are invited.

Where is it best applied?

Co-creation is especially useful in B2B and services markets, where direct contact with customers is essential and where innovation requires a certain degree of coordination between the innovators and the customers it targets. Co-creation is equally effective in highly dynamic, fast-moving markets, exposed to shifting fashions and changes in consumer and customer preferences.

One of the most prevalent methods of co-creation is called Lead User Analysis, developed by Eric von Hippel. It is based on the principle that, if you work with innovative customers, ultimately they will come up with innovative product ideas. The technique involves bringing together users or customers of a company's services or products who are particularly innovative and having them identify problems and solutions. The main challenge is how to identify such customers and convince them to participate in such sessions. 3M is particularly fond of this technique.

A variation on this approach is to invite customers and users to design our new product:

> Bush Boake Allen (BBA), a global supplier of specialty flavors to companies like Nestlé, has built a tool kit that enables its customers to develop their own flavors, which BBA then manufactures. In the materials field, GE provides customers with Web-based tools for designing better plastic products. In software, a number of companies let users add custom-designed modules to their standard products and then commercialize the best of those components.[13]

Co-creation can also be applied in what are known as customer advisory boards or panels, in which the company maintains regular contact with a fixed sample of selected customers, from whom it continually gathers information on new ideas and possibilities. A variation is the "community of enthusiasts," where the sample is made up of customers or users chosen for their level of engagement with the company's product.

Co-creation often takes place in the testing phases of a new product when the company chooses a few loyal customers to try out the product and supply further ideas for improving it.

Case studies

Co-creation occurs at Harley Davidson with devoted motorcycle customers who ask to work alongside the designers. It also occurs in Lego with kids coming in with their ideas. There is also co-creation of advertising ideas. Doritos snack chips by-passed its advertising agency and invited its snack lovers to submit advertising campaign ideas, with prizes going to the best. Starbucks has spent years mining customers for new ideas and exploiting those which online voters want to see on the Starbucks menu or catalog.

On what creative rationale is it based?

Simply, on networking, as a particular type of collaborative work, applied to customers instead of companies specializing in creativity, innovation or design.

Redefining customer value

What is it?

Redefining customer value can be described as modifying the value that customers get out of our products and services. Every transaction consists of two elements: the customer's efforts (the price paid, the time spent informing oneself and making the purchase, the risk associated with the decision and so on) and the product or service he or she receives in return. Value is the ratio of what the customer gets divided by his or her efforts. You can increase customer value in two ways: (a) giving more (quality or quantity) for the same price, or (b) offering the same product for less total effort, facilitating one or more of the elements that go into the sum.

How is it applied?

Its application is very simple. (1) We analyze customer value: what do we deliver? What are all the efforts the customer has to make? (2) Once we know this, we play around with our options for increasing, reducing or eliminating such efforts, in order to see if there is a final increase in the value to customers. (3) Once we have found a new combination, the next step is to connect and develop the idea for turning the new combination into a new product, new service or a new business model.

For example, if we eliminate after-sales services, which are very expensive, and, instead, offer to replace a damaged or defective product with a new one, the customer receives more value at no great extra cost to us, as long as the quality of our product is high enough.

Where is it best applied?

This is a method that works especially well when the aim is to develop a market, to attract potential customers or to redefine the rules of an industry.

Case studies

The most exemplary and illustrative case of the use this technique is IKEA, which completely reshaped customer value by shifting assembly to the customer in exchange for much lower prices.

On what creative rationale is it based?

It uses problem splitting techniques and changes in the factors that comprise the value delivered to the customer.

Which information browsing methods are most useful to the creative technique?

We explained in the previous chapter that information browsing should be directly linked to each creative technique that is to be applied or to the specific needs of developers (D) and executers (E). In Table 5.1, we can see which information browsing methods best fuel each of the techniques we have explored.

Table 5.1 Information browsing techniques suitable for each creative technique

	Synectics	Blue Ocean	Morphological analysis	Lateral marketing	Attributes listing	Scenario analysis	Visits	Co-creation	Customer value redefinition	Brainstorming
Innovation review		X	X	X	X	X				X
Analysis of adjacent categories		X	X				X			X
Internal consulting	X	X	X			X	X			
Social trend/social classes		X		X		X	X			
Market trends		X		X	X	X				X
Buying process			X	X					X	X
Innovation routes		X	X	X						X
Technological solutions	X		X	X		X				X
Design	X	X	X		X		X	X		
Successful strategies and tactics/learning from errors				X	X	X				
Network monitoring					X			X		
Ethnographic		X		X	X			X	X	X
Geolocation					X			X		

When we say "fuel a creative technique" we mean that, in order to be successful, any creativity session, whether it is meant to come up with concepts to develop or to solve problems faced by executors, must be well prepared and organized. Creativity sessions are not informal, disorganized get-togethers. In order for a creativity session to produce positive results and be effective, it requires lots of preparation. You can say that for every minute of generating ideas in a creativity session you need about three minutes of preparation, at least.

In a creativity session, the focus must be well defined and each of the stimuli that the participants will be exposed to must be planned and prepared beforehand. Good creativity sessions are those that achieve a well-planned improvisation.

Assessment of creative techniques and information browsing methods

Faced with so many methods, lots of managers feel lost. Although we have tried in the preceding pages to establish the situations in which they work best, you may still ask yourself: Which are most commonly used in business? Which have proved most useful? Often, the mere mention of an innovation discovered using a particular technique causes its popularity to skyrocket, even though few other companies find it useful. Bob Cooper and Scott Edgett conducted an interesting study, surveying 160 companies that had used some of the methods explained in this book. [14]

The main conclusions are summarized in Figure 5.6. For each method, we compare two factors: how widespread its use is among firms and how the firms rank each technique according to how effective they have found it.

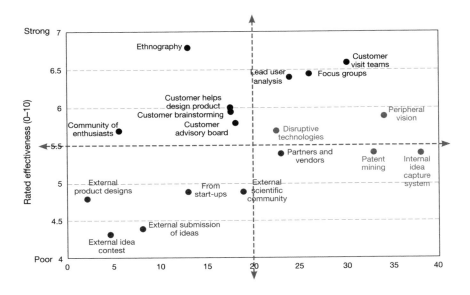

Figure 5.6   **Effective (rated by users) versus popularity for each ideation method**

Source: Adapted from Robert Cooper and Scott Edgett. "Ideation for product innovation: what are the best methods?" PDMA *Visions* Magazine. March, 2008

We can see that there are two preferred categories:

Most effective and popular

▷ Customer visits
▷ Peripheral vision or trend analysis
▷ Focus groups
▷ Incorporation of disruptive technologies in our category
▷ Lead user analysis

Most effective but less popular

▷ Ethnography
▷ Customer advisory boards, community of enthusiasts
▷ Mechanisms to facilitate customer contributions to product design

The others, although ranked lower, should not be dismissed. Their lower rank may be due to a lack of experience or skill in their application or to their lack of suitability to the sector or industry of the company that assessed the technique. Any technique for generating ideas is useful. The secret is knowing how and when to use it.

From idea to concept

Having explored the different techniques of idea generation, we now go on to discuss how creators (together with developers) must transform the best ideas of new products and services or new business models into concepts.

The concept is more developed and defined than the idea. It is not a complete tangibilization of the idea, but it contains the elements and ingredients that fully justify investing in its development.

Applied to new products and services, a concept consists of a brief, but sufficiently explicit, description of how an idea will translate into customer value and why it will capture customer interest and purchase intent.

There is no single way of expressing concepts, rather there are many; each company has its own. The one we present below is another, one that personally we have found useful, and that can also be tested on consumers in the event that the facilitators (F) require this before approving new spending items.

We recommend describing a concept in the following terms: name, images that describe it, the business source it feeds off (source of volume), the insight it appeals to, the basic benefit it covers, the reason why (people would buy it), the end benefit it is aimed at, the social trend in which it is framed, and a subjective assessment of ease of development and market potential. We will examine each in detail and with an illustrative example, under the assumption that we have decided to launch a special cereal to eat with yogurt.

Concept name

This consists of a brief name that in some way describes the product or service we are going to launch. This is something very different from the brand or sub-brand. The intention here is not yet to come up with a catchy brand name. That comes later. Simply put, it's a description that highlights one or more of the following: "what we sell", "to whom", "what need it covers" and "in what situations it will be purchased or consumed."

In the present example, one concept name would be "cereal for yogurt." We can see that the concept name includes neither who it is for nor what need it fulfils, rather we focus on the consumption situation (to go with yogurt, instead of milk). We do this because it is the most distinctive aspect of the concept. In other cases, it may be better to highlight the target market or the need covered: "Cereal for the elderly" or "Cereal for sportspeople" or "digestive cereal" or "anti-aging cereal." In other cases, the concept name might only include the differential characteristic or attribute: for example "red cereal" or "big-sized cereal" or "sugar-free cereal."

Images that illustrate the concept

A picture is worth a thousand words, so one way to have everyone connected to the innovation process share the same vision of the idea that they are going to develop is by using stock photos or images that in some way illustrate the style, color, target consumer and feel that the product or service should have.

In the case of "cereals for yogurt," for example, Figure 5.7 shows the sorts of images that would help describe the concept.

Cereals for yogurt

Figure 5.7   **Cereals for yogurt**

As we can see, the pictures already give us many clues to aspects that we have not yet described: seeing these images it is relatively easy to anticipate what the ingredients, design, packaging, colors, and so on should be. The images tell us that the product is essentially aimed at women who care about their health, who like yogurt and usually eat it with fruit or other complementary foods: basically, healthy people who enjoy natural foods in small quantities. Pictures provide a lot of information that is often difficult to express and communicate, but that is essential in order to "immerse" developers in the idea and opportunity we want to capture.

It is important that creators, browsers and developers take time to select and eliminate images they agree on. It is even useful to share the discarded images. A collage of pictures can be put into two groups:

First group: "This photo **would NOT be** for our concept."

Second group: "This picture **would be** for our concept."

This is a very useful exercise for aligning a lot of people on what we ultimately want to see when the idea has become a tangible product or service.

Source of volume

The identification of the source of volume is central to innovation. This means answering the following questions: Once this product is on the market and, assuming it has gained a certain level of acceptance, from whom will volume be "stolen"? What other products will people stop consuming in favor of our innovation? This is what we call "substitutive items."

The answer, obviously, is a prediction, an assumption and a subjective assessment of what our competitive reference will be. Here are some of the most typical conclusions:

▷ The product or service will produce incrementality; that is, we do not expect it clearly to "steal" sales from any other category, rather that it will generate a net increase in market or increase customer spending.

▷ The product is going to take volume away from some other product or service. In this case, there are three further possibilities:

1 It will take volume away from direct competitors and possibly also some of our own products; in our example, we may consider that the cereal for yogurt will take away volume from the standard cereals we currently sell to go with milk or juices.

2 It will take volume away from adjacent competitors, that is, from related categories with which we compete indirectly. For example, cereal for yogurt can steal volume from nuts and fruit that consumers add to their yogurts.

3 It will take volume away from distant competitors by simply cutting into their share of spending. For example, if we think that sales of cereal for yogurt will lead to a reduction in sales of other supermarket products, from cosmetics to cleaning products.

Locating the competitive reference serves several purposes: it helps frame subsequent commercial development (types of customers, channels and distributors, location in the point of sale, price references, and so on). It also enables the facilitators (F) to estimate the impact on the operating account, since an innovation whose competitive reference is in our portfolio will cause a reduction in the sales volume of such products, an effect known as "cannibalization."

Insight

The next point in the definition of a concept is insight, understood as the main motivation for the customer vis-à-vis the new concept, the inner thoughts, feeling, and latent need we satisfy. For example, in the case of cereal for yogurt, it might be: "I want to give my yogurt a special, healthy touch."

Insight goes beyond need. It's really the "strong" point on which we convince the consumer – what is happening inside them and they wouldn't know how to express. Insight should be validated by research, but we have seen how difficult it is to access customer insights, much less quantify them. Therefore, we do not speak of quantitative but qualitative validation. In this sense, the browsers, using the techniques explained in Chapter 4, should confirm that the insight to which we are appealing actually exists to a relevant degree among our customers and consumers.

Basic benefit

Basic benefit is a conscious approach to insight. It is a verbalization of the need the product fills. Since this is a something the customer or consumer should express, the basic benefit should be formulated in the first person, as if it were the customer who was articulating why he or she would choose this product or service.

For example, in the case of our yogurt, it might be: "This product simply allows me to add a touch of easy-to-eat taste to my yogurt that also provides all the goodness of cereal."

The basic benefit is the essence, the heart of an innovation. Developers cannot and should not lose sight of the basic benefit as they advance in the innovation process. We may find that we have to arrive at the basic benefit in a manner different from the one we originally intended. This often happens when developing an innovation. But what we cannot do under any circumstances is distort, reduce or significantly alter the basic benefit of the product or service we intend to launch.

If we are forced to modify it, the members of the innovation process team should also approve it. The modification or alteration of the basic benefit, even where due to technical requirements or limitations, is not something that developers can do on their own.

Reason why

The "reason why" (also known as "rationale") comes down to the objective reasons why the customer or the consumer will give our proposal credibility. Insight, in fact, is something latent, internal, a motivation. But what stirs that insight is something tangible, objective and also verifiable.

For example, in the case of cereal for yogurt, a reason why might be: "This is possible because the texture of this new cereal melds well with yogurt, which is not the case with cereals meant to be eaten with milk or juice, which are much harder in texture."

The reason why must be something demonstrable. If the consumer or customer cannot verify it for him or herself due to a lack of means or ability, we must offer the evidence and assurances that it is true. If necessary, we can resort to the approval, seals of approval or recommendations of third parties (laboratories, physicians, independent bodies, quality certificates, and so on) or in-store demonstrations and advertising.

There must be no room for doubt in the reason why. It cannot be half-baked. We have to keep in mind that the entire credibility of the basic benefit depends on this factor and, thus, the insight we are going to appeal to. A weak or doubtful reason why is not accessing insight, and thus diminishes our chances of mobilizing the customer or consumer as we intend. When it comes to development, if we don't think that we have sound reasons or arguments or convincing enough rationales it's best to revise the whole concept. Perhaps we have created outsized expectations and, at the moment of truth, we are unable to guarantee the customer what we thought we could deliver.

This is where many new products and services fail. We have found a basic benefit and insight so powerful that we do not want to give it up, even when, in fact, we cannot be sure that we will actually be able to satisfy it. In marketing and especially in new products, there is nothing worse than discovering that your product or service is unable to fulfill its promise. You can fool a customer, but only once. After that, you lose him or her forever.

End benefit

The end benefit is the pinnacle of the pyramid of needs at which the novelty that we are developing is aimed. Let's say that it is the ultimate benefit that our customer is after and that he or she seeks to satisfy, not only with our category or our industry, but with many other products and expenditures.

For example, in the case of "cereal for yogurt," the end benefit might be: "I want to be healthy."

We see that this is a very generic benefit which requires not only healthy eating but also exercise, leading a low-stress life, and so on.

The end benefit helps to frame the product or service within a general outline of customer needs and, therefore, to understand how it relates to other aspects of their lives.

Social trend in which it is framed

In Chapter 4 we emphasized the importance of framing an innovation within a particular social trend and how trend analysis can even be a direct stimulus in creativity sessions.

Defining the social trend that goes with and drives the concept gives us additional assurance that what we are doing makes sense in the real world and in the larger currents that move people's interests and attract the attention of the media.

For example, in the case of "cereal for yogurt," these might be social trends which confirm that the proposed concept has potential and is consistent with current consumption or market trends:

▷ Today, yogurt is the paradigm of healthy food, with a unique, natural taste.
▷ Socially, there is a widespread belief that the healthful qualities of cereals (a food with a high nutritional value, vitamins and minerals) provide a balanced complement to the benefits of yogurt. Cereals in flakes are now a widespread macrotrend.
▷ Among the population there is a concern for health.

Box 5.1 displays a complete concept, which includes everything we have talked about. An output like this, added to the images, can be used in a concept test, both qualitatively and quantitatively.

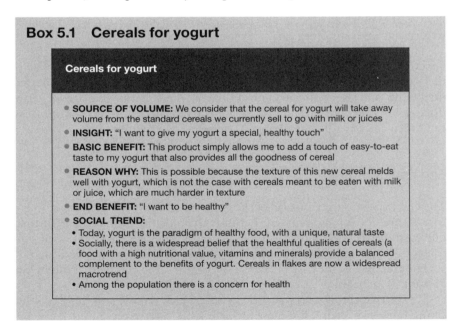

Box 5.1   Cereals for yogurt

Cereals for yogurt

- **SOURCE OF VOLUME:** We consider that the cereal for yogurt will take away volume from the standard cereals we currently sell to go with milk or juices
- **INSIGHT:** "I want to give my yogurt a special, healthy touch"
- **BASIC BENEFIT:** This product simply allows me to add a touch of easy-to-eat taste to my yogurt that also provides all the goodness of cereal
- **REASON WHY:** This is possible because the texture of this new cereal melds well with yogurt, which is not the case with cereals meant to be eaten with milk or juice, which are much harder in texture
- **END BENEFIT:** "I want to be healthy"
- **SOCIAL TREND:**
  - Today, yogurt is the paradigm of healthy food, with a unique, natural taste
  - Socially, there is a widespread belief that the healthful qualities of cereals (a food with a high nutritional value, vitamins and minerals) provide a balanced complement to the benefits of yogurt. Cereals in flakes are now a widespread macrotrend
  - Among the population there is a concern for health

A description such as that in Box 5.1 is equally applicable or readily adaptable to other types of innovations, such as a new business model, a new technology, an upgraded process, and so on. It's simply a matter of gathering the essential information, which includes what the contribution is and what we want to achieve with the proposed change or innovation.

Subjective assessment

In formulating the concept – although we will examine this point in greater detail in our chapter on facilitators (F) – it is useful to include some information on how easy or difficult we anticipate the development of the product will be and the business potential that we see.

This information would help choose from among a large number of concepts we deem worthy of consideration as we move forward in the innovation process (Figure 5.8).

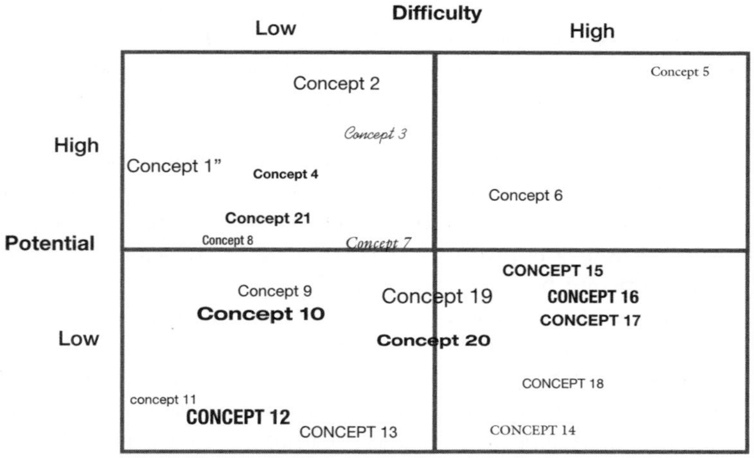

Figure 5.8 **Matrix for new concepts assessment**

The upper left quadrant indicates easily developed, high-potential concepts. We should consider these first.

The upper right quadrant includes high-potential, high-difficulty projects. Here, our recommendation would be to revise the concept in order to simplify its development, and, where this is not possible, to fine-tune as far as possible the manufacturing and marketing costs in order to avoid making a bad financial decision.

The lower left quadrant shows low-potential, low-difficulty concepts. We recommend using them strategically and spread out over time as a means of blocking the competition. Finally, the lower right quadrant corresponds to concepts that should be dropped: we see low potential and high difficulty in development.

Ideally, in the innovation process, companies should develop a large number of alternative concepts, so that they have a choice of which to develop. The combined difficulty–potential analysis is an essential tool in deciding where to invest resources. We will see this in more detail in Chapter 8.

Once you have a matrix like the one shown in Figure 5.8, the developers and facilitators should, based on economic and financial criteria, select a limited number of concepts to continue developing. In Chapter 8 we will examine different methods for assessing concepts. At the same time, and as a basis for taking such a decision, the various limitations that developers will face in developing such concepts should be reviewed. But this concerns the next chapter.

Brand decision

Knowing that the concept is attractive, the next step is to choose the brand under which the innovation will be launched and marketed.

The options are the following. Either we launch the innovation under an existing brand or we launch under a new one. When the innovation is a portfolio extension, it normally makes sense to use the brand of the portfolio.

But, what if we are facing a semi-radical or radical innovation? There exists a general trend towards using existing brands. The reason is clear: to harness current brand awareness, which it takes time and money to reach. For example, Yamaha is a brand applied to motorcycles and also to pianos, and people assume this without any problem. It is true that each piano or motorcycle model has a concrete brand through numbers or letters. But these are not known to many customers and rarely used by consumers. People just tend to say: "My piano is a Yamaha" or "My motorcycle is a Yamaha".

But brands have limits. If we want them to be used for too many products, we may lose force or may produce confusion with our positioning. Al Ries and Jack Trout defend that a product or service within a given category should have its own brand, especially when the innovation is radical because then we have a chance to name the category with our brand name: an iPhone is already more than a brand, it is a type of mobile handset. In this case, iPhone is the brand and Apple, the manufacturer. Or, let's say, the manufacturing brand. Apple is also a brand. In the case of iPhone, Apple acts as a supra-brand. Using brands and supra-brands (manufacturing brand) is a very efficient strategy for new products and services: Actimel by Dannon; Nespresso by Nestlé; iPhone by Apple

This makes it possible to harness the awareness and popularity of the "mother" brand and we can create a new name or brand for the innovation to be launched.

All these decisions concern the CIO (chief innovation officer), CEO, marketing and communication departments. Using existing brands affects current portfolio communication and promotion policies and may change the current positioning of our brands, so this matter must be adequately coordinated in the organization.

TOTAL INNOVATION SYSTEM – Summary Chapter 5

Main person/s in charge of each role

A Activators	B Browsers	C Creators	D Developers	E Executors	F Facilitators
Top management (GM or Chief innovation officer)	Market research department	Advertising agency			
Employees	Market research suppliers	Creativity agency			
Suppliers	Sociologists	Marketing			
Distributors	Marketing	Creative types			
Clients	Sales	R&D			
Investors	Opinion leaders	Clients			
Universities	Watchers' panel	Suppliers			
Scientific community	R&D	Employees with creative profile			
Inventors	Other internal departments	Other suppliers or third parties			
Engineering companies	Other suppliers or third parties				

Up-bottom activation
In-out activation
Bottom-up activation
Out-in activation

Techniques employed by each role

A Activators	B Browsers	C Creators	D Developers	E Executors	F Facilitators
Scope of innovation	Innovation review	Synectics			
Innovation levels	Analysis of adjacent categories	Blue Ocean strategy			
Focus of innovation	Internal consulting	Morphological analysis			
Innovation guidelines	Social trend/ social classes	Lateral marketing			
Innovation checklist	Market trends	Attributes listing			
	Buying process	Scenarios analysis			
	Innovation routes	Visits			
	Technological solutions	Co-creation			
	Design referents	Redefining customer value			
	Successful strategies and tactics/learning from errors	Brainstorming			
	Network monitoring	Concept definition			
	Ethnographic				
	Geolocation				

INNOVATION PROCESS

Innovation framework
Innovation guidelines
Innovation checklist

STRATEGIC PLANNING FOR INNOVATION

Project proposals
Process approval

Browsers ↔ Creators
Activators ↔ Facilitators ↔ Developers
Executors

CREATIVE CULTURE

INNOVATION REWARDS
INNOVATION METRICS

RESULTS

6 Developers

What is a developer?

Developers are people whose job it is to advance from idea to invention –
that is, to translate the idea into something tangible that can be marketed.

It would be both a waste of time and impossible to try to cover everything that is done in the new products or R&D departments. First of all,
this is not a book about engineering and design. It's a book about innovation – basically marketing innovation, where we present a model for
designing and organizing innovation processes. The series of tasks that a
technical department must perform in turning an idea into an invention
or a new service are almost as varied as the number of products on the
market. Anything we could offer on the technical development of, for
example, bicycles would be incomplete or invalid for the development of a
motorcycle, which is very different than an appliance, or a consumer
product or a cosmetic, which are nothing like hair salon or energy distribution services.

There already are books on engineering and processes that deal with such
matters, grouped by industry or type of technology. Here we focus on the
key aspects that characterize the work of a developer in relation to the other
roles that go into an innovation process. We will concentrate on the main
cross-cutting challenges – that is, those common to any industry or product
type. We will particularly emphasize the marketing dimension, something
that technical developments should never lose sight of, and explain in detail
the various techniques and methods that provide insight into how the market
understands and assesses the products and services that come out of a
company's technical department.

We also want to clarify that, in our view, the role of a developer is not
only technical. Just as important as the technical development of an idea is
its marketing development. The next role, that of executors (E), focuses on
execution, understood as the implementation of the total concept. The
executors are responsible for putting things into operation, a role in which
there is little room for new ideas and plans, and, instead, a lot of action.

Traditionally, given their technical skills and expertise, the task of concept
development has been the responsibility of R&D departments. Engineers
and technicians are the ones with the command of the technology and who
can effectively translate the ideas proposed in a company into reality.

We agree on the pre-eminent and fundamental role of the R&D and design department, and that the role of developers should be played mostly by personnel with a technical background. The sales, marketing or advertising staff don't know how to develop technical plans and prototypes or how to organize mass production and logistics. However, we propose that the developers should also include some members from in-house marketing and sales.

A very interesting article,[1] based on research into understanding the management view of the relationship between marketing and R&D during the innovation process, offers revealing conclusions that support and confirm the appropriateness of working with the roles we posit here (A-to-F) in order to ensure collaboration among experts belonging to different departments and functions of the company.

R&D departments focus mainly on new technological solutions, on more disruptive innovations, on the technological possibilities innovation is capable of creating, but they are not in permanent contact with the customer and often their proposals do not necessarily reflect or meet customer needs and concerns.

For their part, marketing departments concentrate basically on marginal innovations, on portfolio extensions, on ensuring that innovations reflect customer needs, but they are not technical experts and are usually unaware of many of the possibilities offered by technology. Thus they look no higher than innovations capable of capturing value, but which are too obvious and often non-disruptive from a technological standpoint.

In fact both roles are complementary, so the interesting and useful way to proceed, as proposed here, is to have R&D personnel helping creators to define the concepts, and marketing experts involved in the development of the innovation. The first will help ensure we don't miss out on the opportunities that technological expertise can contribute to the generation of ideas; the second, that any idea that comes from R&D will be evaluated from the viewpoint of customer needs.

Part of the solution is to recognize how the roles of developers and marketers differ. Developers should be masters of the art of the possible. Marketers should be masters of the art of the valuable – articulating for what people will pay. Knowing what is possible does not tell us what is valuable, and vice versa. It is through the combination of these two questions that we strike the right partnership between marketing and development. These professionals must truly collaborate to turn "valuable possibles", or solutions, into successful new offerings. Both require art and science, and both require each other to ensure the right offering for the available or potentially available demand. These distinct focuses – value and solutions – require different tools and skill sets and result in somewhat different priorities. One can discover many things that are possible but that might have little or no value, while one shouldn't expect to develop the very best offerings if one hasn't yet discovered the most valuable customer needs relative to the competition.

In fact, General Electric has solved this issue on the basis of creating work units in which people from both profiles work. Marketing is required to acquire a certain expertise in technology, and R&D to take time to understand the consumer or customer. Both parties must learn some of the other's technical jargon – that is, a kind of business multilingualism essential for communication between them. For example, the House of Quality is an organizational method where the marketers cite the consumer wants in an automobile and the R&D group turns this into horsepower and other technical statements.[2]

In our A-to-F model, we address this issue, resolving it by assigning people of either profile, and others in the company, to each of the roles and, especially, ensuring that, at points of interaction, the main role in one stage works hand-in-hand with the main role from the next. For example, it is a good thing, as explained in this chapter, to have creators and developers collaborate on the concepts which emerge from the ideas, and likewise, developers and executors should work together on the broad outline of the business plan for the prototype under development.

In any case, the interactive nature of the six roles encourages everyone to be permanently involved in the work and successes, advances and achievements of others, by which means the traditional barriers between departments are broken down and eliminated: R&D develops and marketing launches on the market (typical of technology companies) or marketing proposes an idea and R&D develops it (typical of consumer goods companies).

But we must not count on these two departments alone. The developers could, if necessary, include everything from market experts to engineers, to people from purchasing, logistics or production and sales and design.

As to whether these people should belong to the company or whether the roles can be outsourced, readers should go back to Chapter 3, where we discuss different forms of cooperation, and Chapter 5, where we address the concept of co-creation.

Developers' contribution to concept definition

Developers are not "pack mules" to burden with a brilliant, low-feasibility idea. We made it pretty clear in Chapter 5 that the creators don't come up with just ideas, rather they produce ideas that are relevant, viable, feasible and valuable. We cannot hand a developer an impossible idea along with the responsibility to make it viable, because all we'll succeed in doing is to create conflict, discourage our people and waste money, in addition to wrecking the innovation process.

That is why there are a number of functions that lie midway between the creators and developers, a task they must perform together before moving on to the development of prototypes, models and production plans. We refer to their role in affecting the design of the concept.

Limitations which developers know

Developers are acutely aware of certain business limitations. These limitations can be divided into four groups:

▷ technological
▷ production
▷ marketing
▷ financial

Technological limitations

The first question that arises when developing an innovation is: Do we have the technology? If so, we are way ahead in the game. Having the technological capacities to make an idea possible takes us halfway there. If the answer is "no, we do not have the technology to develop this concept," then developers and browsers must work together to find possible external suppliers to provide us with the technology. This tends to be a long, difficult and costly process, so the benefits of an innovation that requires outsourced technology must be sufficiently attractive. Before continuing with such an innovation process, we should think twice. Perhaps we should stop and review.

Production limitations

In this case, we have a particular technology, but not the production capacities or facilities to manufacture the innovation. That is, our production lines cannot make the product or our structure cannot provide the service. This limitation can be overcome, but again, the implications are important. In this case, there are only two fairly obvious choices: outsource or invest in new facilities. Outsourcing involves the sharing of the profit margin and directly affects the expected return on investment (ROI) and profitability of the project, which is an added difficulty that increases the risk entailed in the project. Investing in new facilities or production lines means money, time and resources, and, above all, requires achieving a minimum sales volume.

Marketing limitations

In this case, we ask ourselves if we have the skills and expertise to market the product or service. It may seem contradictory that we can make something and then find we cannot sell or distribute it, but this often happens in components and raw materials manufacturers. A rubber company specializing in tires, for example, might have the technology and the ability to make kitchen complements and utensils based on the qualities of rubber, yet be so specialized in the automotive sector that it has neither the sales network nor the marketing expertise to enter the household products market. In this case, we might ask ourselves whether we should go ahead or set up partnerships with third parties to distribute what we make. Obviously, there is almost always a solution for something we can manufacture but don't know how to sell, but strategically the company must ask itself whether this diversification is something that enters into its plans.

Financial limitations

And, finally, financial resources. Any innovation has its associated costs and investments (see Chapter 8). Beyond the ROI, an innovation with the potential to produce a lot of money but, given the necessary investment, jeopardizes the whole enterprise is likely to be discarded. This circumstance is the major limiting factor for small and medium enterprises when innovating. SMEs detect more opportunities than they can finance; their financial muscle is not that of a multinational and they drop many of their innovation projects because they entail too much risk.

Summarizing, the key questions are:

▷ Do we have and know how to use the technology this concept needs?
▷ Can we manufacture it?
▷ Can we and do we know how to sell it?
▷ Do we have the resources to develop this innovation?

If the concept doesn't pass this test, there are only three possible solutions: (1) drop the concept. (2) Maintain it as is (making sure in advance that it does not conflict with the general plans or mission of the company) and start looking for suppliers, partners, and so on. (3) Try to modify the concept in order to pass the test.

Conserving the concept

Having picked one or more concepts to translate into products or services with market potential, the developers still face many challenges – the main one being the risk of losing the essence and the potential of the concept as it progresses into something real and marketable.

The world of ideas knows barely any limitations and you can ask for "the impossible": "slimming yogurt" or "a life insurance policy that secures the future of children and grandchildren." On the other hand, the world of real products and services is rife with limitations and restrictions. A creator would say, "Welcome to the world of possibilities and opportunities." A developer would reply, "Welcome to the real world of limitations."

And maybe it should be so. The tension between the two boosts the innovative potential of a company. He who dares not dream does not progress and he who doesn't "keep his feet on the ground" crashes. Both positions are needed in the innovation process.

The challenge is to know how to combine them. Developers should be fully aware that to "land" an idea entails the risk of diluting its potential, blurring its essence, clarity and brilliance. There are countless products and services born with the potential to fill a particular need that, at the moment of truth, either bear little resemblance to what they were intended to be or fail to live up their promise.

As we explained earlier in this chapter, the more realistic, appropriate and feasible the idea, the less pressure on the developers. Additionally, the actual and effective performance of the technical solutions proposed by developers should be accompanied by an assessment of the extent to which the basic benefits and insights of the idea have been maintained.

For this reason, developers should be completely open and honest about their ability to provide answers to what is expressed in the concepts.

In any case, the A-to-F model proposed in this book helps avoid dilution of the concept as it becomes a tangible product or service. Why? Because instead of working in a linear fashion, the different roles relate continuously in all directions. Activators, browsers, creators, executors and facilitators track the concept as it evolves and becomes a product, cooperating where difficulties arise, either with new ideas, information, research or additional resources to help overcome the limitations reality imposes.

How to advance step by step in development

As mentioned, the world of ideas costs a company relatively little money. It's when the developers take charge of the process that the cost issue starts to turn serious. One of the maxims of innovation is proper management of errors and failures: fail soon, fast and cheap. Innovating means managing the errors innovative activity entails.

The way in which developers can advance while facilitators adopt new expenditure and investment items, confident that money is not being thrown away, is using a tangibilization of a product or service that goes from less to more cost over time. In fact, as T. Davila, M. J. Epstein and R. Shelton[3] demonstrate so well, as an innovation project advances over time, the ability to influence the final result diminishes and investment rises. Both factors increase the risk of innovation as time passes (see Figure 6.1).

The way to specify the idea from lowest to greatest cost is:

Concept → Drawings and plans → Model → Prototype → Manufacturing test → Finished product

The process starts with drawings and plans, which is still at low cost. The model is a reproduction (not necessarily to scale) that does not utilize the actual materials with which the product will be manufactured. The prototype is a full-scale reproduction made, if possible, with the materials foreseen for its manufacture. The manufacturing test is one of the first products to come out of the production line, once the latter has been set up. The finished product is what we get when production is fully operational. The difference between the finished product and the manufacturing test is that the former incorporates the learning curve of production to scale and represents the actual item once the production attains the foreseen rate.

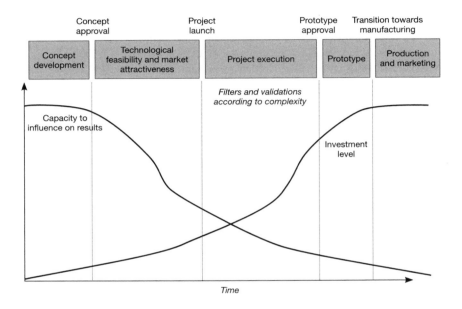

Figure 6.1   **Investment and risk evolution throughout the innovation process**
Source: Adapted from T. Davila, M.J. Epstein, R. Shelton. *Making Innovation Work: How to manage it, measure it, and profit from it.* Wharton School Publishing (2006)

In terms of costs, a drawing requires less investment than a model, which in turn is less expensive than a prototype, which costs less than the first manufacturing tests, which finally, involve less investment than the product that ultimately will be manufactured.

The same goes for services. In this case, the sequence for further controlling costs and investments is:

Concept → Configuration of the service → Demo of the service → Real test → Established service

The service configuration includes the list of deliverables, the customer service sequence, the protocol and how to proceed in case of any eventualities. The demo is a test run, providing the service under fictional, controlled conditions. The real test corresponds to the first deliveries of the service after its launch. The established service is what we offer on an ongoing and non-exclusive basis.

Solutions to the trade-off between key features

In the development of a product, uncertainties do tend to come up about how to weigh its different characteristics, features or qualities. There is a method that has been in use for many years and that nonetheless is little known and even less used in business. We refer to *conjoint analysis*. Its scarce penetration in the business world is due to the fact that its application is complex and, although it is not all that expensive, nor is it cheap.

The conjoint analysis is a type of multivariate analysis and has many applications, since it quantifies the trade-off between different factors or attributes. For example, how much more we can charge for this product if we cut its weight by so many grams? Or: Will the customer go for the product if it weighs a few more grams and, as a trade-off, offers more features?

Conjoint analysis consists in showing a representative sample of customers a number of alternative designs in which each of the key design factors is varied. The customers are asked to order their preferences. For example, do they prefer the heavier product with more features over the lighter one with fewer? One of the largest applications of conjoint was its use in developing the Courtyard hotel chain. It helped the company gauge consumer preferences regarding adding a swimming pool, small or large TV sets, and so on.

Price, features, and so on are examples of factors or attributes. Weight and number of features are different levels or values that these attributes can take and that are within the range of possibilities we are considering in our product development. The same principle applies to services. There is a certain limitation on the number of attributes and levels that can be included in a conjoint. Recently, however, applications have become available for computer-administered interviews where it is possible to include a fairly large number of attributes and factors.

Figure 6.2 shows the results of a conjoint analysis carried out by a cell phone operator in designing its range of handsets for its subscribers. These were the different factors that the company wanted to measure the importance of, with the aim of designing a plan aligned with their customers' preferences:[4]

In this example, most of the factors are related to the design and features of the cell phone, but it also includes some marketing variables such as the price of the pack. This was done because the tool was used for three purposes:

▷ Configuration of the plan (for the developers)
▷ Configuration of the optimal commercial offer (for delivery to the executors)
▷ Estimate of the demand for each of the possible configurations (for the facilitators)

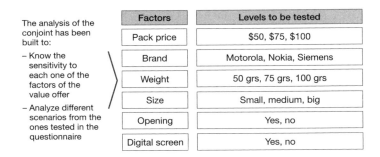

Figure 6.2   **Example of conjoint for a telecom product design**

A conjoint analysis, well thought out, designed and administered, can be tremendously fruitful.[5] Figure 6.3 shows some of the results of this conjoint. For example, it shows the first indicator that this technique provides: the importance of the factors on a scale of 100. Based on total customer feedback, we can calculate the relative weight of the factors that affect design.

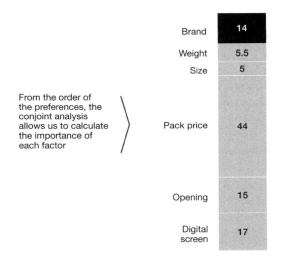

Figure 6.3   **Conjoint analysis (weight or importance of factors according to customers' answers)**

Another output we can derive from conjoint analysis is the prioritization of different configurations, estimating the proportion of customers that would chose a particular option. If, moreover, the design of the conjoint includes the attributes and levels of major competitors, it can even estimate (for the facilitators, in order to evaluate the potential of each configuration) how many customers would prefer our designs versus the ones the competition currently has out on the market. The way to operationalize this analysis is by converting the utilities that the conjoint comes up with into a simple model that can be expressed in a spreadsheet and that allows you to try out different configurations and then verify what percentage of the respondents prefer each one (see Figure 6.4).

Pack price	$50	$60	$65
Brand	Motorola	Siemens	Nokia
Weight	75 grs	75 grs	50 grs
Size	Small	Small	Small
Opening	No	No	No
Digital screen	Yes	Yes	Yes
Estimated share	25%	35%	40%

Figure 6.4 **Conjoint analysis (market share estimation for different design alternatives)**

Quality checks or controls

As the developer moves on, a number of factors for both products and services should be checked over and over again, without fear of being tedious or overly cautious and conservative. Activators, browsers, creators, developers and facilitators should all be involved at this stage, since it is crucial to the innovation process.

From drawing to finished product, between each step, the following checks should be inserted:

▷ *Relative to use:* Does it work well enough? Is it safe to use or consume? Does it meet expectations or fulfill its promise?
▷ *Relative to quality:* Is the product well designed? Will it be as durable as expected? Can this design be manufactured with all its features?
▷ *Relative to the concept:* Are we preserving the basic benefit? Is the reason why clear enough to the customer in our design? Are we mobilizing the customer insight we wanted with the product we have developed? Should we review the difficulties and potential of the concept once we have developed it?

The developer's virtue: patience

Innovation, like creativity, as Picasso and many other artists said, is 1 percent inspiration and 99 percent perspiration, in other words: sweat. Ideas do not simply and easily become realities. This is a task that demands tenacity, going over and over the limitations, difficulties and obstacles that inevitably arise, and never giving up. This is where many companies throw in the towel. They lack the patience or the time, or flexibility in scheduling, or the resources to advance in a slow but sure manner. The authors have seen many companies that, failing to proceed in this way, end up launching products and services that are not ready and that, with no possibility of improvement after coming out on the market, flop miserably.

Tests

One way to go from concept to finished product safely is to do periodic testing. There are companies that test their new products in one way or another, while others, many more than one might think, do not test their new products and services at all. Some fail to do so out of ignorance, others due to lack of habit, and others – the majority – because of the costs involved in testing. This is a critical error because failure is more expensive than testing. In addition, there is a wide range of testing methods, both qualitative and quantitative, of different and varied scope and cost.

Concept
↓   Test of concept
Drawings and plans

Model
↓   Test of product
Prototype

Manufacturing test   Home usage test

Finished product   Area/Market test

These methods are useful to developers in gradually shaping the product as it advances through the materialization and production plan. It is also essential for facilitators in assessing the product's business or market potential; testing the product to ensure that it meets the minimum requirements for launch. Area and market tests are the most developed ways of testing an innovation. And because in each case a certain degree of execution is needed, we will cover both of them in the next chapter.

Many readers will already be familiar with the techniques for concept, product and home usage testing so we will not cover them here, but further details can be found in Annex III of Chapter 9, where we explain what they are, how they are applied and how they help improve the development of the innovation.

TOTAL INNOVATION SYSTEM – Summary Chapter 6

Main person/s in charge of each role

A Activators	B Browsers	C Creators	D Developers	E Executors	F Facilitators
Top management (GM or Chief innovation officer)	Market research department	Advertising agency	R&D		
Employees	Market research suppliers	Creativity agency	New products department		
Suppliers	Sociologists	Marketing	Operations		
Distributors	Marketing	Creative types	Manufacturing		
Clients	Sales	R&D	External suppliers		
Investors	Opinion leaders	Clients	Marketing		
Universities	Watchers' panel	Suppliers	Sales		
Scientific community	R&D	Employees with creative profile	Dedicated engineers		
Inventors	Other internal departments	Other suppliers or third parties			
Engineering companies	Other suppliers or third parties				

Up-bottom activation
In-out activation
Bottom-up activation
Out-in activation

Techniques employed by each role

A Activators	B Browsers	C Creators	D Developers	E Executors	F Facilitators
Scope of innovation	Innovation review	Synectics	Helping in concept definition		
Innovation levels	Analysis of adjacent categories	Blue Ocean strategy	Concept test for improving design		
Focus of innovation	Internal consulting	Morphological analysis	Pictures		
Innovation guidelines	Social trend/ social classes	Lateral marketing	Conjoint analysis for features definition		
Innovation checklist	Market trends	Attributes listing	Drawings		
	Buying process	Scenarios analysis	Mock-up		
	Innovation routes	Visits	Prototype		
	Technological solutions	Co-creation	Product test		
	Design referents	Redefining customer value	Usage/home test		
	Successful strategies and tactics/learning from errors	Brainstorming	Patents		
	Network monitoring	Concept definition			
	Ethnographic				
	Geolocation				

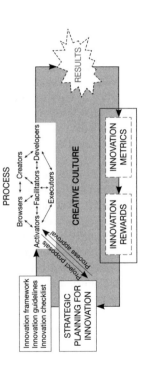

INNOVATION PROCESS

Browsers ←→ Creators
Activators ←→ Facilitators ←→ Developers
Executors

CREATIVE CULTURE

RESULTS

INNOVATION REWARDS

INNOVATION METRICS

Innovation framework
Innovation guidelines
Innovation checklist

STRATEGIC PLANNING FOR INNOVATION

Project proposals

Process proposals

7 Executors

Who are the executors?

The executors are in charge of the practical and effective rollout of an innovation. In other words, executors play the leading role in everything related to implementation.

Execution: a critical factor in success

Notwithstanding the importance of the previous roles, it is precisely in the implementation or execution phase that we find some of the main stumbling blocks and key factors in companies' poor innovation performance.[1]

Vijay Govindarajan and Chris Trimble, leading innovation experts and authors of several books, have devoted an entire book solely to the subject of innovation execution.[2] Commenting in his blog, Vijay Govindarajan describes their views regarding the role of the execution phase:

> We liken innovation to an ascent of Mount Rainier. Most climbers focus their energy and enthusiasm on attaining the summit, leaving very few resources for the less glamorous and more dangerous part of the expedition – the descent. Similarly, companies devote their energies only to reaching the innovation summit – that is, identifying, developing, and committing to a brilliant idea. "Getting to the summit can seem like the fulfillment of a dream, but it is not enough. After the summit comes the other side of innovation – the challenges beyond the idea. Execution. Like Rainier, it is the other side of the adventure that is actually more difficult." In short: There is too much emphasis on ideas, not nearly enough on execution.[3]

Or, in the words of Theodore Levitt:

> A powerful idea can kick around unused in a company for years, not because its merits are not recognized but because nobody has assumed the responsibility for converting it from words into action.[4]

Further testimony supports this thesis:

> More often, the problem is that organizations invest in creative ideation initiatives, such as brainstorming events, idea management, ideas campaigns and the like, but fail to invest in implementing the most creative ideas that come from those initiatives.[5]

In fact, all too frequently companies arrive at the execution phase with their resources and enthusiasm depleted and they make ill-considered decisions on who is best placed to execute the launch of an innovation.

In this chapter we will not tell you how to make a launch plan for a new product or service, given that an extensive literature already exists on that subject. Instead we will devote our attention to the keys to successful execution: who should execute, what execution tools and strategies there are that cut across all industries and sectors, and the factors to consider once execution is underway.

Selecting executors

Who is most suited to be an executor?

This is a question that rarely gets the attention it merits. There is a tendency among companies to assign new product or service launches on a "best-match" basis: either to the department with the most likely portfolio or, failing that, to the one that has the most similar customer base. That is, they decide on the basis of affinities or similarities between the innovation and existing products or customers, though, as we soon shall see, this is not necessarily the best criterion. Figure 7.1 shows the options actually available to a company in a new product launch, from which we can see that we have many more options other than simply having one of the current divisions execute an innovation.

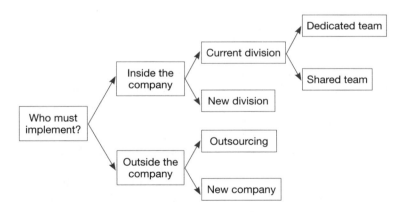

Figure 7.1 **Tree decision to decide where to execute the innovation**

Inside or outside the company?

The first big question is whether to execute inside or outside the company. Obviously, to set up a new company for the exclusive purpose of implementing a launch would be very expensive; expenses that could be shared if we execute within our current structure.

Likewise, having another organization execute means sharing a percentage of the potential gross margins and total benefits, as well as engaging in some sort of medium- to long-term commitment, since, without having secured a share in future profits, the other party can hardly be expected to make the huge effort required to shepherd an innovation onto the market.

The associated costs are one of the main arguments against outsourcing execution. The business world runs on a short-term clock. Many executives stand to reap huge financial incentives if they succeed in increasing company profits or share values. On the other hand, setting up a new business, with a new brand name, personnel structure, and so on, is a venture both risky and involved.

For both these reasons, companies rarely seriously consider the possibility of executing from scratch with a new business project.

Naturally, this statement applies to innovations of a certain magnitude; it does not include portfolio extensions or marginal innovations with low incremental sales. Creating a new company is an option to consider in the following types of innovation: business model, market-level (new customer base), disruptive product or service, or disruptive technology.

Regarding this last type, disruptive technological innovation, Clayton Christensen, one of the foremost authorities on innovation, sees executing innovation by means of a new business project as one of the keys to success:

> With few exceptions, the only instances in which mainstream firms have success-fully established a timely position in a disruptive technology were those in which the firms' managers set up an autonomous organization charged with building a new and independent business around the disruptive technology.[6]

But there is an even more powerful reason to weigh the option of setting up an independent business to execute an innovation. If we examine the statistics on business survival, we find that short-term profitability is not necessarily the most appropriate criterion.

The reason is that, like it or not, companies are doomed, sooner or later, to disappear. Obsolescence is something that rarely can be avoided. The reason is simple. The environment is changing at a rate that rigid corporate structures can't always keep up with. Recent empirical studies show that barely one in ten companies is able to sustain growth in the long term or yield profits on a ongoing basis:

▷ Chris Zook and James Allen, in their study *Profit from the Core*, analyzed 1,854 companies and found that only 13 percent were capable of sustained growth over a 10-year-plus period.[7]

▷ In *Good to Great*, Jim Collins found that out of a sample of 1,435 companies only 9 percent were able to sustain growth for 10 consecutive years over a period of 30 years.[8]

▷ Richard Foster and Sarah Kaplan, in their study *Creative Destruction*, analyzed a sample of 1,008 companies and found that after 35 years the survival rate was just 16 percent.[9]

This last data is supported by the fact that there is only one company in the history of the New York Stock Exchange that has managed to stay in the Dow Jones for more than 150 years. That company is General Electric. The reason is simple: GE isn't one company but a conglomerate. Since in the long term businesses are doomed to disappear, the way to survive is not to be a single business, but to be an aggregate of independent businesses. Thus, when environmental changes cause a company in the GE group to go into decline, it divests of that business in order to invest in its industries that are thriving. General Electric ranks high in the standings of innovative companies. If, for the sake of cost-cutting, it developed its innovations within a single organization, GE probably wouldn't exist today. Were any one of its businesses to go under, it would bring down the rest with it. Despite being more expensive to set up new businesses to undertake innovation, it is a better policy for ensuring long-term survival.

This is equally applicable to small and medium enterprises. Because they are often short on resources, SMEs tend to implement their innovations within their organizations. The result is that when their main business runs into trouble it generates losses so large that, given its relative weight, it drags the whole enterprise down, and the new project with it. Perhaps the project would have survived if they had set up an autonomous organization to implement it.

Thus, our decision on whether to execute inside or outside the company should also be based on sustainability and long-term survival, and not solely on short-term profitability or cost-savings.

If we finally make the decision to go outside our current business, that doesn't necessarily mean we have to set up a new company. We can subcontract or outsource the execution through an alliance with another organization.

The history of innovation abounds in examples of companies that decided it was best not to execute inside their current organization, even by setting up a new one, but rather through joint ventures. Take the case of Nestea, an initiative that a corporation of the size and financial might of Nestlé could have implemented on its own; instead, as everyone knows, it outsourced the project in a partnership with the Coca-Cola company. Another example is provided by Sunil B. Mittal, chief executive officer of Indian telecom company Bharti Tele-Ventures Ltd, whose radical business model, which outsources everything but marketing and customer management, charges 2 cents a minute for calls, and is adding a million customers a month.[10]

Walmart does something similar with proposals from the Walmart Innovation Network. Despite promoting certain projects, Walmart is not obliged to distribute the resulting innovations through its own outlets. When it is in the company's interest to do so, it contacts the appropriate buyers and organizes promotional campaigns for the sale and distribution of the innovation.

The decision as to whether or not to execute inside the company has no bearing on the decision regarding the brand name. There's nothing to say we can't outsource execution under one our current brands.

Below is a summary of the main factors to consider in deciding whether to launch inside the current organization or outside it:

1 *Disruptive level of the innovation.* The more disruptive, the more advisable it is to execute with a new organization.
2 *Expected long-term trajectory of the innovation.* The longer the projected trajectory, the easier it is to execute in a new organization.
3 *Internal obstacles.* In any organization there is a natural resistance to change. Corporate structures and culture can be a drag on innovation execution. The more internal obstacles, the greater the need to execute outside.
4 *Cost savings.* The higher the costs, the more sense it makes to execute inside the organization.
5 *Resources.* The fewer resources you have, the better the reason to execute inside the company.

It is important to consider that delegating execution to a new company does not imply a clean break with the current company. In their book *10 Rules for Strategic Innovators*,[11] Govindarajan and Trimble provide a set of recommendations on how the new company responsible for an innovation can leverage the assets of its parent company. According to the authors, building disruptive or groundbreaking businesses means we must forget, borrow and learn: forget those undisputed truths held in the parent corporation; borrow from the latter whatever assets are useful; and, finally, learn quickly from the market and early results as execution proceeds.

Thus, what we have presented here as a dichotomous decision (to execute either inside or outside the organization) can and should be approached in a much more linear manner, sifting out all the parts of the company that are not going to be involved in execution, even if they came up with the original idea or are financing the project.

Dedicated team or shared team?

Assuming we decide to execute the innovation inside the company, we must then decide whether or not to assign the responsibility to a team dedicated specifically to that task. Although the consequences of this decision are somewhat minor compared to the previous case, either option still has a number of implications, positive and negative.

Dedicated teams mean higher costs in terms of human resources, but they have the advantage of the executors being totally focused and free from other duties, and thus able to concentrate full time on the innovation. Moreover, the message sent out to the organization is that the company is genuinely interested in and committed to the project. If you expect the innovation to acquire a significant volume and are planning marginal innovations to extend the market, we recommend grouping dedicated teams in a new division created for the purpose (see the section *Extending the launch* in this chapter). Putting dedicated teams into a separate division also has the advantage of making it easier to impute costs and giving a much clearer view, from the outset, of the profits earned from the project.

A shared team, by contrast, means that the innovation executors are also in charge of other products and services. They will have to add the new product or service to the portfolio they manage, or the management of a new process or upgrade to the tasks they are responsible for. This is a cheaper way to go, but we must be careful that the execution doesn't fail because our human resources are stretched too thin.

Unified executions option

But there is a third option, which is to unify several innovations in the same team of executors, to be carried out simultaneously. If there is a stage in which various innovation processes can be handled concurrently, it is execution.

It shouldn't be any problem for two independent innovation processes to share executors. The chief innovation officer (CIO), the person responsible for overseeing all of the company's innovation processes, with her or his 360-degree view over innovative activity, is exactly the right person to determine which innovations can be executed by the same departments or teams. In fact, it sometimes happens that ideas executed together reveal more potential than when they are executed on their own.

> Before evaluating ideas generated in an ideas campaign [...], the first step should be to combine related ideas that would likely be implemented together.[12]

Profile of the innovation executor

We can choose the people we want to execute an innovation either before starting the innovation process or when it is has advanced far enough to give a better idea of the best people for the job. We may ask the team leading the process to come up with a list of people who will "buy into" the project and the idea behind it, so that we are certain that execution will be in the hands of motivated people who truly believe in the project. This is the procedure at IBM, for instance. Once an opportunity is detected, management picks a project leader, whose job is to take the idea from square one to execution while ensuring a strong bottom line.[13]

There is a general tendency to assign to successful executives the role of innovation executors. Because they have proven themselves to be good at managing certain businesses, they are also considered right for executing a launch. There is, however, an opposing school of thought which holds that this is not necessarily so. The argument is that managing an ongoing business isn't the same thing as carrying a project starting almost from scratch (as in the case of a new business model, for example). The skills you need in managing an existing business are very different from those required to take on a new project. Those who defend this viewpoint argue that it is better to put at the head of an innovation an executive who has already implemented other innovations, even if that person has a poor track record. The execution of an innovation, especially when it is disruptive or involves a new or independent business, creates new situations in an unfamiliar environment, which requires sharp reflexes: you have to be quick and creative in finding solutions; skills very different from those needed in day-to-day business management, where factors like control or efficiency are more important. Thus the criteria for selecting candidates are of an entirely different order: you want an executor who has already led innovations, someone who is used to reacting to sudden changes in circumstances. Experience in innovation is a better bet than proven success in turning a profit.

Key inputs and features of an ideal execution

Key inputs

When it comes time to execute, there are so many fronts to cover, so many little things to deal with and so many tasks to coordinate, that it's easy to lose our focus on the key components of the innovation, its strengths, the pluses we need to be highlighting.

There is a way to avoid this sort of dispersion: compile a list of the key inputs and keep it for the moment of execution. As each role becomes involved in the innovation process, it will provide inputs, factors of risk and opportunity relevant to execution. We should ensure that all these inputs are recorded and, when we have advanced to execution, that the executors bear them in mind. The activators will stress the requirements that the innovation should meet:

▷ the browsers – the key findings from their research on the target customer, the foundation of business opportunity
▷ the creators – the winning aspects of the concept
▷ the developers – the technological advantages and disadvantages of the innovation and the technological limitations that might impact execution
▷ the facilitators – the risks identified during the assessment stage and the factors that eventually led to the approval of the project

For example, this is how the developers, working from the technical perspective, might set out their most relevant inputs for the executors:

▷ Technical problems encountered during development
▷ Alternative solutions considered
▷ Final technical solution and why it is the best choice
▷ Innovative technologies incorporated in the innovation

Execution means the implementation of the ideas, so the executors need a synthesis of the key ideas that other roles have dealt with over the course of the process.

Value equation

The *raison d'être* of any innovation is its ability to create customer value. There is a very simple equation that reflects the value that a customer seeks in making a purchase (see Figure 7.2).

$$\text{Value of a purchase} = \frac{\text{What consumer receives}}{\text{Costs consumer undertakes}}$$

Figure 7.2 **Customer value equation**

As we saw in Chapter 4, the customer's main effort is the price he or she pays, the outlay. But that's not the only effort. The list also includes: the time spent choosing the article; the time spent acquiring it (trip to the store, finding the item in the store, waiting at checkout ...); the risk, real or perceived, of making the wrong choice; after-sale guarantees, and so on.

When it comes time to execute, it is important to express in the above equation the value proposition of the innovation – that is, how does the innovation create customer value? This can be done either by increasing the numerator (offering higher quality, more features, bigger size, better design, and so on) or by reducing the customer's efforts without changing what he or she gets. All innovations should result in higher value relative to the available substitutive options. This equation's relevance to execution is as a means to simplify and highlight the value inherent in the innovation and, thus, the ultimate objective of execution. Sometimes, the main advantages of an innovation become lost in execution: advertising constraints, a misguided campaign, obstacles at the point of sale, dealers who don't stress the strengths of innovation enough, and so on. In marketing, the unique selling proposition (USP) refers to the main selling points, the core advantages we offer to consumers. In innovation, we need another term, *unique innovation value* (UVI); the factor in the equation that increases customer value. In execution, all efforts should be aimed at communicating the unique innovation value.

Traits of effective execution

Companies should, through the analysis of successful innovations – both their own and those of the competition – build up a log of their common traits. Such traits will, of course, vary from sector to sector and from one sort of customer to another. But in the end, what the company should have is a checklist that acts as a guide for the execution strategy.

Here are some of the common traits of successful innovations:[14]

▷ *Simplicity*. For example, Southwest Airlines focuses on a clear message: "The lowest cost carrier." Bill Clinton took the same approach with his campaign slogan: "It's the economy, stupid." As the saying goes: "Keep it simple."

▷ *Surprise*. An innovation must catch the customer's attention before it can break their inertia and make them change their preferences and buying habits. The only way to do this is to come up with something unexpected. The ability to surprise is directly related to emotions. An execution is more effective when it appeals to emotions than when it appeals to rational arguments – the nature of the product or service permitting, of course. Almost everyone old enough to remember that year can recall precisely where he or she was and with whom the day man landed on the moon. The recall level is high because the event made a huge emotional impact.

▷ *Specificity*. The more specific the stimulus, the better the recall – that's how the human mind works. Which is why it is hard to remember theories in the abstract while it is easy to remember their practical application.

▷ *Credibility*. All marketing innovations introduce some sort of novelty, a change or improvement. The execution must ensure, through communication, distributors, or the product itself, that the value proposition is credible, giving the customer the necessary assurances and evidence.

▷ *Stories*. The communication of an innovation is very effective when we are able to construct a story. In his book *All Marketers Are Liars*, Seth Godin[15] explains that marketing professionals must be able to tell a story, a story that may not be true, but nor is it false. It is similar to the game between the novelist and the reader. The novelist tells a story we know did not happen, but could have happened. It's plausible.

The marketing plan

Basically, this would consist of two elements: the marketing plan and the marketing process. It is not the mission of this book to explain what a marketing plan consists of; there is plenty of literature on this subject and we understand that many of our readers will already be quite familiar with everything that goes into one. Just as a reminder:

Elements of the Marketing Process

1 Definition of market (on the three dimensions: Need – Customers – Situations)
2 Segmentation (criteria for segmenting the current and potential market)
3 Target market (which segment or segments we are going to target)
4 Positioning (attributes that make up differential competitive advantage)
5 4 P's
   Product (basic benefit, physical product and its features, extended product)
   Price
   Place: Distribution and sales strategy, distribution channels
   Promotion: Advertising and communication plan (advertising, public
   relations, social media plan, promotions plan, and so on)

We recommend developing a 4 P's marketing plan and a budget, and to get reactions to this plan.

A useful method for sizing elements of the 4 P's, such as investment in advertising (in money or in GRPs – gross rating points), consists in using statistical models based on historical data. Methods such as time series or multiple regression enable you to estimate the impact on sales of increased investment in advertising or the inclusion of a promotion or gift to beef-up the test. These models are not exact and should not be taken to be a clairvoyant's "crystal ball". But, without being exact, they are very indicative and serve to guide efforts when it comes to launching an innovation.

Elements of the Marketing Plan

I **Executive Summary**
   A summary of the proposed plan for a quick review by management
II **Analysis of the current market situation**
   Relevant data on market, product, competition, distribution and
      macro-environment
III **Analysis of threats and opportunities**
   Identifies, through threats, opportunities, strengths and weaknesses, the key
      issues facing the launch plan
IV **Objectives**
   Defines the objectives that the plan seeks to achieve in relation to sales
      volume, market share and profits
V **Marketing Strategies**
   Marketing guidelines to be used to achieve the objectives
VI **Action Program**
   Answers questions such as: What will be done? Who will do it? When will it
      be done? How much will it cost?
VII **Estimated income account**
   Sets out the foreseen results of the plan. The estimate can be for a 1, 3 and/
      or 5-year term
VIII **Monitoring**
   Indicates how the plan will be monitored

Source: Marketing Management,[16] **Philip Kotler ©**

This document should be accompanied by a detailed explanation of the marketing process, including, as we saw in Chapter 5, the following elements:

▷ Pre-implemenation
▷ Actual execution: the action plan
▷ Post execution: iterate and improve

Pre-implementation

The pre-implementation is a set of actions and tools that are designed to test the appropriateness of some of the decisions regarding execution and to help determine the best mix of marketing investments. The main pre-implementation tools are: experiments and product tests, area tests and market tests.

Companies often use these pre-implementation tools in product and service launches, but rarely in other innovations, such as process or business model innovation, although they would serve equally well to minimize errors in execution.

Experimentation and product testing

One way to pre-implement with a high degree of success is to allow a group of customers to experiment with and test the product or service in real situations.

For example, in 1997 when ExxonMobil launched its *Speedpass* pay-at-the-pump system, which uses a radio-frequency device installed in the customer's car, it decided to offer the device and service for free. Following up what it learned from that first group of users, the company made the corresponding improvements before executing the launch. The results were dramatic: *within a few months of launch, more than 1 million customers had signed up for Speedpass, doubling the number of times people stopped to fill up.*

This is something that Google also does on a regular basis. Prior to the final execution of an innovation, they use the feedback from a product test by a panel of users. In order to facilitate systematic testing of new products among users, Google created the *Google Labs* website (http://labs.google.com), where innovations such as Google Desk Bar and News Alerts were tested.

Area testing

After a product has been launched nationwide, changing your marketing strategy can be very costly. That's why some companies prefer to do area

tests to help shape their marketing strategies. Is it best to focus on advertising? Or on the point of sale? Should we give away free samples? Should
we offer discounts as an incentive to buyers? Area testing is a well-known
resource, yet, generally speaking, it is infrequently used by businesses.

An area test is a small-scale launch in a single city or area with a specific
marketing investment mix. The way to proceed is as follows. We analyze
behavior patterns in a series of areas until we find two that are strongly
correlated (test area and mirror area). The high level of correlation between
the two areas will allow us to test a different marketing investment mix in
each area. Since, historically, with a similar investment mix, they have
behaved in a very similar way (sales correlation), by applying a different
investment mix in each we can determine which mix is better.

Having found our two areas, we execute the launch with two different
strategies. We wait a while, then compile the sales data and compare them
against the above correlations to see if we have performed better in the area
with a different investment mix (test area) than in the other (mirror area).
Since all correlations have a given level of error, the conclusion is valid only
if the results for the test area fall outside the statistical confidence interval for
the mirror area. In Figure 7.3 we illustrate this analysis in a very simple and
intuitive manner.

Despite all the pluses of being able to try out different marketing investment mixes for the execution of an innovation, area testing is rarely used.
The main reasons why include:

▷ It reveals our cards to the competition, who get an advance look at
what our innovation consists of and the main points of our marketing
strategy. In many markets there is a tendency for competitors to come
out with the same innovation and we may lose the benefits of being
the first mover.
▷ In the real world, distribution has become concentrated into large logis-
tical platforms, making localized campaigns difficult.
▷ There are relatively few market research firms specialized in this type of
analysis.
▷ Area testing requires investing a large chunk of a company's marketing
resources. We may be launching in just two areas, but we still have to
carry out a marketing campaign, buy media space, distribute the product,
locate it at the point of sale, and so on. Since resources are always scarce,
companies tend to prefer to allocate them directly to the final release and
then adjust the investment mix in accordance with the results as they
come in.

However, where the final launch is going to take place over a large
geographical area (for example a global launch) and where marketing investment is high enough, area testing is a very effective and profitable pre-
implementation tool.

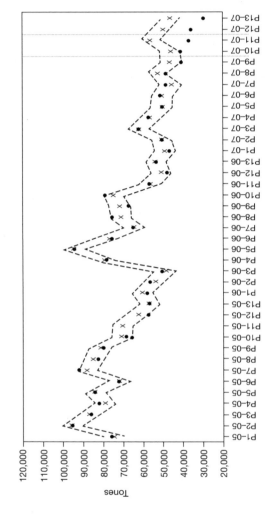

Black bullets indicate real sales on test city

Crosses indicate estimates sales on test city calculated through the mirror city

Dotted lines represents 95% confidence interval for estimated sales on test city through the mirror city

During the last 4 periods a new marketing configuration was tested in the test city

Results (bullets) show a worst performance, even out of the confidence interval, versus theoretical sales calculated through mirror city, where marketing mix remained as before

Conclusion: we reject the new marketing configuration

Figure 7.3   Area test results (test city versus mirror city)

Market testing

Market testing differs from area testing in that, rather than testing various marketing investment mixes, you choose just one, judged to be the definitive one. It resembles area testing in the limited scale of the launch, although the options for defining the scope of the launch are different:

▷ A certain geographical area
▷ A certain channel
▷ A certain set of distributors
▷ A certain set of customers

Depending on the results, information is collected (based on key performance indicators – KPIs – for example) on areas for improvement or, possibly, as discussed in the next chapter, in order to assess whether or not to go ahead with a national launch, or roll-out.

Market testing suffers from disadvantages similar to those of area testing, so its use is recommended in cases of high-risk innovations. The best way to cut risk is with a small-scale launch as a trial run for final execution.

Although many people argue they are only applicable to consumer products, market tests are actually much easier to do in the service sector. IBM uses just such a strategy in developing its EBOs (emerging business opportunities).

> The EBO leader starts selling the new service through pilot (small) projects, trying them out on the company's major customers (forming a kind of intellectual-service joint-venture). If the pilots work, the company can decide to allocate more resources, and other customers can start buying these services. This strategy gives IBM just enough time to show that the concept makes sense, establish key relationships in the market and position itself as a leader before exploiting the segment.[17]

The fact that, since 2000, IBM has launched twenty-five EBOs and just three have failed is ample evidence that this execution system increases the probabilities of a successful innovation.

Actual execution: the action plan

According to the organization of tasks we suggest in this book, the executors must sketch the outlines of the business plan in the form of two strategic elements: the marketing plan and the marketing process. Both must be translated into a set of concrete actions. The practical and effective embodiment of the marketing plan comes in the form of the action plan.

The action plan is a list of specific activities, tasks or actions to be carried out by a specific date by individuals, service providers or departments within the resources allocated.

The action plan is the basic manual for the executors in organizing and coordinating the efforts, investments and actions in the marketing plan for the innovation. The basic points of an action plan are:

▷ List of actions and activities
▷ Start date for each action or activity
▷ Budget allocated to each action or activity
▷ Leader of each action
▷ Aims and scheduling of each action
▷ Risks of failure in carrying out the execution and contingency plan

The implementation of the action plan is monitored to ensure that the execution is carried out as planned. Not only do we check that each action has been done in the way and within the timeframe stipulated in the plan, but we also gauge the extent to which it meets its aims.

Post-execution: iterate and improve

Here we are talking about a set of indicators and tools a company can use to help it execute successfully, to understand how to improve its product and adapt, eliminate or include activities related to the launch. Increasingly, given the difficulty of getting the innovation execution right the first time, companies are adding iterate-and-improve to their strategies. This is a very effective means of carrying out a market launch while being prepared to quickly detect the parts of the execution that fall short of the expected results and to provide the resources to improve on them, in accordance with the information and feedback received.

Purchase funnel

A certain time after an innovation has been launched, it is essential that we diagnose what marketing variables need adjusting in order to improve our results. For this purpose, there is a little known tool of extraordinary simplicity and usefulness: the purchase funnel. It starts from the premise that any loyal customer we might have must go through the following stages in relation to us:

▷ Awareness
▷ Consideration
▷ Trial
▷ Repeat

This is obvious enough, but not so if we turn it around. The reasons people do not buy from us today are:

▷ They are not aware of us
▷ They are aware of us, but haven't considered us
▷ They have considered us, but haven't tried us
▷ They have tried us, but haven't repeated

In a hypothetical situation in which we held 100 percent of the market, all the customers would be aware of us, have considered us, tried us and repeated. Therefore, if we do not hold 100 percent of the market it's because, starting from the 100 percent scenario, we have been losing customers. And the four reasons for this are: lack of awareness, lack of consideration, lack of trial and/or lack of repeat.

This seems theoretical, but is actually easy and cheap to put into practice. We have to do a market study in order to obtain the data, but we only need to ask a representative sample of our target market four questions: Do you know about us? If so, have you considered us? If so, have you tried us? And, if so, have you repeated? In the event of budget constraints, we can save money by including these questions in a multi-customer (omnibus-type) study.

Let's have a look at all we can get out of this information in order to correct our marketing efforts in an innovation execution. Suppose we have launched an on-call taxi service. We have conducted an advertising campaign on the radio and on billboards outside airports and train stations, informing people that we have a fleet of new vehicles and are so committed to punctuality that, if we are more than two minutes late, the trip is free. We have offered a 10 percent discount to the first 10,000 customers as an incentive to try us out and have gotten a number of customers to respond to a brief satisfaction survey to get an idea of our quality of service and areas for improvement. After a few months, we want to know how our marketing campaigns have performed so we do a small market study, which gives us:

▷ Awareness of our taxi service brand: 70 percent
▷ Have considered us: 65 percent
▷ Have tried us: 40 percent
▷ Have repeated: 10 percent

With these four figures, we can now calculate where we are losing potential customers. Out of the potential 100 percent, we have lost 30 percent due to lack of awareness (subtracting the 70 percent awareness rate from 100 percent of the market). Out of the 70 percent that could be our customers (since they are aware of us), we've lost 5 percent due to lack of consideration (subtracting the 65 percent consideration rate from the 70 percent awareness rate.) We've lost 25 percent due to lack of trial (65 percent–40 percent) and another 30 percent due to lack of repeat. Figure 7.4 shows this in illustrated form.

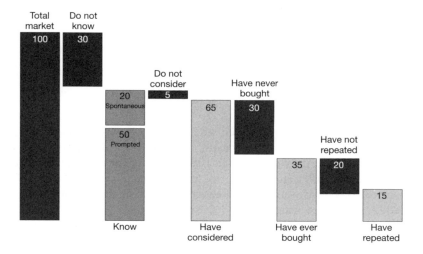

Figure 7.4 **Purchase funnel**

The diagnostic of the innovation execution is clear. After several months of marketing campaign we can safely consider a 70 percent awareness rate as optimal. We see that almost everyone who was aware of us, considered us. However, we lost a big share at the trial level. Either our incentives were a poor fit or the discount we offered wasn't enticing enough. Another possibility is that the incentives were correct and we simply need to invest more in getting people to try our service. To find out, we have to examine the reasons why these customers didn't try it (ideally, introducing questions about this in our market study). We also lost a lot of customers who tried our taxi service, but did not repeat. This points to a possible problem in the quality of service. We have to examine the satisfaction surveys we did and find out what's happening in order to make corrections. Box 7.1 shows the most common scenarios.

One example of the effective use of the purchase funnel tool is a case much lauded in the business world and often mentioned in management books: 3M's Post-it note. The story of the product's invention is oft-told, but few people know that the execution of the launch got off to a rocky start. The company found that it was losing potential customers, not because of lack of awareness, but because people weren't giving the product a try. The Post-it was so novel that customers weren't sure whether it had any real use. 3M changed its marketing strategy and invested millions in free samples, even handing them out at football stadiums. Everyone had to get a free pad of Post-its. The company was convinced that anyone that tried the product would repeat, so the focus of the launch execution turned to getting people to try it. The rest is history.

The purchase funnel, also known as ATR (Awareness, Trial and Repeat), is a basic diagnostic tool a few months after the execution of a marketing innovation.

Box 7.1 Satisfaction surveys

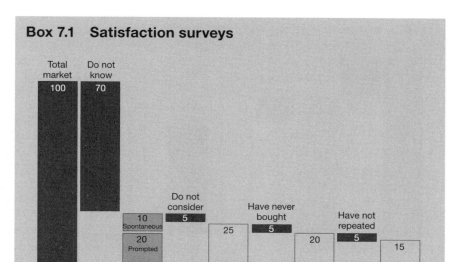

This scenario is associated with companies that skimp on advertising. They have limited market presence, and customers barely know they exist.

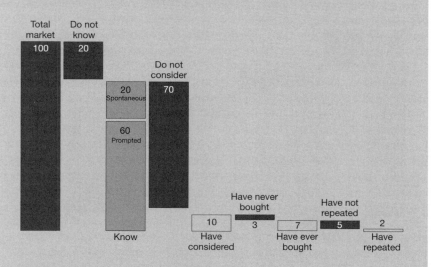

Brands with decent recognition, but with unclear or unconvincing positioning. They may also suffer from a lack of presence at the point of sale or sellers that don't push their product.

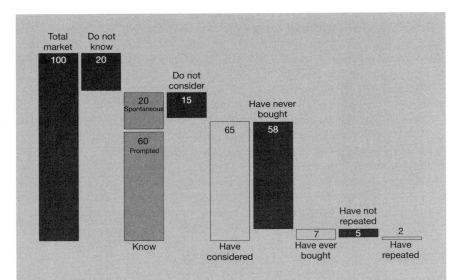

Brands that are taken into account, but that don't convince customers. They often have problems with pricing or perceived quality.

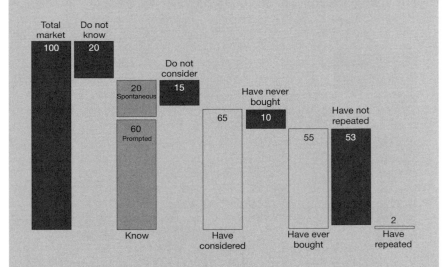

Brands that disappoint customers due to poor quality or to having created expectations they can't deliver.

KPIs evolution

The execution of an innovation is the execution of its strategy. A strategy whose results cannot be measured is of little use. The monitoring of KPIs serves both to determine whether the innovation is meeting our objectives and to determine whether the execution will lead to the accomplishment of our plans.

In order to get the execution right, it is essential that we monitor key aspects of the innovation. In order to do that, we need to define our key performance indicators. KPIs relate to the strategic objectives of the innovation, marketing plan objectives, the facilitators' assessment systems and everything that goes into the value proposition. KPIs must be specific, measurable and quantifiable. Table 7.1 gives some examples of KPIs that a company might monitor in the launch of, for instance, a new upgraded version of a product from its portfolio.

Table 7.1 Examples of KPIs to monitor for a product upgrade

• **Market KPIs**
▷ % penetration in the target market
▷ Market share in units
▷ Level of satisfaction relative to the original product
• **Channel KPIs**
▷ Numerical distribution (% of outlets where the product has been distributed)
▷ Weighted distribution (% that these outlets represent out of domestic sales)
▷ Outlet position (% of outlets where the product is in a prime position)
• **Financial KPIs**
▷ Commercial margin in %
▷ Profit/Loss in dollars
• **Innovation KPIs**
▷ % of customers with the older product that have moved up to the superior version
▷ % of new customers captured from the competition, thanks to the new version

For example, Tesco uses a very simple KPI: sales. If a new product does not meet the company's sales objectives, it is removed from the shelves. The life cycle for new products is 18 months.

Extending the launch

Launch extension means taking all the lessons learned and improvements of a launch and broadening the scope of the project.[18]

ExxonMobil's *Speedpass*, which we have already mentioned, is the perfect example of how extension policies for an innovation can produce profits very quickly and with much less risk. Speedpass had a somewhat fitful introduction. But once it got off the ground – once the system had proved to be a success with a high level of acceptance and penetration among customers – this is what ExxonMobil did:[19]

▷ *Extended the payment system from the pump to the filling station store.* Contrary to the concerns of ExxonMobil management, Speedpass users kept coming into their stores to buy the consumer products on offer there.
▷ *Developed marketing campaigns to encourage the use of corporate Speedpass tags* for companies with sales staff and transporters.
▷ *Set up an agreement with the Timex company* to develop a Speedpass device built into a wristwatch.
▷ *Created the Speedpass Network Unit to extend the system to other service sellers,* such as carwashes, parking lots, fast food restaurants, vending machines, and so on.

An innovation can be extended in the following ways:

▷ Entering new geographical markets (countries or areas)
▷ Adapting our message to capture new customers
▷ Adjusting our prices to increase penetration
▷ Incorporating new sales channels not included in the launch
▷ Modifying the makeup of the core product
▷ Extending our portfolio with marginal innovations

This last point is fundamental. If you examine the history of any market, you will find that it was a disruptive innovation that created the market, but that it was marginal innovations that built it up. In our previous book, *Lateral Marketing*, we explained that lateral innovations create new markets, but it's the vertical innovations that develop them. There are some companies with the ability to create markets; companies that exceed at disruptive innovations (Apple is an obvious case). There are others that lack the capacity to reinvent markets and that are nonetheless quick and efficient in the development of variations on and extensions of disruptive products launched by other companies. Such companies are called *fast second* companies.[20] For a time, Microsoft was a fast second company. In the software market, Apple was more creative and groundbreaking, it was the one that introduced disruptive innovations; but Microsoft was faster and better at extending and improving on them, so it ended up capturing a larger market share. All that has changed. Apple learned its lesson. With the iPhone, for example, it didn't launch the disruptive innovation (the new terminal) until it had a well-defined post-launch extension strategy: iPhone Apps. Apple no longer simply does the groundwork for the competition. Since the life cycles of products and services are becoming shorter and shorter, in innovation it is essential to act in this way. We need to have the marginal or vertical follow-up innovation ready to succeed a radical or lateral innovation. If a radical innovation is successful, we must act very, very quickly and extend the market with variations on the product. That's the way to optimize the risk and investment entailed in all disruptive innovations.

Morphing

This type of execution has become very fashionable of late. It consists in assuming that we will never achieve the perfect innovation or execution strategy, and that the best way to go about things is to launch the new product or service in the knowledge that we will have to adjust both its makeup and the marketing strategy.

> Applying the usual techniques of market research to radically new products (with which we seek to discover or create markets that do not exist) can have a paralyzing effect, insofar as they require detailed estimations, plans and budgets that are impossible to define. In this case, the conventional approach based on gathering all possible information to increase the likelihood of success not only consumes a lot of time and effort, but due to the particular scenario of volatility and uncertainty of these projects this information will never be valid or sufficient.
>
> In recent years quick-launch approaches have gained acceptance, since they enable you to reap the benefits of early entry and quickly gain real experience in the market. [21]

Since it is assumed beforehand that the product will have to be modified, the company prepares itself to innovate in a radically different way. Warning mechanisms are put in place in order to identify the necessary changes based on customer and user feedback, and the developers and engineers are ready to make the appropriate modifications.

This type of strategy means a radical shift in innovation process design by putting the entire focus on the company's ability to learn from the market and act accordingly.

Morphing is based on the premise that markets change so rapidly that it makes no sense to wait until an innovation is perfect because we'll still need to modify or improve it in the short term. Thus, innovation is an ongoing, market-sourced improvement of a product or service. Instead of thinking in terms of innovation, we think in terms of continual redesign based on feedback from customers and the market.

Google uses morphing in a manner that is both surprising and intelligent. When they launch an innovation, they let external developers and programmers make improvements on an ostensibly developed product, thus exploiting the programmers' universe as a giant team of potential product improvers.

On the new Web 2.0, many products and services are provided in "perpetual beta", the functionality of which is continuously evolving based on the use that users (who are treated as co-developers) make of them.

The similarities between area testing, test marketing and morphing can be confusing. Table 7.2 should help differentiate them.

Table 7.2 Differences between area test, market test and morphing

	Execution alternatives (investment mix)	Execution scope
Area test	Several alternatives	Partial (test cities or regions and control cities and regions)
Market test	One (the definitive plan)	Partial (by areas, cities, regions, channels, distributors or customers)
Morphing	One (the definitive plan)	Total

TOTAL INNOVATION SYSTEM – Summary Chapter 7

Main person/s in charge of each role

A Activators	B Browsers	C Creators	D Developers	E Executors	F Facilitators
Top management (GM or Chief innovation officer)	Market research department	Advertising agency	R&D	Current marketing department (shared team)	
Employees	Market research suppliers	Creativity agency	New products department	Current sales department (shared team)	
Suppliers	Sociologists	Marketing	Operations	Dedicated marketing team	
Distributors	Marketing	Creative types	Manufacturing	New division	
Clients	Sales	R&D	External suppliers	New company	
Investors	Opinion leaders	Clients	Marketing	Third party alliances	
Universities	Watchers' panel	Suppliers	Sales		
Scientific community	R&D	Employees with creative profile	Dedicated engineers		
Inventors	Other internal departments	Other suppliers or third parties			
Engineering companies	Other suppliers or third parties				

Up-bottom activation
In-out activation
Bottom-up activation
Out-in activation

Techniques employed by each role

A Activators	B Browsers	C Creators	D Developers	E Executors	F Facilitators
Scope of innovation	Innovation review	Synectics	Helping in concept definition	Marketing plan and launch plan	
Innovation levels	Analysis of adjacent categories	Blue Ocean strategy	Concept test for improving design	Morphing	
Focus of innovation	Internal consulting	Morphological analysis	Pictures	KPIs' evolution	
Innovation guidelines	Social trend/ social classes	Lateral marketing	Conjoint analysis for features definition	Next marginal evolution	
Innovation checklist	Market trends	Attributes listing	Drawings	Area testing	
	Buying process	Scenarios analysis	Mock-up	Market testing	
	Innovation routes	Visits	Prototype	Product testing	
	Technological solutions	Co-creation	Product test	Intensity on ATRs	
	Design referents	Redefining customer value	Usage/home test	Experimentation	
	Successful strategies and tactics/learning from errors	Brainstorming	Patents		
	Network monitoring	Concept definition			
	Ethnographic				
	Geolocation				

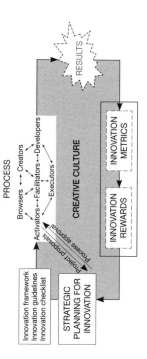

INNOVATION PROCESS

Browsers ←→ Creators
Activators ←→ Facilitators ←→ Developers
Executors

Project proposals
Process approval

CREATIVE CULTURE

RESULTS

Innovation framework
Innovation guidelines
Innovation checklist

STRATEGIC PLANNING FOR INNOVATION

INNOVATION REWARDS

INNOVATION METRICS

8 Facilitators

What do facilitators do?

Facilitators have the following functions:

▷ Approve the related investments
▷ Select the best options for innovation
▷ Advance the innovation process
▷ Jumpstart the group when it gets bogged down
▷ Give the definitive "go" for a launch or innovation execution

The role of the facilitators is essential to ensure that the process moves forward efficiently and does not cause the company unnecessary costs. Facilitators are also responsible for terminating a process before costs get out of hand or for putting it back on course when it goes awry, such as when it diverges from the objectives or budget. We should remember that one of the secrets to successful innovation is to fail fast, early and cheaply. The facilitators are responsible for anticipating failures, and weeding out overly ambitious or low-potential ideas as well as for adopting the most promising ones, encouraging the group to advance the process and supporting it with the necessary resources.

The facilitators' engagement in the innovation process is less constant than that of any other role. They should always be ready to make decisions and, if appropriate, approve investment items, but it's healthy to have them keep a certain distance from the process so that they can act more objectively than if they were involved on a day-to-day basis.

Who they are

The following people can act as facilitators at any given point in the innovation process (from lower to higher hierarchical level in the organization):

▷ Employees
▷ Team in charge of the innovation process
▷ Middle management

▷ Department heads (marketing, R&D, sales, operations, and so on)
▷ Financial director
▷ Chief innovation officer (CIO)
▷ Managing director
▷ Chief executive officer (CEO)
▷ Board of directors
▷ Shareholders

External facilitators include:

▷ Experts
▷ Stakeholders
▷ Investors

During an innovation project, the facilitator may be more than one of these people and, moreover, the person may change over the course of the process. For example, in the early stages of a process, when the role of a facilitator is to shortlist projects, the facilitator may be the company's employees who rate the best ideas. On the other hand, when it comes to approving investments, the role can be assigned to senior management. Typically, there is a correlation between the stage of the innovation process and the facilitator's rank in the hierarchy. As an innovation process moves forward, a more senior facilitator with greater decision-making power within the organization is usually required.

How high in the hierarchy do we go? Let's recall Chapter 3, where we established a relationship between type of innovation and hierarchical level. Ideally, in the closing stages of an innovation process the facilitator should be the top position in the area of innovation: the CEO or shareholders in the case of a new business model; the managing director in a process innovation; the marketing director or managing director in a market-level innovation; the marketing director in a product innovation (line extension). Figure 8.1 shows this relationship and the top levels corresponding to the role of facilitator according to the type of innovation.

In some cases, the facilitators' role coincides with that of the activators of the process, but this is not necessarily so. For example, at Google, employees use part of their free time to act as innovation activators or to vote for good ideas, but they are not the ones who approve the investment items. In the case of Tesco, process activation was once delegated to researchers and universities, but the financing and facilitation of processes remained in the hands of company management.

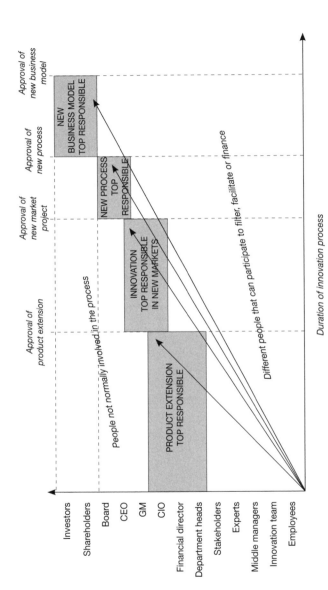

Figure 8.1 **Filters, facilitators and financers**

Types of facilitation

There are three types of facilitation, according to the point in time and stage of the process:

1 Assessment and selection of alternative ideas or concepts
2 Jumpstarting the innovation process in the event of a breakdown
3 Approval and allocation of financial resources and investments

Below we describe in brief the tools and systems of facilitators, organized by the three types of facilitation mentioned above.

Systems for assessing and selecting alternative ideas or concepts

Subjective assessment

Subjective assessment is a very basic tool often used to prioritize ideas or concepts. It is ideal for small groups and something the team in charge of an innovation process can use in a timely manner at various stages of the process.

The aim here is to expedite decision-making without losing time in discussion, and thus it is used in less critical decisions, at less critical points in time or at the start of the process; that is, where there are too many ideas or suggestions, in order to discard the least attractive options.

Subjective assessments are made with simple rankings (from 0 to 5, or 0 to 10) and a small number of dimensions (1 to 3 dimensions). Dimension refers to an aspect of the idea to consider. For example, if we are assessing an array of concepts for a product or service, assessment typically focuses on just one or two of these dimensions:

▷ Market potential
▷ Difficulty of development business risk
▷ Appeal of the idea
▷ Synergy with existing business
▷ Strategic priority
▷ Consistency with current business
▷ Current competitors

The results are tabulated in a simple manner and equal weight is given to each person's score, such that more senior people have the same impact as everyone else (at least at this stage).

In dealing with a larger number of ideas, subjective assessment can be done in several rounds, eliminating in each round the worst, and voting again on those which remain. You proceed in this way until you have reduced your options to a manageable number for moving ahead in the process.

Sometimes it is advisable to analyze the spread of the scores, since there are two types of policies that can be adopted in choosing concepts based on group-sourced ratings. The first option is based on mean scores. This has the advantage of accounting for all the scores, and the disadvantage that it does not discriminate between one concept that scores, for example, 8 forty times (with a mean of 8) and another one whose score is split evenly between 10s and 6s. Here the mean would also be 8, but there is a substantial difference between the two outcomes. In the first case, we could say that this is an idea everybody "quite" likes. In the second case, some like it "a lot" while others give it just a passing score. This leads to another type of analysis: standard deviation. A concept with high scores and higher than mean deviations, it is a polarizing concept; that is, it has ardent fans and equally ardent opponents. Some companies prefer to take the risk and focus on these sorts of concepts rather than those that everybody "quite" likes. It all depends on the company's innovation policy and the level of risk it wants to assume.

When the scores are very similar and the differences are incremental (decimals) a point distribution system can be used. For example, you award 10 points to the highest-rated option, 9 to the second, 8 to the third, and so on.

Company-wide rating

This is similar to the previous system, but it involves almost the entire organization. It is an ideal system for screening the ideas and suggestions that emerge from all corners of the organization, even prior to the innovation process, as a tool for deciding which ideas are suitable for inclusion in a process.

It is a tool used by innovation-intensive companies with a strong creative culture. At the same time, since the ideas to be rated come from within the organization itself, people should obviously have the opportunity to assess the ideas of their peers.

Google uses this system routinely, exploiting its intranet as a very simple means for everyone to be exposed to and vote on ideas.

Popular voting systems are not limited solely to the filtering or screening of ideas. They are also used to rate alternative final projects, where staff opinions and voting are an additional factor in decision-making, along with, for example, expert opinions or demand estimations.

It is not a technique exclusive to large organizations. In small and medium enterprises, where innovation requires the support and involvement of all staff, it is a very effective tool for involving everyone in the project. It also helps to build a creative culture.

Levels of concept screening and tests

Once we have chosen highly rated new product ideas to work on, we might need to look at the potential of different product concepts. In Chapter 6, we saw the different methods for testing concepts, products and uses. In addition to being used to refine and improve the design of innovation with the help of the views of consumers and customers, tests include a series of questions formulated for representative samples of the market to help us prioritize ideas and concepts, and to estimate, albeit very roughly, the potential demand for the innovation.

Concept screening is a tool in which respondents are shown a large number of concepts and given little information about them, so as not to wear them out too quickly during the interview and so that they can rate a large number of ideas. Concept screening can be done *qualitatively* (focus groups) or through structured questionnaires with sufficient statistical bases. Qualitative screening helps us to determine which concepts are rated lowest and which are rated highest. Although this does not lend itself to discriminating among intermediate concepts, it does help us to decide what to discard and what customers seem to like most.

In the case of *quantitative* screening, the most common way to proceed is with two questions in order to decide among an overwhelming number of possibilities which concepts to eliminate and which to keep. Respondents are asked about purchase intent and how much they like the idea. For purchase intent, we use either of two scales: 7 points or 5 points, with the latter becoming increasingly preferred. In the 5-point model, the respondent is given the following options:

Would you buy this product?

▶ **Definitely**
▶ **Probably**
▶ **Maybe**
▶ **Probably not**
▶ **Definitely not**

Companies that employ this tool frequently end up building a benchmark: that is, as they launch products on the market and get the results, they compare the latter with the data obtained in consumer-assessment studies. This enables them to establish a set of baselines that a concept must attain in future tests in order to be launched. For example, in the food industry it is estimated that a new concept, in order to be launched, needs to score 20 percent " definitely" in terms of purchase intent (called Top Box Score; that is, the best response) and a 60 percent aggregate of "definitely" and "probably" responses (called Top Two Box Score).

Screening is designed to prioritize among a large number of concepts. When fewer concepts remain, the most common method is a concept test or, if the product is already developed, product test, where it can also be tried out and touched physically.

In concept and product testing, in addition to purchase intent, we also take into consideration other useful questions for estimating demand. For example, respondents who say they would definitely buy the concept or product are asked to estimate how the purchase of this product would impact their current buying habits: that is, out of every 10 future purchases in this product category how many do they think would be the new product or concept? Since the interview also includes any competing products that the respondent regularly buys or acquires, we can make estimates, very rough but indicative of the market share a concept can aspire to.

We do these tests for the overall market as well as target segments. A concept might obtain average scores in the market as a whole yet have a lot of appeal among certain segments. In order to identify this sort of situation, we need a sample broad enough to yield a sufficient statistical base in certain subsamples. Since this raises the costs of market research, it is advisable to predetermine segments of the population in which we think the concept will find greater acceptance and have the research firm doing the test skew its sample towards that target group, then weigh the results in order to ensure representativeness.

Some companies also run concept screening and tests among their own employees.

Delphi method

The Delphi method is a means for making prognoses and predictions, something that is very useful for assessing alternative innovation concepts. The Delphi method seeks to achieve a consensus based on interaction and discussion over a time period among a panel of specialists and experts in the field in which we seek to make forecasts.

A limited number of people with relevant experience in the product and service to be innovated are given a questionnaire. The results of the questionnaire, which combines qualitative and quantitative assessments, are then given to all the participants, and they are asked to revise their assessments and forecasts in light of what their colleagues have said. They are also encouraged to come up with solutions to problems or setbacks that others foresee will arise in the launch of innovation. The anonymity of the participants is ensured and, after two or three rounds, the results are exploited statistically.

By working in successive rounds, the assessments tend to converge. That is, as the experts learn the scores of others and respond to doubts and concerns about the new project under assessment, the standard deviation of the scores is reduced. It comes to a point where the process converges towards a mean score with very low variability. It is assumed that this consensus will be sufficiently valid. In his book *The Wisdom of Crowds: Why the Many Are Smarter Than the Few and How Collective Wisdom Shapes Business, Economies, Societies and Nations*, James Surowiecki highlights the benefits of combining information in groups, arguing that decisions arising from a group are usually better than those taken by a single individual alone.[1]

Research by Basu and Schroeder[2] showed that the Delphi method was able to forecast sales of a new product during the first two years with a margin of error of 3–4 percent compared to actual sales. Other quantitative methods produced errors of 10–15 percent and unstructured traditional methods had errors of about 20 percent.

One of the advantages of the Delphi method is that it uses each member of the panel to encourage opinions among the rest. Another advantage is that it does not require physical presence, so the panel can include people from different places around the world, ensuring the sort of diversity that is essential to the method. Anonymity also prevents the most powerful, most influential, best-known or strongest personalities from dominating the rest. Today, this method can be applied very efficiently, given the Internet's potential for information processing, selecting experts, maintaining anonymity, and online presentation of results as the process advances.

Other subjective methods

There are times when the assessment of ideas and concepts is not as dependent on a quantitative baseline as it is on a series of insights that lead to the conclusion that a particular innovation makes sense. This is especially true in the case of disruptive innovations or startups, where it is difficult to define the market.

Assessments of new concepts in these cases are based on qualitative information and market indicators that arise from observation and contact with the customer, of the habits and trends seen among heavy users and earlyvangelists, "enthusiasts who recognize the potential of the product and can help spread the good word, customers who take risks on new products."[3]

Systems and tools to jumpstart a stalled innovation process

The facilitators should not confine themselves to being mere financers or resource providers. The role of the facilitators is to ensure that the process keeps moving forward efficiently and avoids unnecessary costs especially when its leader lacks the formal authority to do so on his or her own. Obviously, this function does not fall to shareholders, stakeholders or the board of directors. These are tools that are employed by the CIO, the head of the group in charge of the innovation process, the managing director or the like.

Let's examine the methods.

Nominal group techniques

The nominal group technique (NGT) provides a means of overcoming the typical problems groups have in decision-making and searching for solutions, where, due to the members' varying levels of responsibility and power, an imbalance occurs when making judgments and voting. It is useful for making quick decisions by voting, and allows everyone's opinion to be taken into account, without the need for a majority.

The nominal group technique, or any of its derivatives (for example Phillips 66), can be used in the innovation process in two ways:

▷ To jumpstart the process when the group gets bogged down due to disagreement or other challenges that may arise at any given time
▷ As a way to prioritize among different options or concepts that the group is assessing

Nominal group technique is structured in the following steps:

Step 1 – Introduction

The participants meet and the leader explains the purpose of the meeting. The participants are divided into small groups (four to ten people). The leader explains the problem to be solved or the decision to be made.

Step 2 – Ideas

Individually, without any discussion, each participant jots down useful ideas and possible solutions to the problem. In the case of project assessment, each participant, also working individually, lists the risks and opportunities that he or she foresees.

Step 3 – Presentation of ideas

The director of the meeting presents all the ideas generated by each person. There is no discussion of them yet; rather they are simply recorded in summary fashion.

Step 4 – Analysis

The ideas are analyzed, but without discussing them in depth. Then they are discussed, not with aim of rejecting ideas, but rather in order to enrich them, avoiding judgments and criticism. Finally, all the participants vote anonymously.

Step 5 – Ranking

Based on the above results, the ideas receiving the fewest votes are discarded and best ones ranked. Further discussion of the best ideas is encouraged and there is another round of voting with the aim of selecting a single idea.

Step 6 – Solution

The agreed solution is further defined and the plan of action is set out in detail. When prioritizing innovation concepts, projects are ranked according to the voting.

For example, at the Nutrexpa food company, NGT is used to decide on the promotional gifts for each year. First they determine what class of gift is best suited for a particular product category. Having established this focus, the product manager then initiates a search for the most appropriate gift for the promotion. All the product managers from the marketing department take part in the NGT.

Six Thinking Hats[4]

This is a technique developed by Edward de Bono, based on parallel thinking (in turn, based on eastern cultures-type of discussion). It is a form of nominal group technique for solving problems that need to be addressed in groups. It can be used also as a way to rank competing projects.

The technique seeks to avoid discussion going on too long or getting stalled due to participants holding different attitudes at the same time. The individual members of a group carry an attitude determined by the structure of their personality and their inclination toward or against the object of the discussion. A person with a markedly critical character will look for faults and problems, which can be useful at times, but can also cause the discussion to come to an impasse. Similarly, a person who is set against a proposal will adopt a destructive or negative attitude. Although this behavior can be beneficial to identify the risks entailed in a project, it can also disrupt the group dynamics.

The Six Thinking Hats technique deals with this problem by defining six attitudes or states with regard to a particular issue. The six states are:

▷ Objectivity (white hat), which presents figures, established facts and objective information about the innovation
▷ Creativity (green hat), which applies fertile thinking, new ideas and possibilities
▷ Emotions (red hat), which lets flow the intuitions, the feelings that the innovation stirs in the person, although they are not based on data
▷ Optimism (yellow hat), which stresses the opportunities and possibilities offered by innovation, thinking constructively
▷ Pessimism (black hat), putting the innovation to the test and thinking about the dangers and risks, asking oneself why the innovation is not going to work
▷ Control and organization (blue hat), which raises factors related to the process and its organization: thinking about thinking

During group discussion, the individual members as a group assume each of these roles or states in turn and in an organized manner. For example, while thinking or working with the red hat for half an hour, everyone must examine and judge the innovation with the same attitude, regardless of whether one's personal inclinations toward the project are positive or negative. Then, the group "changes hats" and the discussion continues with everyone thinking in a different state, for example creatively (green hat), and so on.

This working technique – based on eastern countries' thinking, on alignment rather than confrontation – enables the group to work in a highly organized manner and to address the dimensions of an innovation in an orderly way, free from the dominant part of each person's personality and their personal feelings about the project.

At the end of the session, if no consensus has been reached, some sort of vote can taken, but for the most part this nominal method tends to produce an overall alignment of positions and consensus.

Phillips 66

This is a nominal group technique for breaking deadlocks or choosing among options very quickly and efficiently. The technique was devised by J. Donald Phillips and consists in dividing a large group into 6 small groups of 6 people each. Each group discusses the problem for 6 minutes. The 6 minutes can also be given by turns to each person, who suggests a possibility or solution to the problem under discussion. When the 6 minutes are up, the participants vote individually for their preferred options. Then the representative from each group takes the best solutions and the 6 representatives form a new group, which, for 6 minutes, assesses the highest-rated options.

This system works well in innovation processes when the need arises to find quick solutions to less important problems that, nonetheless, due to a lack of consensus, remain a stumbling block for the group. It is also very useful for choosing in an organized and democratic manner among an unmanageable number of options or ideas up for consideration.

Six Sigma

Companies that continuously innovate and keep multiple innovation processes going simultaneously acquire such experience that, over time, they can determine whether an innovation process is progressing normally or a warning light should start flashing. Such companies base this assessment on a series of deviations in scheduling, costs or incidents. The Six Sigma methodology can serve to do the same thing.

As a company gains experience in starting up innovation processes, it can relate certain variables indicative of future problems with the final outcome. Once a correlation has been established, it is possible to, in a certain sense, "automate" the facilitators' assessment of the innovation process. Instead of focusing solely on the expected results of the innovation, here the attention is shifted to indicators related to the efficiency and effectiveness of the process, in the understanding that, when innovation processes deviate too far from such indicators, the process will run into difficulties in the future.

Six Sigma is actually a methodology and strategy aimed at improving processes related to quality, seeking to minimize the defects in a product or service. But it has many applications:

> The original purpose of Six Sigma, as developed by companies like Motorola and General Electric, was to identify and eliminate causes of manufacturing defects within large-scale industrial projects. Over the past few decades, a legion of managers in a variety of industries have adapted Six Sigma methodologies to suit their own uses. For example, some project management professionals rely on Six Sigma tools to measure team effectiveness.[5]

The Six Sigma philosophy is adaptable to continuous assessment of a company's innovation processes. The idea is to approach innovation processes in the same way as you would with any other process in the company, whether it be production processes, materials supply or administrative processes.

The Six Sigma method strives to minimize the defects and deficiencies in a process to 3.4 chances per million of a defect arising. Naturally, it is impossible to achieve such a ratio in innovation, but it is possible to enumerate the factors that cause defects and problems in the innovation process. For example, a company may determine that when an innovation process …

▷ runs behind schedule by over 30 percent
▷ shows a budget deviation greater than 20 percent
▷ shows more than 25 obstacles in the process
▷ is questioned by over 25 percent of management
▷ shows different volume projections with variability higher than $\pm$ 40 percent

… a warning light should start flashing and it's time to revise the design of the process or even the viability of the project.

The factors and level of tolerance can be adjusted to suit all sorts of innovations: marginal or disruptive, technological or business model.

Exceeding these tolerances does not necessarily mean we must put an end to a process, but it does warn us of potential problems regarding its feasibility and costs. It also signals the need for a higher-than-normal profit projection, since the number of defects in the process is directly related to the level of risk of failure.

Systems and tools for approving and allocating financial resources and investments

The tools that we are going to examine now serve to give the "go/no go" to an innovation and approve or refuse the investment it entails.

Cost (or risk)–benefit analysis[6]

From any business decision there derive a number of costs and benefits that must be enumerated and assessed in economic terms. It is understood that those activities or initiatives whose benefits outweigh their costs are worthwhile and the rest will fail. This method is perfectly applicable to assessing whether or not to proceed with an innovation, although it can also be used for innovation in political and social projects. In some cases, instead of costs, it is the risks that are gauged.

This method takes into account absolutely all of the benefits and costs of an innovation, regardless of whether they are imputable to its operating account (for example any potential loss of sales in other divisions of company caused by an innovation). This is what differentiates it from other economic or financial methods, such as profit and loss or ROI (return on investment) analysis, which include only earnings and operating costs, and do not take into account other secondary costs associated with but not directly part of the profit and loss account of an innovation.

We particularly recommend cost–benefit analysis for product improvement projects or quality upgrade processes, because it measures quite clearly whether the benefits of a change are commensurate with the costs of carrying it out. It enables you to determine which among various options offers the best ROI. This is calculated by the ratio of profits (expressed in monetary terms) to development and execution costs (also in monetary terms). Based on that ratio, you can calculate how long it will take for your profits to outweigh your costs; that is, payback time.

Here's an example. A market research company is assessing the desirability of introducing an online system for administering questionnaires for its quantitative research department.

Its costs are $94,000:

▶ Computer equipment: $45,600
▶ Staff training: $14,400
▶ Loss of efficiency during the introduction of the working method: $34,000

The expected profits are $109,000:

▶ Increased capacity: $32,000
▶ Reduction in errors: $21,000
▶ Capture of new customers: $56,000

As a result, the payback time is: $94,000/$109,000 = 0.86 of a year, or roughly 10 months.

We can see that the method takes into account both direct and indirect costs and profits.

Secondary cost–benefit analysis is especially useful in the case of public-sector innovation. For example, if a city government were assessing the feasibility of a new museum concept with a cost–benefit analysis, it would include the social costs and benefits of the innovation:[7]

▷ Social costs: the assessment may be based on the loss to society of the shift of assets from their alternate optimal use (for example, the social opportunity cost of the personnel employed equals the product of these people in alternative employment)
▷ Externalities: loss of land and other raw materials, potential road or urban congestion due to public works, and so on
▷ Induced increase in tourism sector income (higher flow and increased average length of stay)
▷ Additional increases in income due to other potential induced activities (stores, restaurants, leisure, and so on)

Companies establish go/no go criteria based on three factors:

▷ Minimum profit (for example, the innovation must earn a minimum of $100,000)
▷ Minimum payback time (for example, profits must outweigh costs within one year)
▷ Minimum ratio by which profits must outweigh costs (for example, final profits of the project must exceed total costs by a factor of three)

Although some estimates of costs and profits are based on subjective assumptions, this is a very useful system for identifying all the expected impacts of a given innovation. This tool forces us to ask the question: "Which of the solutions offers the greatest benefits in relation to the resources invested?" instead of "What is the cheapest solution?"[8]

Demand estimation[9]

Estimating the demand (existing or potential) for a proposed service or product is the first step to determining whether or not an investment is viable.[10]

The measure of the demand for a product or service is the number of people who buy or make use of it. For demand to be considered effective there are three requirements:

1 There must be people with a need met by the product or service.
2 There must be people ready to pay to satisfy this need.
3 They must have the purchasing power to actually pay for it.

Demand is usually estimated in two ways. One, by multiplying the following variables:

▷ Quantification of the potential market (number of customers)
▷ Foreseen penetration (percentage who will buy it)

▷ Acts of purchase per month (or year)
▷ Average units per act of purchase

The second way is to multiply these other variables:

▷ Quantification of the annual market (in units, value)
▷ Estimated market share (percent)

Clearly, it is difficult to estimate the demand for goods and services that do not yet exist.

> For the Nintendo Wii, despite the strong market success of this leading video game console, poor demand planning and mismatched pricing cost them at least $680 million, as well as six market share points. Nintendo was loosing hundreds of millions of dollars in profit on the Wii based on a two year long shortage, and an inability to foresee demand. According to Nintendo's president for North America, their supply curves and demand curves did not intersect.[11]

How can demand be predicted? The answer depends on the type of innovation. When it comes to marginal innovations, the common method is to use information on similar launches from the past or make estimates based on the sales of other products in the portfolio. When it comes to disruptive innovations, given the absence of references in the market, sales figures for substitutive products and services can be used as a reference, such as those identified in the definition of the concept in the section "source of volume" (see Chapter 5).

In either case, one possibility is to use the results from product tests indicating how many consumers say they will definitely buy the product when it is released on the market and the customers we expect to impact with communications and promotional campaigns. To do this, we multiply the following variables:

▷ Quantification of the potential market (number of customers)
▷ Estimated awareness percentage that we will attain with advertising
▷ Estimated trial percentage over the public impacted by trial incentive promotions and advertising
▷ Estimated percentage of repeats over the public impacted in trial, based on the "likeness" scores in product tests
▷ Average number of units purchased (frequency) among the public that repeats, based on normal consumer habits as determined by market research

When making estimates of demand, if we are using past information to predict future sales, it's a good idea to check a number of variables known to be strongly correlated with changes in demand:[12]

1   Annual growth rates for the industry
2   Price elasticity for our category

3 Income elasticity for our target market
4 Cross elasticity with substitutive products
5 Growth trends in GDP
6 Expected growth in consumer credit or investment
7 Consumer sentiment (for example University of Michigan Consumer Sentiment Index)
8 Population and income growth and changes in their distribution
9 Changes in the overall price levels
10 Changes in consumer preferences
11 Emergence of substitutive products
12 Changes in economic policy
13 Changes in the evolution and growth of the economic system

Profit and loss

The profit and loss account is an accounting tool that reflects economic performance for a given period (usually one year), yielding a positive (profit) or negative (loss) result. It is one of the most commonly used tools in innovation, at either the product or market level, as companies will normally have an operating account for each of their products.

It is also used in the case of business model innovations, although equal or greater importance is usually given to return on investment (see section on ROI below). In an innovation to upgrade processes, as we have seen, cost–benefit analysis is commonly used.

The analytical profit and loss account is a very basic tool with which the reader will be quite familiar. Regarding the imputation of costs, profit and loss accounts for innovations usually give a good deal of weight to the concept of *depreciation*, given that innovation tends to entail significant investment that is imputed in the first years in the form of depreciation.

The same applies to the costs of launches and marketing campaigns. That is why the profit and loss account for an innovation, in its initial years, does not reflect future profits in a situation of stability. The depreciation of the initial investment, along with marketing investments for the launch, represents additional costs in what will become, over time, the operating account for the new product or service. The common way to deal with this is to draw up a profit and loss account for the coming three to five years, such that the true future contribution of the innovation can be properly assessed.

With respect to the imputation of overheads or fixed costs, some people like to impute a very low proportion of overhead to the new product, assuming that the company's fixed costs remain largely unchanged with the new launch (depending on its magnitude, of course). The second option is to estimate the additional investment in increased company structure and impute only this additional cost. The third option, which is the most common, is to treat the new product like the any other, imputing overhead based on volume.

The operating account is a step beyond assessments related to potential (estimation of demand, product testing or Delphi methods, for example), given that it incorporates the costs of manufacturing and launch. It is therefore the most crucial tool in the innovation process. It is usually done in the later stages of the process. Since it requires calculating, in addition to the necessary investments and variable costs, the costs derived from the marketing plan to be drawn up, the profit and loss account is usually done and redone at several points, as information comes in regarding the costs of and earnings from the innovation. There is also the provisional profit and loss account, where, in order to assess whether or not to proceed with an innovation, the variable costs, overheads, depreciation and advertising investments are calculated based on the direct billing rates for other products by the same company.

ROI

ROI (which stands for return on investment) is a measurement of the performance of an investment, and is thus used to assess how effective our spending is, whether current or planned. It measures the effectiveness of the money invested, rather than the size of investment, and is expressed in terms of a rate of return on invested capital: in this case, in innovation. ROI is applicable to almost any kind of innovation, from a process upgrade to the design or launch of a new product or service, as well as the costs of that improvement.

ROI has several advantages over other methods. The first is that it is useful as a benchmark for measuring levels of risk. ROI is normally compared to an alternative interest rate or cost, called opportunity cost: if the company put the money into another project, what would the ROI be? And if we simply invest it in the bank or a financial product, how much would we earn?

That is why ROI is perhaps the favorite method among shareholders and investors: it quantifies the value of the project in terms with which they are comfortable, narrowing their decision to two factors: profitability and risk. In general, when they back a particular project, shareholders want to see what the value of their dollars is going to be. That is what ROI allows you to do. Moreover, being a purely quantitative tool, this method is also useful for prioritizing among the different alternatives that arise during the innovation process.[13]

In this regard, the following are commonly used in setting the criteria for approving or rejecting investments based on ROI:[14]

▷ *Set ROI to the level of other investments:* With information from the finance and accounting departments on the average return on other investments, we set our sights on equaling or beating those levels.

▷ *Set ROI at the point of equilibrium:* This means setting ROI at a percentage that means getting our money back. For example, if we invest $100,000 in upgrading a product and our return is $100,000, we do not get any profit, but we recover the investment. Such an approach is typical of non-profit organizations.

▷ *Set ROI according to the demands of the financers:* In this case, the financers or shareholders determine beforehand the minimum return on investment for the approval of new projects. Projects that meet the standards set by shareholders or investors get the green light. (This is a very common approach in innovations funded by venture capital funds and Business Angels.)

A very interesting case of return of investment is the movie *Avatar*, which achieved an incredible ROI:

> *Avatar* was officially budgeted at $237 million. Other estimates put the cost at between $280 million and $310 million for production and at $150 million for promotion.
>
> The film earned $27 million on its opening day, and $77 million over its opening weekend. Seventeen days after its release, it became the fastest film to earn 1 billion dollars and, after three weeks, was ranked the second highest grossing film of all time, surpassed only by *Titanic* (1997), also directed by James Cameron. *Avatar* managed to beat that mark in less than six weeks, becoming the highest grossing film in cinema history to date, as well as being the first film to overcome the barrier of 2 billion dollars in earnings.[15]

ROI is also used in complex and large-scale innovation projects. Euro Disney or Eurotunnel, for example, are typical of the types of innovations or initiatives assessed with this tool. In both cases, due to the difficulty of estimating future demand and controlling investment costs, the true ROI was very different from the forecast.

That brings us to the caveat that the calculation of an ROI can be quite subjective and even manipulable, and a project's backers can modify whatever is necessary to suit their needs. Therefore, in calculating ROI, just as important as the level of risk and expected return are the details of the assumptions behind the calculations.[16]

ROI is usually based on two well-known financial indicators: NPV and IRR. NPV (net present value) is the present value of a number of future cash flows (both positive and negative). When NPV is positive, it means that the total investment will be offset in future expected income. IRR, or internal rate of return, is the percentage that is discounted from all future cash flow rates in order to equal total investment, and is thus the indicator of the profitability of a project.

Scenario analysis and intervals

We saw in Chapter 5 that scenario analysis can be used as a creative technique. It can also be used as a means to assess and decide whether to proceed with a particular innovation. In these cases, scenario analysis takes two different forms:

▷ The first is to weigh the project not only in terms of its expected return, but also the expected changes in the environment and competition. It may happen that one innovation shows a higher ROI than another but is more exposed to changes in the environment and, given possible movements by the competition, is not the best option. Here, scenario analysis acts as a filter that conditions the quantitative estimates of management, which draws up budgets based on the market *ceteris paribus*. Often, the shareholders, the board of directors or CEOs of large companies have inside information that management is not aware of in making such estimates. This tool is used to refine these estimates.
▷ The second way to apply scenario analysis is by setting intervals: pessimistic, realistic, optimistic. In this case, we do not use the changing legislative or competitive environment; rather we seek a spectrum, a broad interval in which to frame quantitative estimates and business plans. The aim is to analyze what would happen to the innovation if things don't go as expected (worst case scenario) or if everything goes off without a hitch (best case scenario). It is another way of getting a perspective on the risks of the innovation.

Some companies, such as IBM, assign different probabilities to each scenario and use them to weight the expected profitability of each scenario. The final weighted result is considered a single rating to be compared with other alternatives.

Market tests

In Chapter 7, we saw the market test as a way of pre-launch. Market testing is probably the surest way to assess the suitability of an innovation. You simply release the product or service on a small scale in a limited geographical area or within a predetermined set of sales channels. Of all the ways to quantify the potential of innovation, market testing will give the most realistic picture. It has many advantages, but also many drawbacks. To begin with, it assumes that investment in innovation (production lines and product development, for example) is relatively low, because, if not, a small-scale launch costs nearly as much money as a full-scale launch. This technique is used when industrial investment is much lower than commercial investment. In other words, the risks are largely associated with the resources to be invested in communications, advertising, product testing, distribution and creating the sales channel and network, and so on. In this case, market testing makes a good deal of sense, given that, by restricting the scope of the launch, marketing investment is low and we can estimate, based on the results, whether or not it makes sense to move on to a national or international roll-out.

The next problem is that we unveil the innovation at an early stage, which means we give the competition time to react. So market tests should be done only after we have shielded an innovation with patents or when we are prepared to green-light the full-scale launch faster than the competition can steal it from us.

Finally, we should be very careful when choosing the geographical area (or, alternatively, channel or customer type) for the market test. Choosing an unrepresentative area, or customers particularly inclined to buy the innovation, can render the results worthless. One reason to launch in the "best" market is: "If you fail in that market, kill the project."

Combination of criteria and levels of approval or rejection

The tools and systems we have presented here are not mutually exclusive, but rather complementary. We do not recommend relying solely on a single one in adopting an innovation, but rather that you combine them to get as broad and varied a perspective as possible, with alternative views, and that you use all that information to make the best possible decision. This goes against the human penchant for simplicity: we tend to prefer one figure, a single result on which to base a decision, rather than having to deal with conflicting evidence. In real life, however, this is a form of self-deception, because there is no method that can, with a single number, ensure the right decision. And even less so in the world of innovation.

We must remember that the work of the entrepreneur, the manager or businessperson involves a certain amount of risk. If there were a tool able to predict the outcome of the launch of an innovation, success in the business world would come easily. And it does not.

The tools we have seen should be considered as a complement to two traits inherent to successful businesspeople: intuition and risk-taking.

The history of business innovation is littered with products and services where early assessments failed to reflect what actually happened next. Some fell short of the mark, others surpassed it. There are numerous cases of innovations that, after all indications pointed to weak performance, proved to be a tremendous success; and others where lofty expectations were met with disaster.

This is not to deny the usefulness of these tools or the need to evaluate an innovation before investing in it. Decision-making must combine intuition and risk-taking with scientific, empirical methods. True ability to predict is found in leaders who combine both talents, and that requires being able to deal with systems of innovation assessment and evaluation in which the disparity of results enriches the analysis. Let's look at an example of how to combine these tools.

A company is going to approve an innovation if:

▷ The concept has a purchase intent (Top Box Score) of 30 percent in the target market
▷ Company staff rates the concept with an average score of over 8 points on a scale of 0–10.
▷ Product testing indicates a 60 percent purchase intent (Top Two Box Score)
▷ Estimated demand is equivalent to a turnover in excess of $3 million
▷ Estimated market share exceeds 2 percent
▷ The profit and loss account is a positive before the third year
▷ ROI is over 7 percent

If innovation meets all these benchmarks, we proceed with the launch. Otherwise, the process is brought to a halt. Each criterion must have its justification; in the above example, minimum test levels are required to ensure a high level of market acceptance. The minimum turnover of $3 million is required because a minimum volume is needed to justify the project; a market share of 2 percent, because, otherwise, the distributors won't include it in their portfolios; profits before the third year because that timeframe is the industry standard; an ROI of 7 percent because it is the opportunity cost of money at average risk, below those returns, shareholders will go for financial investments.

The combined use of tools, nevertheless, should not yield to an over assessment which may create a paralysis in decision:

Care should be taken not to over-evaluate ideas. For many organizations, evaluation is about avoiding risk. However, the most innovative ideas with the biggest potential returns on investment inevitably are the most risky. If a highly innovative idea has to go through multiple evaluations and reviews by multiple committees, it is almost certain to be rejected for perceived risk or so heavily modified in attempt to limit risk, that it looses its innovativeness.[17]

The tools for setting the objectives of the launch

These tools can also be used to set objectives for an innovation, once we are in the launch phase. In this case, we must:

▷ Choose one or more objectives
▷ Determine timeframes for verification
▷ Then, set limits or minimum values

Let's look at an example of how to use the tools we've enumerated to set objectives.[18] A company determines that innovations must account for at least 5 percent of its total billing (with margins similar to those currently being recorded) three years after launch and that after eight years it must account for 15 percent of sales (with equal or similar margins). An innovation that meets such requirements would be considered successful.

Type of innovation versus facilitators' tools

There is a certain relationship between the types of tools used and whoever assumes the role of facilitator. For example, shareholders regularly use ROI as a means to approve and allocate resources for a project but are hardly likely to take the time required for a nominal group technique, which, in contrast, the members of the team in charge of the innovation process would use.

Figure 8.2 shows the relationship between types of facilitators and the most common techniques.

	Subjective assessment	Company-wide rating	Test levels	Delphi method	Nominal group techniques	Six Thinking Hats	Phillips 66	Six Sigma	Cost-benefit	Demand estimation	Profit and loss	ROI analysis	Scenario analysis	Market test
Investors									X	X	X	X	X	X
Shareholders									X	X	X	X	X	X
Board				X					X	X	X	X	X	X
CEO	X		X	X				X	X	X	X	X	X	X
General manager	X	X	X	X	X	X	X	X	X	X	X	X	X	X
Chief innovation officer	X	X	X	X	X	X	X	X	X	X	X	X	X	X
Financial director		X									X	X		
Department heads	X	X	X	X	X	X	X				X			
Stakeholders	X	X												
Experts	X			X										
Middle managers	X	X	X			X	X	X						
Innovation team	X	X	X	X	X	X	X	X		X	X	X	X	X
Employees	X	X												

Figure 8.2 **Facilitators tools by company hierarchical levels**

There is also a relationship between the types of innovation and the tools we have presented (Figure 8.3).

	Subjective assessment	Company-wide rating	Test levels	Delphi method	Nominal group techniques	Six Thinking Hats	Phillips 66	Six Sigma	Cost-benefit	Demand estimation	Profit and loss	ROI analysis	Scenario analysis	Market test
Line extension	X	X	X			X	X			X	X	X		
New product for a new market		X	X	X	X	X				X	X	X	X	X
New process	X	X		X	X	X	X	X		X	X	X		
New business model			X	X	X	X	X			X	X	X	X	X

Figure 8.3 **Facilitators tools by innovation levels**

Finally, here there is a matrix evaluating each technique in terms of how much companies use it and how much effort each technique requires (Figure 8.4).

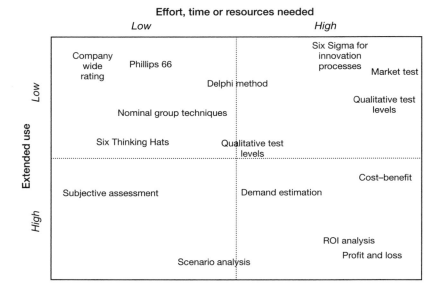

Figure 8.4   **Facilitator tools according to use and required effort**

TOTAL INNOVATION SYSTEM – Summary Chapter 8

Main person/s in charge of each role

	A Activators	B Browsers	C Creators	D Developers	E Executors	F Facilitators
Up-bottom activation	Top management (GM or Chief innovation officer)	Market research department	Advertising agency	R&D	Current marketing department (shared team)	Top management (GM or Chief innovation officer)
	Employees	Market research suppliers	Creativity agency	New products department	Current sales department (shared team)	Financial director
	Suppliers	Sociologists	Marketing	Operations	Dedicated marketing team	New projects committee
	Distributors	Marketing	Creative types	Manufacturing	New division	Chief innovation officer
In-out activation	Clients	Sales	R&D	External suppliers	New company	Board
	Investors	Opinion leaders	Clients	Marketing	Third party alliances	Shareholders
Bottom-up activation	Universities	Watchers' panel	Suppliers	Sales		Employees
	Scientific community	R&D	Employees with creative profile	Dedicated engineers		Innovation team
	Inventors	Other internal departments	Other suppliers or third parties			Middle management
Out-in activation	Engineering companies	Other suppliers or third parties				External: experts, stakeholders or investors

Techniques employed by each role

A Activators	B Browsers	C Creators	D Developers	E Executors	F Facilitators
Scope of innovation	Innovation review	Synectics	Helping in concept definition	Marketing plan and launch plan	Subjective assessment
Innovation levels	Analysis of adjacent categories	Blue Ocean strategy	Concept test for improving design	Morphing	Purchase intention according to test levels
Focus of innovation	Internal consulting	Morphological analysis		KPIs' evolution	Delphi method
Innovation guidelines	Social trend/ social classes	Lateral marketing	Conjoint analysis for features definition	Next marginal evolution	Nominal group techniques
Innovation checklist	Market trends	Attributes listing	Drawings	Area testing	Company-wide rating
	Buying process	Scenarios analysis	Mock-up	Market testing	Phillips 66
	Innovation routes	Visits	Prototype	Product testing	Six Sigma
	Technological solutions	Co-creation	Product test	Intensity on ATRs	Cost-benefit analysis
	Design referents	Redefining customer value	Usage/home test	Experimentation	Demand estimation
	Successful strategies and tactics/learning from errors	Brainstorming	Patents		Profit and loss
	Network monitoring	Concept definition			
	Ethnographic				ROI analysis
	Geolocation				Scenario analysis
					Market test

Innovation framework
Innovation guidelines
Innovation checklist

STRATEGIC PLANNING FOR INNOVATION

INNOVATION PROCESS

Browsers ←→ Creators
Activators ←→ Facilitators ←→ Developers
Executors

Project proposals / Process approval

CREATIVE CULTURE

INNOVATION REWARDS

INNOVATION METRICS

RESULTS

9 The Advantages of Designing Innovation Processes with the A-to-F Model

Advantages of the A-to-F model

Some people might think the A-to-F model is much the same as the traditional, well-worn stages of the innovation process, where:

Traditional stages or steps of the innovation process
Objectives → Research → Ideas → Evaluation → Development → Launch

It is true that the A-to-F model moves in the direction A, B, C, D, E, as shown in Figure 9.1 below ...

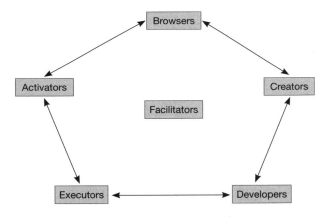

Figure 9.1   **Natural sequence of the A-to-F model**

The definition of objectives is associated with activation, research with information browsing, the generation of ideas with creativity, assessment with financing, and development and launch are equivalent to what in our model the developers and executors would do. Where, then, are the differences and what is the added value of our model? Let's take a look:

1 In the paradigm shift of talking in terms of roles rather than stages

Each stage is tied to a particular role, with the result that each role operates inside a bubble, isolated from the people in charge of the previous and subsequent stages. It has been shown that allocating stages in this manner generates a "this stage is my baby" sort of attitude. The result is that the main role in each stage is responsible for just one part of the process. So, should the innovation flop, the people who generate ideas claim that their ideas were great, but the folks in charge of tangibilizing them screwed up, or that the executors got their strategy wrong.

On the other hand, operating by roles, we go from "this stage is my baby" to "these stages belong to all of us, so let's see how each role can give them some added value." Thus you get everybody involved throughout the innovation process. Naturally, this can be achieved simply by designating dedicated teams. But if the dedicated team is also structured on the A-to-F roles, that will ensure that the key functions of a process of stages are represented in a process without stages.

Let's insist on this, one of the main advantages of our model:

> **THE KEY FUNCTIONS OF A PROCESS OF STAGES
> ARE REPRESENTED IN A PROCESS WITHOUT STAGES**

Stage-based processes tend to be quite rigid. The fact that the stages are a result of group dynamics among six types of roles leads to a natural and spontaneous flexibility, freeing those responsible for the innovation process from having to stick to a prescribed script and from feeling that when they move forward and backward in the process they are acting inefficiently or simply abandoning a stage-based method whose inflexibility makes it hard to follow.

By saying goodbye to the rigidity of stages and letting the process flow as a result of group dynamics, this sequence does not occur linearly, but rather can go forward and backward as often as needed, as we pointed out in Chapter 2, where we discuss the flexibility of the model and we argue that the natural sequence:

A–B–C–D–E(F)

could change to:

A–B–C–A–F–D–B–D–F–E–C–E

Or to something as simple and brief as:

A–D–E

2 In the engendering of new collaborative formulas

It is a well-known fact that when the innovation process is a set of stages, backtracking to previous stages is seen as a setback or failure. People are reluctant to return to departments that have already done their bit for fear of losing decision-making power or influence in the process. Here are some very common scenarios:

▷ If the research phase comes up with information that doesn't satisfy the creators, the latter will feel justified in their belief that market information and research only reflect the past and that creativity is the only field able to envision the future. They are unlikely to ask for new information and, instead, will go ahead and start generating ideas relying solely on their own resources.

▷ The new product design and development departments lament the impossibility of developing the ideas that land in their "inbox". Knowing that this is the common fault among the creators, they choose not to ask them to review or think of new ideas and simply mold the concept to what they believe is its true scope and potential. The creators will, as so often happens, say that their idea has been gutted by the technicians.

▷ Those in charge of launching new products and services tend to be the final victim of these sorts of disagreements or conflicts as things move along the pipeline. Their view is likely to be that the innovation doesn't have enough potential, resulting in a product or service that fails to consider either the customer and his or her needs or the commercial reality of the market. Many innovations are a threat to a marketing and sales department, so the involvement and commitment of resources will be minimal, in the belief that the innovation threatens the relationship with the sales channel and/or customers. They would prefer to "sabotage" the innovation commercially before asking for improvements in it.

But these departments need each other:

▷ The activators, in defining objectives, need technical experts in order to know what possibilities technology can offer, and they need the market research, marketing and sales departments in order to narrow down where the opportunities lie.

▷ The research department needs the marketing department's knowledge of the customer; the sales department's knowledge of the channel; the R&D department's knowledge of technology.

▷ The R&D and design departments need, as discussed in Chapter 6, marketing's ability to capture value.

▷ The marketing department needs the engineer's expertise on technological possibilities.

We have seen throughout the previous chapters how each role can provide, by its very nature, additional help to the other roles, something that, due to the closed nature of stages, rarely occurs in innovation processes. In our model, as we move forward and back through multiple interactions, new collaborative stages, which we call *cross-cutting inputs*, emerge.

The cross-cutting input is a secondary task that sometimes one role can perform in collaboration with another. This is not the main thing expected of a role, but the latter's expertise permits the development of new skills that can help advance the innovation process

Each role has a primary function, which is shown on the diagonal of the chart (Figure 9.2).

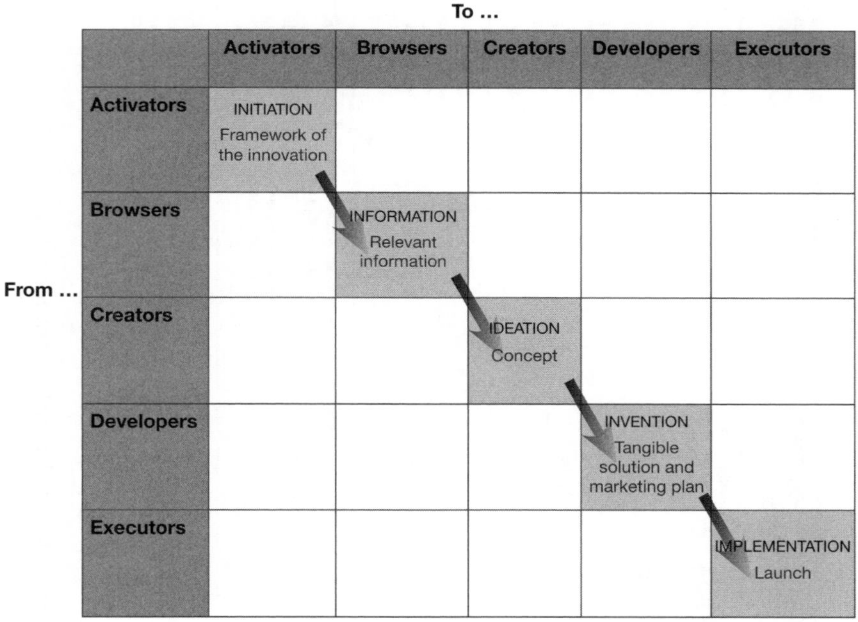

To ...

		Activators	Browsers	Creators	Developers	Executors
	Activators	INITIATION Framework of the innovation				
	Browsers		INFORMATION Relevant information			
From ...	**Creators**			IDEATION Concept		
	Developers				INVENTION Tangible solution and marketing plan	
	Executors					IMPLEMENTATION Launch

Figure 9.2   **A-to-F model: matrix of roles interaction**

In Figure 9.3, the cross-cutting inputs are outside the diagonal of the chart and indicate the collaborative tasks they can offer to other roles. The chart is read across. For example, what the creators (C) can offer the activators (A) corresponds to the third box in the first column: "Discarded Ideas."

These sorts of cross-cutting activities or collaborative tasks are hardly rare in companies, but they tend to emerge spontaneously and are not always part of a formal process. Using the A-to-F model, many of these practices can be organized within the context of a process and implemented deliberately. In Annex I of this chapter we look at each of these collaborative tasks in more detail.

To ...

From ...	Activators	Browsers	Creators	Developers	Executors
Activators	INITIATION — Framework of the innovation	Definition of the research framework, according to the process goals, levels and guidelines	Focus to be used in creative sessions – Objectives and framework of the process they initiated	Assurance of alignment with the overall business strategy	To ensure the executors that the final implementation of the innovation remains within specified guidelines
Browsers	Cataloging of learnings from errors or failures of innovation – Detection of opportunities that can lead to new activations	INFORMATION — Relevant information	Stimuli and material for creative sessions, obtained out of their research	Analysis of products that use same technology to help Developers to define usability and design – Possible suppliers search	To document and flag the tactics and strategies of market references and learn from errors in the implementation of similar innovation – Monitoring of KPIs during launch
Creators	Discarded ideas that do not proceed in the process, but with potential to start a different innovation process	Devise new ways to capture information or combine existing methods, appropriate to and tailor-made to the process	IDEATION — Concept	Creative problem-solving tools in tackling the series of obstacles, difficulties or bottlenecks found during development	Creative sessions to come up with new and original ideas for the new product or service
Developers	New possibilities or applications for the same technology in innovations other than those of the process	Complete information on technological trends in the analysis of social and market trends	Help to define concepts that evolve out of creative sessions – Technical constraints of concepts defined	INVENTION — Tangible solution and marketing plan	Shaping the product as it is being tested and used, even after launch, as it is required in morphing
Executors	Ideas of marginal innovations after executing a radical innovation	Understanding of the market and sales channels	Ways to capture value as creators generate ideas	To foresee potential marketing problems before they are built into the innovation in its final physical form	IMPLEMENTATION — Launch

Figure 9.3   Crossed tasks and collaborative tasks between roles

3 Roles, not departments

We have seen that interaction occurs among people with different fields of expertise, each taking a role. However, it is also possible to have a multidisciplinary composition of each role. Obviously, the developers will be made up largely of engineers and designers, and most of the browsers will be researchers. But it is feasible, depending on the size of the company and the scale of the project, to include among the personnel assigned to a given role a certain number of people from other departments, which is much trickier to do when we work by stages assigned to specific departments.

Designing innovation processes with the A-to-F model

A huge plus of the model is that it enables us to design totally different innovation processes that respond to objectives and specific innovation strategies. We proceed to build the innovation process by addressing the four dimensions:

1 Main person/s in charge of each role
2 Techniques employed in each role
3 Total time and time allocated to each role
4 Resources allocated to each role

We now illustrate these four dimensions.

Dimension 1: Main person/s in charge of each role

Table 9.1 includes all the possible options regarding who can perform each role, as we outlined in the preceding chapters. These are the different options to choose from (you can choose one or more).

We see that there are many possibilities, ranging from internal to external resources. How do we choose the best makeup? The answer depends on the combination of the following factors:

▷ Type of innovation (disruptive, marginal, upgrade, portfolio extension, and so on)
▷ Type of sector or industry (mass consumption, B2B, services, industrial, and so on)
▷ Type of product (in terms of capabilities and complexity)
▷ Innovative capacity and innovative culture of the company (less innovative firms will tend to subcontract and outsource some of these roles)

Table 9.1   Main person/s in charge of each role in the innovation process

A Activators	B Browsers	C Creators	D Developers	E Executors	F Facilitators
Top management (GM or Chief innovation officer)	Market research department	Advertising agency	R&D	Current marketing department (shared team)	Top management (GM or Chief innovation officer)
Employees	Market research suppliers	Creativity agency	New products department	Current sales department (shared team)	Financial director
Suppliers	Sociologists	Marketing	Operations	Dedicated marketing team	New projects committee
Distributors	Marketing	Creative types	Manufacturing	New division	Chief innovation officer
Clients	Sales	R&D	External suppliers	New company	Board
Investors	Opinion leaders	Clients	Marketing	Third party alliances	Shareholders
Universities	Watchers' panel	Suppliers	Sales		Employees
Scientific community	R&D	Employees with creative profile	Dedicated engineers		Innovation team
Inventors	Other internal departments	Other suppliers or third parties			Middle management
Engineering companies	Other suppliers or third parties				External: experts, stakeholders or investors

Dimension 2: Technique(s) employed by each role

Once we have decided who, we can move on to how. Obviously, each of the roles will have a great deal to say about what techniques they want to employ in each project.

Committing oneself to a certain method before starting the innovation process may be inadvisable. In any event, based on their accumulated experience, companies that innovate on a recurring basis often draw up a short list of techniques, whether or not each role then proposes modifying or incorporating the techniques that best suit the project (see Table 9.2).

However, subsequent analysis of the performance of techniques and methods is always interesting. You gradually build up a typology of projects based on their results, efficiency and costs, as a means of, over time, designing into the innovation process the techniques you want to apply.

Table 9. 2 Techniques employed by each role in the innovation process

A Activators	B Browsers	C Creators	D Developers	E Executors	F Facilitators
Scope of innovation	Innovation review	Synectics	Helping in concept definition	Marketing plan and launch plan	Subjective assessment
Innovation levels	Analysis of adjacent categories	Blue Ocean strategy	Concept test for improving design	Morphing	Purchase intention according to test levels
Focus of innovation	Internal consulting	Morphological analysis	Pictures	KPIs' evolution	Delphi method
Innovation guidelines	Social trend/ social classes	Lateral marketing	Conjoint analysis for features definition	Next marginal evolution	Nominal group techniques
Innovation checklist	Market trends	Attributes listing	Drawings	Area testing	Company-wide rating
	Buying process	Scenarios analysis	Mock-up	Market testing	Phillips 66
	Innovation routes	Visits	Prototype	Product testing	Six Sigma
	Technological solutions	Co-creation	Product test	Intensity on ATRs	Cost–benefit analysis
	Design referents	Redefining customer value	Usage/home test	Experimentation	Demand estimation
	Successful strategies and tactics/learning from errors	Brainstorming	Patents		Profit and loss
	Network monitoring	Concept definition			ROI analysis
	Ethnographic				Scenario analysis
	Geolocation				Market test

Dimension 3: Total time and time allocated to each role (a priori)

The design of an innovation process must also include an anticipated or recommended scheduling. We have made it clear that the A-to-F model does not specify or commit to specific stages; rather the latter should be an outcome of the interaction among roles. However, based on the objective and nature of an innovation process, the amount of time it will require from each role can be anticipated quite accurately.

For example, a company seeking to expand the range of flavors for a product in its portfolio requires little time from the developers in comparison with a company that is going to launch a disruptive innovation.

To a large extent, the sector or industry will determine the total time required. The time needed for a new piece of furniture is not of the same order as that needed for a new car, for example.

The same goes for the level of the innovation, as expressed in the terms set out in Chapter 3. Innovation in business models entails more time than innovation in processes, which entails more or less the same time as innovation in new markets, which usually entails less than product innovation.

Dimension 4: Resources allocated to each role (a priori)

The same principle applies to the estimated budget for the process. Evidently, the facilitators are already there to oversee the allocation and approval of new spending items, but knowing about how large a slice of the resources is foreseen for their role helps each of the participants in the innovation process to locate their expectations. Obviously, the amounts of time and financial resources are not necessarily related.

Table 9.3 Resources allocated to each role in the innovation process

	A Activators	B Browsers	C Creators	D Developers	E Executors	F Facilitators
Total estimated time X months	X% of working hours	X% of working hours	X% of working hours	X% of working hours	X% of working hours	X% of working hours
Estimated resources $XXX,XXX	Y% of budget	Y% of budget	Y% of budget	Y% of budget	Y% of budget	Y% of budget

Let's look at an example of a complete design. Let's imagine an innovation process for a new fragrance line for teenagers in a company that is already present in the perfume sector, but with fragrances for adults.

The activator of the innovation process is the general manager. Since the company does not have its own research department, the role of browsers is outsourced to its regular market research firm; the creators' role will be played by the marketing department and other in-house people chosen for their creative character; the facilitators will be the general manager with the support of the chief financial officer; the execution will be carried out by a new teenage perfumes division, which is to be created for this purpose (see Table 9.4). The objective of the innovation process is to create two new teenage fragrances with which to launch the new division.

With regard to dimension 2 (technique to use, see Table 9.5), the activators will use the framework of the innovation, the level of the innovation (innovation in markets) and the guidelines for the process. For their part, in this sort of innovation process, the browsers will be using tools such as adjacent category analysis, exploring new developments, not necessarily fragrances, in teenage products and an analysis of social trends among young people. This is because the company wants the perfume line to be quite innovative in its approach, distancing it from the mainstream fragrances on the market. The creators are expected to use attributes listing and visits to other countries as a means of developing new and differentiated concepts; and, together with the developers, must tangibilize the proposal with a concept definition. The latter will develop a prototype and a product test with consumers. The executors will establish a new division, and will sketch out the marketing plan, which will be monitored through a series of key performance indicators (basically, unaided and prompted awareness and market penetration and share). And finally, the facilitators will assess the feasibility of project using ROI and cost–benefit analysis.

With respect to dimensions 3 and 4, time and resources, the company gives itself four months and a budget of $600,000, and estimates the following share of total time and budget for each role (see Table 9.6)

Table 9.4 Design of an innovation process for a new fragrance for teenagers – dimension 1 (main people in charge of each role)

A Activators	B Browsers	C Creators	D Developers	E Executors	F Facilitators
Top management (GM or Chief innovation officer)	Market research department	Advertising agency	R&D	Current marketing department (shared team)	Top management (GM or Chief innovation officer)
Employees	Market research suppliers	Creativity agency	New products department	Current sales department (shared team)	Financial director
Suppliers	Sociologists	Marketing	Operations	Dedicated marketing team	New projects committee
Distributors	Marketing	Creative types	Manufacturing	New division	Chief innovation officer
Clients	Sales	R&D	External suppliers	New company	Board
Investors	Opinion leaders	Clients	Marketing	Third party alliances	Shareholders
Universities	Watchers' panel	Suppliers	Sales		Employees
Scientific community	R&D	Employees with creative profile	Dedicated engineers		Innovation team
Inventors	Other internal departments	Other suppliers or third parties			Middle management
Engineering companies	Other suppliers or third parties				External: experts, stakeholders or investors

Table 9.5 Design of an innovation process for a new fragrance for teenagers – dimension 2 (techniques employed)

A Activators	B Browsers	C Creators	D Developers	E Executors	F Facilitators
Scope of innovation	Innovation review	Synectics	Helping in concept definition	Marketing plan and launch plan	Subjective assessment
Innovation levels	Analysis of adjacent categories	Blue Ocean strategy	Concept test for improving design	Morphing	Purchase intention according to test levels
Focus of innovation	Internal consulting	Morphological analysis	Pictures	KPIs' evolution	Delphi method
Innovation guidelines	Social trend/ social classes	Lateral marketing	Conjoint analysis for features definition	Next marginal evolution	Nominal group techniques
Innovation checklist	Market trends	Attributes listing	Drawings	Area testing	Company-wide rating
	Buying process	Scenarios analysis	Mock-up	Market testing	Phillips 66
	Innovation routes	Visits	Prototype	Product testing	Six Sigma
	Technological solutions	Co-creation	Product test	Intensity on ATRs	Cost–benefit analysis
	Design referents	Redefining customer value	Usage/home test	Experimentation	Demand estimation
	Successful strategies and tactics/learning from errors	Brainstorming	Patents		Profit and loss
	Network monitoring	Concept definition			ROI analysis
	Ethnographic				Scenario analysis
	Geolocation				Market test

Table 9.6 Design of an innovation process for a new fragrance for teenagers – dimensions 3 and 4 (time and resources)

	A Activators	B Browsers	C Creators	D Developers	E Executors	F Facilitators
Total estimated time 4 months	5% of working hours	30% of working hours	20% of working hours	30% of working hours	10% of working hours	5% of working hours
Estimated resources $600,000	5% of budget	20% of budget	10% of budget	30% of budget	30% of budget	5% of budget

We can see how the A-to-F model has enabled us to design an innovation process in full (Table 9.7).

Table 9.7 Design of an innovation process for a new fragrance for teenagers using the A-to-F model

	A Activators	B Browsers	C Creators	D Developers	E Executors	F Facilitators
Assigned to ...	General manager	Market research agency	Marketing department and 4 creative types within our company	R&D and our manufacturing department	New division	General manager and financial director
Deliverables (Techniques and tools to be used)	Scope of innovation – Innovation levels – Innovation guidelines	Analysis of adjacent categories – Social trends analysis – Social classes study	Attributes listing – Visits to Paris, Milano, New York	Concept definition – Prototype development – Product test – Development of marketing guidelines	Launch and track through KPIs (awareness, penetration, trial and market share during first year)	Return on investment analysis – Cost/risk analysis
Load of hours (24 weeks)	5% of working hours	30% of working hours	20% of working hours	30% of working hours	10% of working hours	5% of working hours
Resources	$30,000	$120,000	$60,000	$180,000	$180,000	$30,000

Coordination of the process

Finally, although the dynamics of the roles themselves determines the process, we recommend having someone who oversees the entire series of roles, from A to F, a sort of project manager. His or her function, perhaps different from those in other, more controlled processes, would be to intervene at critical moments when the group dynamics, rather than adding value, are hindering the progress of the process.

In all projects there are key moments at which you need someone to put an end to an ongoing discussion or, given a lack of consensus, to make a decision for the group. At the same time, it makes things easier to have one person as an intermediary, representing the other departments, members of the company and even the people on one's own team.

But the project manager is not an autocratic figure or someone that holds all the responsibility, but rather a person who, in key situations, ensures the innovation process does not get stalled. This person could be the activator of the process, in situations where the project manager is someone from within the organization.

In order to illustrate the versatility of the A-to-F model and its applicability to any company, whatever its size or business, Annex I provides several designs using the model. We have taken two of those discussed in this book: Shell's GameChanger Panel and IBM's EBOs (emerging business opportunities). And we have also included three theoretical examples covering different types of industries and types of innovation: a new product in the industrial sector, a processes upgrade in the retail sector and a new business model in the services sector.

From processes to schemes

The A-to-F model allows not only for designing processes, but also for incorporating innovation schemes, such as the recently developed ones of reverse innovation, co-creation or open innovation.

Notice that by including in dimension 1 (roles) external agents (clients, suppliers, collaborators or channel) in each of the roles, from activators to executors, recent innovation approaches and schemes can be perfectly represented with the model.

See, for example, how the roles in Apple's iPhone applications open innovation scheme can be represented with the A-to-F model (Table 9.8).

Table 9.8   Open innovation scheme roles represented with the A-to-F model

A Activators	B Browsers	C Creators	D Developers	E Executors	F Facilitators
Top management (GM or Chief innovation officer)	Market research department	Advertising agency	R&D	Current marketing department (shared team)	Top management (GM or Chief innovation officer)
Employees	Market research suppliers	Creativity agency	New products department	Current sales department (shared team)	Financial director
Suppliers	Sociologists	Marketing	Operations	Dedicated marketing team	New projects committee
Distributors	Marketing	Creative types	Manufacturing	New division	Chief innovation officer
Clients	Sales	R&D	External suppliers	New company	Board
Investors	Opinion leaders	Clients	Marketing	Third party alliances	Shareholders
Universities	Watchers' panel	Suppliers	Sales		Employees
Scientific community	R&D	Employees with creative profile	Dedicated engineers		Innovation team
Inventors	Other internal departments	Other suppliers or third parties			Middle management
Engineering companies	Other suppliers or third parties				External: experts, stakeholders or investors

Conclusion

As we have seen, this design is perfectly adaptable to any situation and industry. We also believe that the A-to-F model, given its completeness with respect to the functions required in an innovation process, is suited for incorporating new techniques, tools and formulas developed by other authors, researchers or innovators in the world of innovation. Similarly, companies who enter the field of innovation will gradually develop their own methods and tools.

Just as in their day the 4 P's of marketing were a good system for organizing, locating and bringing coherence to the marketing activities of a company, we believe the A-to-F model is an equally valid scheme in the field of innovation for organizing, situating and coherently applying the vast and varied literature that appears every day on innovation.

Annex I

Examples of process design using the A-to-F model

We have taken two of those discussed in this book and briefly described in Chapter 3: Shell's GameChanger Panel and IBM's Emerging Business Opportunities. We recall our example of Shell from Chapter 3:

> Shell, for example, in the mid 1990s created the "GameChanger" panel, a small group of creatively minded mid-level executives who could also draw on other technical resources across the company. They were given the task of developing new ideas and a $20-million budget to implement ideas that would break with existing rules and conventional wisdom. The GameChanger panel, in turn, created several more dedicated teams to perform some of the basic functions of the innovation process: an innovation lab, whose job was to refine and improve their ideas; an action lab to explore ideas in a controlled environment; and a board of entrepreneurs [venture board] to assess and finance the best projects. The GameChanger experiment started in one division: exploration and production. Now it has spread throughout the company and each division has its own GameChanger panel process. There is even a special GameChanger team dedicated to radical projects that fall outside the boundaries of Shell's existing businesses.

We can see that the initiative lies with management (activators), which is limited to checklisting the resources for innovation, leaving open its field, focus and scope. Based on our information, it seems that the company uses its own research departments (browsers), who examine technological trends and possibilities; the creators, in this case the Innovation Lab, also come from the organization itself (no creativity or development techniques are specified). The developers, too, come from Shell (R&D and New Products Department), and the execution is either handled by a dedicated team (which Shell calls the Action Lab) or, in the case of a disruptive innovation, a new division created for the purpose (called the Special GameChanger Panel). We found that the initiatives result from a subjective assessment of new products by a special group (in Shell parlance, the Venture Board).

We can see, then, that the names of each of the figures assigned to the roles vary, but they are in essence the same as those found in the different options in the table of our model.

Table AI1   GameChanger panel at Shell Corporation (roles)

A Activators	B Browsers	C Creators	D Developers	E Executors	F Facilitators
Top management (GM or Chief innovation officer)	Market research department	Advertising agency	R&D	Current marketing department (shared team)	Top management (GM or Chief innovation officer)
Employees	Market research suppliers	Creativity agency	New products department	Current sales department (shared team)	Financial director
Suppliers	Sociologists	Marketing	Operations	Dedicated (The action lab) team	New projects committee
Distributors	Marketing	Creative types	Manufacturing	New division (Special game changer)	Chief innovation officer
Clients	Sales	R&D	External suppliers	New company	Board
Investors	Opinion leaders	Clients	Marketing	Third party alliances	Shareholders
Universities	Watchers' panel	Suppliers	Sales		Employees
Scientific community	R&D	Employees with creative profile	Dedicated engineers		Innovation team
Inventors	Other internal departments	Other suppliers or third parties			Middle management
Engineering companies	Other suppliers or third parties				External: experts, stakeholders or investors

Table AI2 GameChanger panel at Shell Corporation (techniques)

A Activators	B Browsers	C Creators	D Developers	E Executors	F Facilitators
Scope of innovation	Innovation review	Synectics	Helping in concept definition	Marketing plan and launch plan	Subjective assessment
Innovation levels	Analysis of adjacent categories	Blue Ocean strategy	Concept test for improving design	Morphing	Purchase intention according to test levels
Focus of innovation	Internal consulting	Morphological analysis	Pictures	KPIs' evolution	Delphi method
Innovation guidelines	Social trend/ social classes	Lateral marketing	Conjoint analysis for features definition	Next marginal evolution	Nominal group techniques
Innovation checklist	Market trends	Attributes listing	Drawings	Area testing	Company-wide rating
	Buying process	Scenarios analysis	Mock-up	Market testing	Phillips 66
	Innovation routes	Visits	Prototype	Product testing	Six Sigma
	Technological solutions	Co-creation	Product test	Intensity on ATRs	Cost–benefit analysis
	Design referents	Redefining customer value	Usage/home test	Experimentation	Demand estimation
	Successful strategies and tactics/learning from errors	Brainstorming	Patents		Profit and loss
	Network monitoring	Concept definition			ROI analysis
	Ethnographic				Scenario analysis
	Geolocation				Market test

This is how in Chapter 3 we described IBM's innovation system, based on EBOs (emerging business opportunities):

In order to identify business areas that might hold opportunities, IBM calls on customers, external observers and venture capitalists to propose areas of business where IBM does not have a presence and that have potential for the future (IBM calls them EBOs, emerging business opportunities). IBM doesn't look to its own R&D department for such proposals because the latter is focused on current areas of business and therefore lacks the outsider perspective to think about new business opportunities. IBM's strategy manager picks the most promising proposals out of the lot and then identifies company executives with long experience and, at the head of major divisions, with responsibility for a large team of people, but with little room for maneuver to invest in new, higher-risk projects within their own unit. They are then designated to build the future. At the height of their careers, they are called on to put their experience to work on an internal startup. Since launching this system in 2000, IBM has generated twenty-five EBOs, of which only three have failed. Four of them, Digital Media, Life Sciences, Linux and Persuasive Computing, obtained earnings of over one billion dollars each in 2003 and 2004.

We can see that here the activators are investors and customers, and essentially make proposals at a certain level of innovation (new businesses, new markets). The information browsing, then, is performed by these same actors, who, in a certain way, act as opinion leaders, indicating the most important market trends. In principle, there is no eminently creative phase, since a business area of interest is indicated directly. Development and creativity go hand in hand and are not assigned to R&D, but to specific managers who will be taken away from their normal jobs and will be fully dedicated to develop the new business units (EBOs). They will have to present a separate profit and loss account, monitored through selected KPIs. All investments must be approved by IBM's strategy director, who assesses each initiative, both qualitatively (subjective assessment) and quantitatively (ROI analysis).

Table AI3   Emerging business opportunities (EBOs) at IBM (roles)

A Activators	B Browsers	C Creators	D Developers	E Executors	F Facilitators
Top management (GM or Chief innovation officer)	Market research department	Advertising agency	R&D	Current marketing department (shared team)	Top management (GM or Chief innovation officer)
Employees	Market research suppliers	Creativity agency	New products department	Current sales department (shared team)	Financial director
Suppliers	Sociologists	Marketing	Operations	Dedicated marketing team	New projects committee
Distributors	Marketing	Creative types	Manufacturing	New division	Chief innovation officer
Clients	Sales	R&D	External suppliers	New company	Board
Investors	Opinion leaders	Clients	Marketing	Third party alliances	Shareholders
Universities	Watchers' panel	Suppliers	Sales		Employees
Scientific community	R&D	Employees with creative profile	Dedicated engineers		Innovation team
Inventors	Other internal departments	Other suppliers or third parties			Middle management
Engineering companies	Other suppliers or third parties				External: experts, stakeholders or investors

Table AI4 Emerging business opportunities (EBOs) at IBM (techniques)

A Activators	B Browsers	C Creators	D Developers	E Executors	F Facilitators
Scope of innovation	Innovation review	Synectics	Helping in concept definition	Marketing plan and launch plan	Subjective assessment
Innovation levels	Analysis of adjacent categories	Blue Ocean strategy	Concept test for improving design	Morphing	Purchase intention according to test levels
Focus of innovation	Internal consulting	Morphological analysis	Pictures	KPIs' evolution	Delphi method
Innovation guidelines	Social trend/ social classes	Lateral marketing	Conjoint analysis for features definition	Next marginal evolution	Nominal group techniques
Innovation checklist	Market trends	Attributes listing	Drawings	Area testing	Company-wide rating
	Buying process	Scenarios analysis	Mock-up	Market testing	Phillips 66
	Innovation routes	Visits	Prototype	Product testing	Six Sigma
	Technological solutions	Co-creation	Product test	Intensity on ATRs	Cost–benefit analysis
	Design referents	Redefining customer value	Usage/home test	Experimentation	Demand estimation
	Successful strategies and tactics/learning from errors	Brainstorming	Patents		Profit and loss
	Network monitoring	Concept definition			ROI analysis
	Ethnographic				Scenario analysis
	Geolocation				Market test

Using the A-to-F model, any type of company, of any size and in any business, can design its innovation processes. Now, we'll examine three theoretical examples: a new product in the industrial sector, a processes upgrade in the retail sector and a new business model in the services sector.

Design for a medium-sized company in the industrial sector

Imagine a medium-sized company that manufactures small components for large textile machinery. The company has about 30 employees, but has no marketing or innovation department. It has a CEO, a sales manager with four representatives, a technical department which combines the tasks of manufacturing and new product development, with five engineers and ten workers at the plant. The rest of the personnel are staff. The company decides to launch an innovation process to improve the quality and cost of the components it manufactures for its customers. The components are long blades for fabric cutters on digital looms. The company doesn't have a great deal of resources to innovate with, so it is not considering a radical innovation, but rather wants to improve its current components enough to increase customer satisfaction and loyalty.

Using the A-to-F model, the design of their innovation process might be as shown in Table AI5.

Table AI5   Design of an innovation process for an industrial company (SME)

A Activators	B Browsers	C Creators	D Developers	E Executors	F Facilitators
Top management (GM or Chief innovation officer)	Market research department	Advertising agency	R&D	Current marketing department (shared team)	Top management (GM or Chief innovation officer)
Employees	Market research suppliers	Creativity agency	New products department	Current sales department (shared team)	Financial director
Suppliers	Sociologists	Marketing	Operations	Dedicated marketing team	New projects committee
Distributors	Marketing	Creative types	Manufacturing	New division	Chief innovation officer
Clients	Sales	R&D	External suppliers	New company	Board
Investors	Opinion leaders	Clients	Marketing	Third party alliances	Shareholders
Universities	Watchers' panel	Suppliers	Sales		Employees
Scientific community	R&D	Employees with creative profile	Dedicated engineers		Innovation team
Inventors	Other internal departments	Other suppliers or third parties			Middle management
Engineering companies	Other suppliers or third parties				External: experts, stakeholders or investors

The process starts at the initiative of the manager, who asks his major customers for a range of indications on the improvements that they would like to see in the components the company provides. The manager asks (see Figure AI1) the technical department for inputs in order to focus the objectives of the process. The search for information on past innovations and possibilities is entrusted to the sales director, who is assisted in this task by the developers (see Figure AI1). The generation of ideas (creators) will be conducted by personnel from the technical department and a major supplier of the steel with which the company manufactures its components. The developers are assigned to assess the technical feasibility of the ideas proposed by the creators. The company's technical department is responsible for development, the sales director for the execution of the plan and the general manager for approving investments.

We find, thus, that the participants in the process are limited to management and the sales and technical departments, and that inputs come from customers and suggestions from suppliers.

Figure AI1 provides a table of envisaged collaborative tasks. Although during the process any of them can be activated, should the need arise, it is foreseen that, basically, the developers should provide support to the other roles.

Main tasks of A-to-F and crossed contributions

To ...

From ...		Activators	Browsers	Creators	Developers	Executors
	Activators	INITIATION	Research framework	Creativity focus – Concept validation	Strategic alignment	Guidelines – Extra resources
	Browsers	Learning – Findings	INFORMATION	Stimuli for creativity sessions	Technological analogies – Suppliers or third parties search	KPIs' tracking – Successful strategies and tactics
	Creators	Discarded ideas	Innovation in new research techniques	IDEATION	Problem solving techniques	Ideas for marketing and sales plan
	Developers	Technological new inputs	Technological trends	Concept technical validation	INVENTION	Morphing
	Executors	Marginal innovation possibilities	Market understanding	Value capture	Sales and marketing limitations	IMPLEMENTATION

Figure AI1   **Design of an innovation process for an industrial company (SME)**

The tools and outputs that the process is designed to produce are seen in Table AI6. We can see that it is a very basic and simple process, aimed at improvements, and that it consumes few resources. Management clearly defines the focus of innovation and hands out a checklist of what must be done. The browsers (the sales department, in this case) come up with a report on trends in the industry (cutting components) and provide promising technological solutions that have been detected in other companies. All this information is given to the technicians, who, in their role as the creators, we recommend use a morphological analysis technique in order to find new combinations that will help improve the components. The creative sessions are organized by means of co-creation techniques – in this case, in partnership with the suppliers. The adopted ideas are given to the developers, who are asked only to produce drawings of the plans and then to build prototypes. The launch is planned for before the improvement of the component is complete. One customer will test it and improvements will be finalized according to the results. The investments will be assessed by the company's technical and sales management and by the customers participating in the development of the component, as well as through ROI analysis, under the responsibility of the manager.

Table AI6   Design of an innovation process for an industrial company (SME)

A Activators	B Browsers	C Creators	D Developers	E Executors	F Facilitators
Scope of innovation	Innovation review	Synectics	Helping in concept definition	Marketing plan and launch plan	Subjective assessment
Innovation levels	Analysis of adjacent categories	Blue Ocean strategy	Concept test for improving design	Morphing	Purchase intention according to test levels
Focus of innovation	Internal consulting	Morphological analysis	Pictures	KPIs' evolution	Delphi method
Innovation guidelines	Social trend/ social classes	Lateral marketing	Conjoint analysis for features definition	Next marginal evolution	Nominal group techniques
Innovation checklist	Market trends	Attributes listing	Drawings	Area testing	Company-wide rating
	Buying process	Scenarios analysis	Mock-up	Market testing	Phillips 66
	Innovation routes	Visits	Prototype	Product testing	Six Sigma
	Technological solutions	Co-creation	Product test	Intensity on ATRs	Cost–benefit analysis
	Design referents	Redefining customer value	Usage/home test	Experimentation	Demand estimation
	Successful strategies and tactics/learning from errors	Brainstorming	Patents		Profit and loss
	Network monitoring	Concept definition			ROI analysis
	Ethnographic				Scenario analysis
	Geolocation				Market test

The estimated costs of this process (the bulk of which is foreseeen for development) are not high.

Table AI7 Design of an innovation process for an industrial company (SME)

	A Activators	B Browsers	C Creators	D Developers	E Executors	F Facilitators
Total estimated time 3 months	5% of working hours	10% of working hours	20% of working hours	40% of working hours	10% of working hours	5% of working hours
Estimated resources $100,000	5% of budget	10% of budget	10% of budget	50% of budget	20% of budget	5% of budget

Design for a retailer

Imagine a company in the retail sector that is not thinking of re-inventing itself, rather it wants to upgrade its processes to increase customer satisfaction: more comfortable access and parking, easier to find products, faster checkout and a greater range of payment methods.

The process is activated by management, which defines only the focus of the innovation (improving processes to increase customer satisfaction). The search for information is performed by the retailer's research department, which is asked to provide a review of levels of customer satisfaction and dissatisfaction through market research and a series of interviews with in-store employees and salespeople to get their opinions on possible improvements in processes that, from their experience, they believe it would be worth considering. An analysis of recent social trends in relation to user satisfaction for different products and services will be outsourced to a sociologist. The generation of ideas will come from creative sessions with the in-store employees and salespeople, using two creativity techniques: brainstorming and redefining customer value. The operations department will develop the best ideas, and be offered the opportunity to fund a study using conjoint analysis to prioritize potential improvements. The execution will be up to the sales department, which will be asked to implement the new process in five stores. This will serve as a test, comparing customer satisfaction with the remaining outlets, where, for now, the improvements will not be instituted. In either case, key performance indicators will be analyzed and, if substantial improvement is found, the financial director, through cost–risk analysis, will approve the appropriate investment. Let's see what this looks like (Tables AI8 and AI9).

Table AI8   Design of an innovation process for new process in a retailer

A Activators	B Browsers	C Creators	D Developers	E Executors	F Facilitators
Top management (GM or Chief innovation officer)	Market research department	Advertising agency	R&D	Current marketing department (shared team)	Top management (GM or Chief innovation officer)
Employees	Market research suppliers	Creativity agency	New products department	Current sales department (shared team)	Financial director
Suppliers	Sociologists	Marketing	Operations	Dedicated marketing team	New projects committee
Distributors	Marketing	Creative types	Manufacturing	New division	Chief innovation officer
Clients	Sales	R&D	External suppliers	New company	Board
Investors	Opinion leaders	Clients	Marketing	Third party alliances	Shareholders
Universities	Watchers' panel	Suppliers	Sales		Employees
Scientific community	R&D	Employees with creative profile	Dedicated engineers		Innovation team
Inventors	Other internal departments	Other suppliers or third parties			Middle management
Engineering companies	Other suppliers or third parties				External: experts, stakeholders or investors

Table AI9 Design of an innovation process for a new process in a retailer

A Activators	B Browsers	C Creators	D Developers	E Executors	F Facilitators
Scope of innovation	Innovation review	Synectics	Helping in concept definition	Marketing plan and launch plan	Subjective assessment
Innovation levels	Analysis of adjacent categories	Blue Ocean strategy	Concept test for improving design	Morphing	Purchase intention according to test levels
Focus of innovation	Internal consulting	Morphological analysis	Pictures	KPIs' evolution	Delphi method
Innovation guidelines	Social trend/ social classes	Lateral marketing	Conjoint analysis for features definition	Next marginal evolution	Nominal group techniques
Innovation checklist	Market trends	Attributes listing	Drawings	Area testing	Company-wide rating
	Buying process	Scenarios analysis	Mock-up	Market testing	Phillips 66
	Innovation routes	Visits	Prototype	Product testing	Six Sigma
	Technological solutions	Co-creation	Product test	Intensity on ATRs	Cost–benefit analysis
	Design referents	Redefining customer value	Usage/home test	Experimentation	Demand estimation
	Successful strategies and tactics/learning from errors	Brainstorming	Patents		Profit and loss
	Network monitoring	Concept definition			ROI analysis
	Ethnographic				Scenario analysis
	Geolocation				Market test

A new business model for the services sector

Let's take a slightly more complex case. We are an insurance company that sells policies online and decides to develop a new business model. We sell automobile insurance, but want to switch from selling via the Internet, as we are doing currently, to a new sales channel: driving schools and car dealerships. This means a radical change in the whole margin structure, given that we must establish sales agreements in which the profits from each policy sold are shared. This business model is completely different from our present one, and thus we have to look for innovative formulas on multiple fronts. We are facing a long innovation process requiring large investments and an entire series of negotiations with third parties. The design of our insurance policies and liabilities is going to change, since our prospective customers will now be first-time drivers, on the one hand, and new-car buyers, on the other.

Let's see how we can use the A-to-F model to design an innovation process in the services sector and to define a new business model.

The activation of our innovation process is a joint initiative between car dealerships, driving schools, the insurance companies that provide us with risk coverage and our own general management. The scope and level of innovation is clearly defined (a new business model), the innovation guidelines will specify the maximum investment available and minimum billing and profits for the first three years of the new business. Since the process is long, there will also be a checklist including questions about the resources, people and so on needed for the process.

The role of the browsers is assigned to our marketing department, who must thoroughly analyze the procurement process followed by insurance underwriters for first-time drivers and new-car buyers. Our market research department is charged with the analysis of adjacent categories, such as roadside assistance insurance and after-sales guarantees or repair packages. There will also be an innovation review that describes all the innovations in the automobile insurance industry, to ensure that we are offering something new to the sector. Additionally, we will seek information from five opinion leaders (a professional from the financial sector, two driving school managers, a car dealership manager and the manager of a drivers club), who will assess the initiative through in-depth interviews led by our market research provider. Additionally, a panel of observers will be set up to inform us, over the course of a month, about what is happening currently in the car insurance sector.

The generation of ideas will be assigned to an external creative agency, which must form a team that integrates, in addition to its own personnel, two people from our marketing department, two people from the financial institutions that supply our risk coverage and two creatively inclined salespeople from our current network. The creative techniques envisaged are: Blue Ocean strategy (ideal for identifying new businesses), visits to different insurance distributors and co-creation sessions with customers who meet the following conditions: they have taken out insurance in the past year; they have held a driver's license for less than one year and/or own a car less than nine months old.

The creative team will work together to define a new business model, the details of which will be specified in working sessions with staff from the in-house operations department. The service will be tested through market research and a summary of the marketing plans set out prior to the creation of the new business, the responsibility for which will be assigned to a dedicated marketing team and a new company or partnership created for the purpose. The executors are also expected to be prepared to adapt the design of the insurance, prices and the sales strategy based on what happens in the first few months (morphing). Moreover, and in the event of positive results, they should have an insurance portfolio development strategy ready with at least five additional products.

Based on the demand estimate derived from the service test, ROI analysis and assessments of members of the board, the initiative will be presented to shareholders for their approval.

Table AI10   Design of an innovation process for a new business model in the insurance market

A Activators	B Browsers	C Creators	D Developers	E Executors	F Facilitators
Top management (GM or Chief innovation officer)	Market research department	Advertising agency	R&D	Current marketing department (shared team)	Top management (GM or Chief innovation officer)
Employees	Market research suppliers	Creativity agency	New products department	Current sales department (shared team)	Financial director
Suppliers	Sociologists	Marketing	Operations	Dedicated marketing team	New projects committee
Distributors	Marketing	Creative types	Manufacturing	New division	Chief innovation officer
Clients	Sales	R&D	External suppliers	New company	Board
Investors	Opinion leaders	Clients	Marketing	Third party alliances	Shareholders
Universities	Watchers' panel	Suppliers	Sales		Employees
Scientific community	R&D	Employees with creative profile	Dedicated engineers		Innovation team
Inventors	Other internal departments	Other suppliers or third parties			Middle management
Engineering companies	Other suppliers or third parties				External: experts, stakeholders or investors

Table AI11 Design of an innovation process for a new business model in the insurance market

A Activators	B Browsers	C Creators	D Developers	E Executors	F Facilitators
Scope of innovation	Innovation review	Synectics	Helping in concept definition	Marketing plan and launch plan	Subjective assessment
Innovation levels	Analysis of adjacent categories	Blue Ocean strategy	Concept test for improving design	Morphing	Purchase intention according to test levels
Focus of innovation	Internal consulting	Morphological analysis	Pictures	KPIs' evolution	Delphi method
Innovation guidelines	Social trend/ social classes	Lateral marketing	Conjoint analysis for features definition	Next marginal evolution	Nominal group techniques
Innovation checklist	Market trends	Attributes listing	Drawings	Area testing	Company-wide rating
	Buying process	Scenarios analysis	Mock-up	Market testing	Phillips 66
	Innovation routes	Visits	Prototype	Product testing	Six Sigma
	Technological solutions	Co-creation	Product test	Intensity on ATRs	Cost–benefit analysis
	Design referents	Redefining customer value	Usage/home test	Experimentation	Demand estimation
	Successful strategies and tactics/learning from errors	Brainstorming	Patents		Profit and loss
	Network monitoring	Concept definition			ROI analysis
	Ethnographic				Scenario analysis
	Geolocation				Market test

Annex II

Detail of collaboration tasks and examples

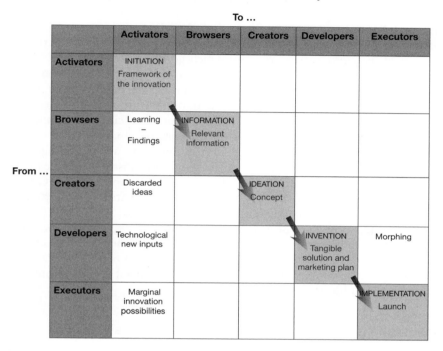

Figure AII1   **Main tasks of A-to-F and crossed contributions**

Input from browsers to activators: Feedback and findings

Because they monitor the launch of the new product, the browsers are in a position to enrich the knowledge of innovation by means of the proper cataloguing of information learned from the errors or failures that arise both in the process and in the development and implementation of the innovation. Or, to look at it from the opposite angle: there is no doubt that a thorough information search process by means of the innovation review or the methods discussed in Chapter 4 will result in the detection of market opportunities, niches and insights that can lead to the activation of new processes for different teams. This is essential feedback that can be passed on to the activators or to a CIO (chief innovation officer), a figure explained in Chapter 3 who has a 360-degree view of all innovation projects planned, underway or past.

For example, at Tesco many innovations arise as a result of the ongoing analysis of loyalty card data, the changes in which are used to decide on new assortments. In this case, browsers within Tesco act as finders of possible new innovation processes for activators – consider that loyalty cardholders (11 million customers) account for 80 percent of purchases at Tesco.

Input from creators to activators: Discarded ideas

We believe in exploiting everything that comes out of an innovation process. Experience shows that creative sessions produce a large number of ideas that must be discarded because they stray too far from the objective of the project. We are talking about anything from simple marginal improvements or innovations to disruptive ideas for consideration by management. The creators can set off new innovation processes which go directly from A to D. Let's imagine an idea that has been discarded but which seems to have potential. This idea, once valued and assessed, might be the starting point for a new innovation process that doesn't require a lot of input from the browsers and creators, instead going directly to development, financing and execution, and limiting the role of the browsers and creators to support or collaborative tasks such as those described here. As a rule, one idea leads to another, and so on, such that if a record is kept of the good ideas discarded in creativity sessions, one innovation process is likely to give birth to another – the C-to-A collaborative relationship being an exceptional generator of projects and contributions to the innovative culture of the company.

For example, the Puig Beauty & Fashion company, which markets Carolina Herrera, among many other brands, took an idea that it had discarded for being out of the scope of the innovation process, an oat-based shampoo, that became a new innovation project. Out of a recycled idea, the company came up with a hit product.

Input from developers to activators: Technological inputs

In the development of the technological possibilities of an innovation, it is likely that new possibilities or applications will arise for the same technology in innovations other than those contemplated in the process, or simply for improvements in other products in the portfolio.

Input from executors to activators: Marginal innovations

A disruptive innovation should be thought through for associated marginal innovations. The executors are probably best suited to propose to the activators the start of a new innovation process, in this case marginal, to develop the portfolio of a disruptive product or service.

For example, every year PepsiCo's snacks division launches several new flavors under existing brands. The proposals for such marginal innovations come from the marketing and sales department based on what they observe in their markets.

Input from activators to browsers: Information-browsing framework

The activators, by defining objectives, the desired level of the innovation, the guidelines and the type of process, provide an ideal framework for those who must collect information in the first phases of the process. In fact, this may not be considered a collaborative task, but actually part of their main function (it goes from A to B).

	To ...				
From ...	**Activators**	**Browsers**	**Creators**	**Developers**	**Executors**
Activators	INITIATION Framework of the innovation	Research framework			
Browsers		INFORMATION Relevant information			
Creators		Innovation in new research techniques	IDEATION Concept		
Developers		Technological trends		INVENTION Tangible solution and marketing plan	
Executors		Market understanding			IMPLEMENTATION Launch

Figure AII2 **Main tasks of A-to-F and crossed contributions (research framework)**

Input from creators to browsers: Innovation in information browsing

The creators can, thanks to their creative techniques, help the browsers to devise new ways of capturing information or combining existing methods, thus providing methods fully focused on, appropriate to and tailor-made to the process at hand.

Input from developers to browsers: Technological trends

The technicians and engineers can offer browsers complete information regarding technological trends for incorporation in their analysis of social and market trends. This information is useful for instilling, from the very start of the innovation process, the art of the possible – all that is offered by technical possibilities.

For example, the designers at Sacha London, an Anglo-Spanish women's footwear firm, study the different technological possibilities available, then ask social researchers about their relevance to the fashion world. This partnership bore fruit in the innovative use of laser technology to get the exact three-dimensional foot sizes of customers. From the exact model of each foot, a last is made for a shoe designed by the customer herself. In this case, the technological possibilities of laser imaging of three-dimensional shapes were validated because they connected with a social and market trend: personalization of products and services.

Input from executors to browsers: Understanding of the market

Innovation executors, who basically consist of people linked to sales and marketing, offer the browsers an understanding of the market and sales channels. The browsers often have a perspective highly focused on the final customer, which is good, but this view isn't yet complete until it is framed in the context of the market in which we compete.

A practical application of this collaborative task comes from Internet forums and blogs. Marketing departments have turned the opinions expressed on the Internet into genuine information tools, to the extent that, today, their management and monitoring has been transferred to research departments, constituting a new research technique. The technique emerged out of the mechanisms executors set up to communicate with customers.

Thus far we have seen what sort of input the browsers get from the other roles. In the case of the creators it works as follows.

To ...

From ...	Activators	Browsers	Creators	Developers	Executors
Activators	INITIATION Framework of the innovation		Creativity focus – Concept validation		
Browsers		INFORMATION Relevant information	Help for preparing creativity sessions (stimuli)		
Creators			IDEATION Concept		
Developers			Concept technical validation	INVENTION Tangible solution and marketing plan	
Executors			Value capture		IMPLEMENTATION Launch

Figure AII3 **Main tasks of A-to-F and crossed contributions (relationships with creators)**

Input from activators to creators: Focuses and checking of concepts

The activators provide the creators with a proper formulation of the so-called creative focuses we saw in Chapter 5, and the assurance that creative sessions are not focused on generating ideas outside the limits established at the start of the process. For example, at General Electric each area head, based on his or her portfolio, must propose to the board of directors a minimum of five innovations that provide at least 100 million dollars of growth in three years. They call them "Imagination Breakthrough Projects." It is a way for the activators to establish objectives for the creators.

Another area of collaboration can emerge during the concept definition phase: the activators can validate that the concepts developed, and which are going to be evaluated, fall within the objectives and framework of the innovation process they initiated.

Input from browsers to creators: Stimuli

Browsers are responsible for performing relevant research, some of the outputs of which should either be direct information in itself or contain stimuli for creative sessions. The browsers can work with the creators in preparing material for such sessions. However, this may be considered a fundamental task of the role, rather than collaborative (it goes from B to C).

For example, at Nestlé, during an innovation process for the chocolate category, the market research department examined recent innovations in five countries, using such innovations as direct stimuli for their creative sessions.

Input from developers to creators: Concepts and constraints

The technicians and engineers can (or rather, should) collaborate in the definition of the concepts that evolve out of the ideas generated in creative sessions, in order to ensure as far as possible that the ideas are translated into concepts that are viable from a technical standpoint. As regards constraints, they may apply to what we can and cannot specify in terms of the features, specifications and benefits of the innovation. Without playing the naysayer or the relentless blue-penciling censor, the technical personnel can contribute those doses of realism that good ideas need as they enter the defining phases.

Input from executors to creators: Ideas–value

The executors offer the creators ways to capture value as they generate ideas. For example, the IKEA sales departments realized that there were a number of products considered almost unnecessary, impulse purchases, even though they were for the home. Customers bought them to increase the perceived value of having made the effort to travel to IKEA and walk through its large stores. They call them Hot Dog products. It is unlikely that the creators would have come up with such a concept without an analysis of how to capture value with the customer, an analysis that came from the executors.

In the context of the creative sessions described in Chapter 5, it is advisable to have people from all roles participate in such sessions. People's creative potential can be very high when given exercises designed to elicit easy displacements and provocations. Similarly, the creators should invite all roles to try to make connections individually or in teams. By having a representative sample of all the roles throughout the innovation process, each working from their perspective, we get a rich diversity of connections and solutions for the same provocation. Out of this mix, the creators can design winning solutions that they may not have thought of on their own. Let's now look at the relationships with the developers.

From ...	To ...				
	Activators	**Browsers**	**Creators**	**Developers**	**Executors**
Activators	INITIATION Framework of the innovation			Strategic alignment	
Browsers		INFORMATION Relevant information		Technological analogies – Suppliers or third parties search	
Creators			IDEATION Concept	Problem solving techniques	
Developers				INVENTION Tangible solution and marketing plan	
Executors				Sales and marketing limitations	IMPLEMENTATION Launch

Figure AII4   **Main tasks of A-to-F and crossed contributions (relationships with developers)**

Input from activators to developers: Strategic alignment

As the idea is developed in the form of plans, models and prototypes, and as the business strategies are established, the activators, in the event that they are drawn from management, give the developers the assurance and peace of mind of knowing they are aligned with the overall business strategy.

Input from browsers to developers: Technological analogies

Browsers can help overcome technical difficulties regarding design and usability in the application of new technology by detecting and analyzing products and services that, either within or outside our industry, sector or category, incorporate the same technology. They can also help in the search for industrial suppliers, in case of technological constraints, or for partners, in case of marketing constraints. For example, Google, considered one of most innovative companies in the world, give its employees time to dedicate to searching the Web for opportunities in the form of small companies that have developed interesting technologies that Google can incorporate. In 2004, following this strategy, it bought Keyhole, which includes the technology that now enables Google to offer sophisticated maps with satellite images.

Input from creators to developers: Solutions

The creators provide their creative problem-solving tools in tackling the series of obstacles, difficulties or bottlenecks – in production, logistics, procurement or marketing – that are likely to arise over the difficult and often prolonged development phase, especially when it comes to a complex product like an automobile or an engine.

For example, at the Motorola factory in Penang (Malaysia) there is a room with over 2,000 notes posted on the walls. Each of them starts with the words "I recommend ..." and together they constitute a cornucopia of suggestions for resolving technical problems that arise in new developments.

Input from executors to developers: Marketing factors

Executors can help anticipate problems that may arise later, by which time it would be costly or simply too late to fix them. The sorts of problems we're talking about include those related to logistics in the sales channel, usability for customers or acceptance by distributors. In other words, the executors can foresee the whole range of potential marketing problems before they are built into the innovation in its final physical form. For example, at Starbucks it is standard practice to use outlets for validating the innovations developers are working on. In this way, the executors (who will have to implement each new initiative) can advise the developers of marketing factors they should be taking into consideration.

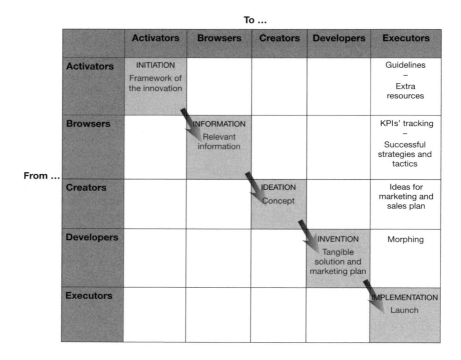

Figure AII5   **Main tasks of A-to-F and crossed contributions (relationships with executors)**

Input from activators to executors: Guidelines and resources

Having specified a series of guidelines, the activators should make certain that the executors ensure the final implementation of the innovation remains within those guidelines. Since the activators are often mobilizers of resources, it often happens, when it comes to execution, that the collaboration or assistance of other areas or divisions of the company is required.

Input from browsers to executors: Strategies, KPIs

Browsers have the ability to document and flag the tactics and strategies of market references and learn from errors in the implementation of similar innovations. For example, at Google, when a new product is launched, the company analyzes the errors users make in its use, sometimes asking for their feedback. These errors are communicated to the executors, who then request improvements from the programmers.

Likewise, at the time of launch, the browsers can handle the monitoring of KPIs (key performance indicators) such as market placement (numeric and weighted distribution) and levels of awareness, testing and repetition. The KPIs could include the changes in the product or service suggested by the opinions of early adopters, in order that such changes can be introduced rapidly (if possible). This activity would be key in the case of a morphing strategy as we explain it in Chapter 7. For example, Tesco's information analysis departments continually analyze the strategies of small local outlets and try to adapt their neighborhood supermarkets' offer on the basis of the successful products in a given neighborhood.

Input from creators to executors: Marketing ideas

The creators can conduct brief, concise creative sessions to come up with new and original ideas for the launch plan for the new product or service. This is a sort of miniature creative project where the focus of displacement is the marketing and sales plan for the innovation that has emerged from the process.

Input from developers to executors: Morphing

The strategy of launching an innovation on the market and shaping the product as it is being tested and used (known as "morphing") requires very close, rigorous and flexible cooperation between the developers and the executors, since the former must redefine, perhaps more than once, the design of the innovation according to the latter's suggestions. For example, 3M has three innovation centers where customers can try out their technologies and the company can see how effective they are in real situations. In doing so, the company gains the customer insights it needs in order to gradually make improvements in its products. Thanks to this policy, 3M has upgraded leading products like Scotch Tape and Scotchlite reflective tape.

In short, we can see that working with roles rather than stages produces fresh interactions that exploit the full potential of all the people involved in the innovation process. The interaction among the different professional profiles involved in an innovation process is now considered a critical factor in the success of innovation processes.

Annex III

Testing techniques – from concept to finished product

Concept tests

A concept test is normally carried out when we want to validate a new concept, to measure the potential in the market and to what extent it fits with the brand. At the same time we use a concept test to validate the features that the customer values the most, and those that the customer is not interested in, so we can adequately focus the development phase efforts. A concept test is carried out through personal interviews (recently, however, Internet-administrated tests are being employed). In concept tests, the customer or the consumer does not use, touch or try the product; he or she will just evaluate the idea. On some occasions, information about the price is given to the respondent, but this is normally done after the concept has been evaluated, in order to avoid price information influencing the concept perception. The interviewee is also asked about concept understanding (the concept is shown on paper, sometimes with a graphic design and with a brief written description): about what he or she likes and dislikes, the aspects that generate attraction or refusal, the fitness with the brand (in case an existing brand is going to be used), about the packaging (if there is any), about the product name and about the elements that he or she would modify.

Product tests

A product test is done when we already have a prototype or some units produced that we can test. The interview takes place in special settings where the product will be tried (or used). Sometimes, prior to trial, the concept is explained in the same terms as in the concept test and the same types of evaluations and questions are made. Once the product has been tried, the interviewee is asked about: the purchase intention; to what extent he or she believes the product to be something unique or distinct to what already exists in the market; and also, whether what has been tried fits the concept description made before the product trial. After all that, we normally move on to the interviewee's opinions on physical features and characteristics, so that we can improve the development. If, say, it is a consumption good, this consists of a flavor assessment. We try to identify what's missing or what's wrong, what are the likes and dislikes, which aspects need to be improved and, finally, to assess if it makes sense moving forward in the innovation process (see Chapter 8, Facilitators). Additionally, after product usage or trial, we facilitate information about prices, so we can estimate minimum and maximum prices we can charge.

All this information is vital to developers, who will proceed to make changes and adjustments before definitive industrial production.

In some cases, after product trial, more quantity is given to the interviewee, so he or she can continue using or consuming it at home. This is what we call home usage test.

Home usage tests

In this case, customers or consumers take with them one or more samples of the tested products (if it is a service, we give them the opportunity to use it). We are interested in detecting potential problems when the customer is within his or her natural environment, without an interviewer, and far away from an interview setting. After some days of extended usage or consumption, normally one or two weeks, the person is interviewed again. This second interview is done either personally or through the telephone and it repeats the questions on liking, fit with brand, purchase intention and aspects to be improved. We want to know how the repeated use or consumption changes compared to the first trial. Apart from this objective, we also gather information about usage or consumption situations: which household members have used/consumed it? Where? Why? What activities were performed while consuming? All this information is vital to developers, and also to executors if, finally, the innovation is launched.

Area test and market tests

These are the most developed ways of testing an innovation. And because in each case a certain degree of execution is needed, both techniques are discussed in Chapter 7.

PART TWO

10   Planning Innovation

There is ample evidence of the relationship between planning and the results of innovation. The companies that use the tools described in this chapter perform better than those that do not.[1] At one time Procter & Gamble (P&G) had no innovation strategy. Innovation efforts were wasted; projects were launched in non-priority categories and segments. When P&G instituted innovation planning, its innovation processes started to meet the company's goals, targets, strategies and metrics. Its results improved and it began to come up with breakthrough innovations.[2]

Planning, however, it is not easy. Academics who have studied the factors that determine success in the area of innovation have emphasized the need for a high degree of "discipline" during the innovation planning process.[3]

The elements of innovation planning

Planning is the first factor in the Total Innovation System. Planning enables us to align our efforts with corporate strategy, allocate resources efficiently and feed the innovation process pipeline in an orderly manner.

Planning for innovation should be the joint responsibility of the CIO and CEO. In the absence of someone directly responsible for innovation, senior management should take charge of innovation planning, since it is a strategic area and critical to the survival of any organization.

Innovation is planned for a period of three to five years, with annual revisions of strategy and resource allocation. The reasons we should revise our plans annually are:

▷ Changes in the market (customers, channels and suppliers)
▷ Technological changes
▷ Regulatory changes
▷ Movements among the competition
▷ Results achieved with innovation

Innovation planning tools include: business diagnostic, mission, corporate goals and strategy, and innovation goals and strategy.

Let's start with the first.

Corporate business diagnostic

A corporate business diagnostic is a general analysis of the various forces both involved in and that determine the current status of a company, and that will determine its future (industry dynamics, competitive landscape and economic and regulatory environment). The diagnostic aims to identify what has made a company successful so far and what needs to be changed or modified in order to sustain that success in the future. Management commitment and growth opportunities will depend on the diagnostic.

The diagnostic is used to formulate corporate goals and strategy, out of which will arise, in turn, the goals and strategies across functional areas and business units, and the criteria and processes for decision-making.[4]

There is a series of management tools for carrying out diagnostics. These tools are outside the scope of this book (for example value map,[5] industry evolution,[6] Porter's 5 Forces,[7] the McKinsey 7's framework[8] or the Marketing Audit[9]) but they are very useful in the area of innovation, thus we recommend that managements share them with the people responsible for innovation.

Fit with company mission, goals and overall strategy

As we explained when talking about the activators, innovation management does not operate autonomously, independently from the rest of management. Innovation must be aligned with corporate strategy and arise from it.

Some experts argue that such dependence can hinder the emergence of disruptive innovations or restrict the number of opportunities. Their rationale is that many disruptive innovations resulted not from a goal but rather from a (perhaps accidental) discovery or idea, and thus the idea forces the company to revise or redefine its mission, goals and strategies. Their conclusion is that the discovery could come before the strategy.

There is some truth in this. But we also need to plan innovation. How can we plan and at the same time not limit the search for opportunities? The answer is with idea campaigns or projects "free" of restrictions.

We should distinguish between predictable and exploratory innovation. Exploratory innovation means that an organization can allocate time and resources to search for opportunities freely, without the restrictions of corporate strategy and without the pressure of the need for their discoveries to be implemented. This means an investment in time to produce new possibilities that, even if they fall outside the corporate mission, merit consideration and assessment. About 42 percent of companies carry out such exploratory innovation processes.[10] A good number of these companies also plan innovation. This proves that "innovation planning" is not an oxymoron.[11] The dual tasks of innovating and planning are not incompatible.

The relationship between innovation and corporate goals and strategies

In the first place, in planning innovation we should not include goals, strategies or policies inconsistent with our corporate goals and strategy. Companies that don't plan innovation are likely to run into that very problem.

Second, corporate goals should be "shared" across all departments and functional areas: human resources, marketing, sales, and so on. Innovation is also a functional area, and, as such, it should pursue its corresponding share of corporate goals. Additionally, the overall corporate strategy determines the weight and role of each area, including innovation.

Imagine that a corporate goal of company X is a 20 percent increase in profitability within five years and the strategy to achieve this is to improve processes and supply. Supply concerns the purchasing department and process improvement concerns the innovation department. The strategy reveals the weight of these two departments in meeting the corporate goal. The next step would be to establish the specific goals of both departments.

This is a simple example of how corporate strategy and goals become the goals of a functional area.

The mission: a general framework

In the case of the mission, the approach is different. The company mission is a much more open statement of intentions which covers a large number of strategic possibilities. When an innovation clashes with the company mission, there's not a lot of room for maneuver. In an innovation process, a company specializing in the use of silicone in the manufacture of kitchen and household products wanted to detect opportunities for innovation at all levels. Silicone is a versatile material with countless applications. The first ideas (silicone components for electronic products, for apparel, and so on) fell outside the company's mission. The company did not want to get into these areas. They were beyond its scope. The innovation team had to swiftly adapt the creativity sessions to focus on ideas within the mission.

The way you ensure that innovation conforms to your mission is by marking boundaries for innovation (see "Innovation framework", Chapter 3) between the markets and regions where the company wants to compete and those it has ruled out.

Let's take a look at a theoretical example for a rent-a-car company:

Corporate mission: Provide solutions for private transport, land, air and sea, in and from the major cities in our country with vehicle rentals.

Corporate goals:

▶ Be the brand of choice for anyone who needs to rent a vehicle for private use in our country.

> ► Achieve a market share of 40 percent in our country within five years.
>
> ► Grow from a turnover of 35 million to 50 million dollars within five years with an average return of 10 percent.
>
> ► Be present in all cities, ports and airports with a minimum of two customer service **centers per city of over 75,000 inhabitants.**
>
> **Corporate strategy:** Development of a franchising system with private investors or entrepreneurs and use of fleets through partnership with vehicle manufacturers.

Innovation goals

Innovation goals comprise the things a company seeks to accomplish with the launch of new products, process improvement, a new business model or entry into new markets; that is, with all that entails a substantial change in the status quo.

We should distinguish between resolutions and goals. Let's look at a non-business example. On the first of January, when a person says "this year I'm going to lose weight," he or she is not setting a goal, but rather making a resolution. Now, if that person says "in the next six months I am going to lose eight kilos," that's a goal. Generally speaking, resolutions are mere declarations of intent. Some executives dictate resolutions in the belief that they are setting goals, and they are wrong. In the innovation field this problem is magnified by the relatively scarce use of specific metrics (see Chapter 11). Here are some examples of resolutions concerning innovation:

▷ We want to improve the efficiency of customer services
▷ We want to increase margins
▷ We want to be more aggressive in our new product policy

Now let's see them reformulated as goals:

▷ We want to innovate to reduce customer service time by 10 percent within the next year
▷ We want innovation in industrial processes to attain a five-point increase in margins within the next two years
▷ We want new product sales to reach 5 percent of sales within two years

Goal setting has been a subject of much study and it has been shown empirically that the more specific the goals, the more likely people are to meet them.[12] For example, with this in mind, at Tesco, at the beginning of each year, a team of 10 people decides how many new products will be introduced and sets the specific goal for each one of them.[13]

Innovation metrics are concrete and specific, and hence their close relationship with goal setting. Innovation metrics are the set of variables used to measure the results of innovation, which in turn enables you to manage innovation over time and to see if your policies are bearing fruit. We deal with metrics in detail in the next chapter.

The following are examples of innovation goals defined in terms of metrics:

▷ Billing generated by new launches must rise from 10 percent to 30 percent of total billing
▷ Profits from new launches must rise from 5 percent to 15 percent of total profits
▷ The success rate for new products must rise from 30 percent to 50 percent
▷ The percentage of employees who contribute ideas must rise from 5 percent to 30 percent

The most effective means to ensure that project proposals and ideas submitted will be consistent with the innovation goals is to use innovation guidelines, as we saw in Chapter 3. Recall that the guidelines provide a framework for all innovations that will be considered. For example, a large company might say that it will only invest in innovations that will generate in excess of one million dollars in profits within two years. The innovation guidelines are not quite the same thing as goals; rather they define the minimum requirements for a project to be approved and for a process to get the green light for activation.

Linking goals to metrics does not necessarily mean that all innovation goals must be quantitative. Qualitative innovation goals are perfectly valid too. The common way to proceed is to qualify first and then quantify.

Imagine a company that wants to set a qualitative innovation goal: the level of risk in launching new products. The qualification is made with subjective criteria: a group of executives assesses the level of risk for new products, with each participant ranking them on a scale of 1 to 5 based on his or her personal criteria. The ratings reach an average of 2.64. The minimum score the company wants to achieve is, say, 3 out of 5. We can already set a target for next year (for example achieving a 3, at least).

People responsible for achieving innovation goals

Responsibility for meeting the innovation goals ultimately lies with the CIO (see Chapter 12, culture). However, given that innovation occurs by means of projects and processes, the goals are divided among departments (for example marketing, R&D, logistics, production, and so on) or teams in charge of the processes.

Therein lies one of the difficulties of meeting innovation goals. The CIO delegates part of the goals to members of the organization over which he or she has no direct authority. Therefore, the CIO or head of innovation should occupy a position of certain power in the hierarchy.

Time horizons, number of goals and resource allocation

Innovation goals are usually specified according to two time horizons: one short term (goals for next year) and one medium-to-long term (three to five years). Except for some very specific industries where technological developments require several years (for example aeronautics, the space industry, energy, and so on), goals for terms longer than five years are not usually fixed. Some innovation goals (for example getting to the moon, a flying car, and so on) may be set as a long-term goal but usually specific goalposts are set in three to five years to get closer to the ultimate goal. The reason is the speed of technological and environmental change. That is also why the three-to-five-year goals are set by means of innovation strategy and resource allocation.

How many innovation goals should you set? The answer depends on the resources available for innovation, company size and speed of change in your industry. In general, management sets a relatively small number of goals (one to three), such as: "percentage of sales that must come from new products" or "number of innovations to implement" or "increase in billing generated by innovation." These goals are defined for the entire company and are usually divided among the business units. Below is an example of innovation goals for the rent-a-car company that we used before:

> ▶ Launch of services related to vehicle rental attaining 5 percent of total turnover.
> ▶ Process upgrades that will achieve a 3-percentage-point improvement in cost structure.
> ▶ Marketing innovations to capture 20,000 new customers.
> ▶ Development of a new business unit to attain a minimum of one million dollars within three years.
> ▶ The maximum budget for innovation will be $1 million.

When you have more than one innovation goal, you should rank each according to its importance in order to reflect the priorities of management. Prioritizing goals is also used for resource allocation.

Defining the innovation strategy

Once we have defined our goals, we can move on to our strategy. Our innovation strategy should be defined within the innovation framework. Management's selection of markets and regions is part of the innovation strategy and helps the activators narrow down their proposals.

The innovation strategy also includes: how much innovation is desired, what kind of innovation we want, how we want to compete, levels of innovation required, the pace of approval for the projects that feed the innovation pipeline, and resource allocation. Let's examine each of these items in turn.

Quantity and type of innovation

There are three types of innovations: marginal or incremental innovation, radical or disruptive, and semi-radical.

The classification is based on two variables: the degree of transformation in the business model and the use of either new or existing technologies. Combining these two variables, we have the matrix shown in Figure 10.1.

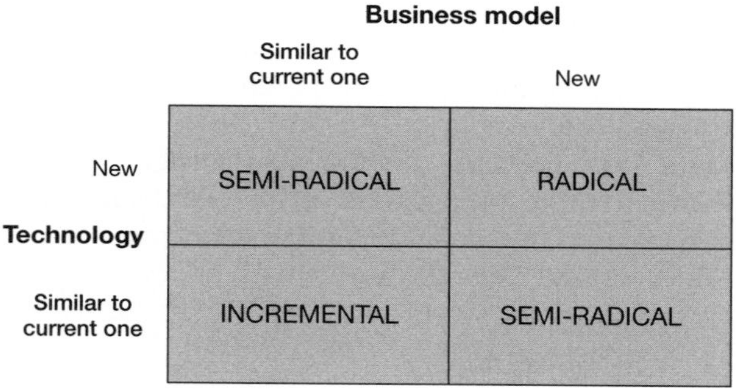

Business model

	Similar to current one	New
New Technology	SEMI-RADICAL	RADICAL
Similar to current one	INCREMENTAL	SEMI-RADICAL

Figure 10.1   **Matrix of types of innovation**

Evidently, of these three types, a marginal innovation entails lowest risk and usually the least investment, a radical one the highest, with semi-radical lying somewhere in between. Determining the type of innovation is a way of limiting the level of risk and, in turn, indicating whether you want to change technologies, your business model, both, or neither.

By classifying all possible projects in these three categories we can see how much innovation we can set in motion and what type. If we carry out a lot of disruptive projects, our strategy is aggressive and risky. If we carry out just a few marginal projects, that would define a conservative strategy.

How we want to compete

T. Davila et al.[14] summarize attack strategies according to two types: playing not to lose and playing to win. In the first case, the priority is to minimize losses; in other words, a defensive strategy with marginal innovations. In the case of "playing to win," we're talking about risk-taking and aggressiveness: we are willing to take losses for the sake of large potential profits. In this latter sort of strategy, the company would go for radical or semi-radical innovations. These two innovation strategies are also called "reactive" and "proactive," respectively.

Many companies focus too much on the short term and thus risk losing out in the long term. Reactive companies assume the environment determines the strategic possibilities and that their duty is to know how to adapt to changes. They act once the changes have taken place.

Proactive companies, in contrast, seek to shape the market according to their own interests. Instead of being the top competitor in the status quo, they prefer to change the rules. They act before the market changes. Firms with a proactive strategy are willing to take risks and make mistakes, and they have a high capacity for innovation.

The way of competing is also called the attack strategy or entry strategy,[15] in which you define in greater detail your strategic possibilities, whether it's playing to win (proactive) or playing not to lose (reactive):

▷ Proactive (for example Apple)
   Innovator: tries to change the rules of the market
   Differentiator: tries to introduce new purchasing attributes
▷ Reactive (for example Nokia)
   Fast follower (also called *fast second*): makes quick copies of innovators
   Defender: tries to protect the market share or/and customers' base
   Niche: the company concentrates on small segments
   Low cost: the company tries to compete with prices

Levels of innovation required

We also saw in Chapter 3 that management can specify for the activators the levels at which the company wants to innovate. We are now ready to expand a little further on the strategies that can be followed within each of these levels.[16]

Level 1: Business model innovation

▷ Channel (how you connect your offering to your customers, for example NikeTown)
▷ Business model (how the enterprise makes money, for example Dell)

Level 2: Process innovation

▷ Networking (enterprise value chain structure, for example Walmart)
▷ Enabling process (assembled capabilities, for example Siebel)
▷ Core process (proprietary processes that add value, for example General Electric)

Level 3: Market innovation

▷ Brand (how you express your offering's benefit to customers, for example Virgin)
▷ Customer experience (creating an overall experience for customers, for example Lexus)
▷ Serving new needs for existing customers (for example Wii fitness)
▷ Serving new customers with existing portfolio (for example Nestlé coffee for seniors)

▷ Introducing the product or service in new situations (for example, in France, a company offered human resources recruiters using cafeterias for open and free interviews without previous filtering of CV)

Level 4: Innovation in products and services

▷ Product performance (features, performance and capabilities, for example Intel Pentium)
▷ Product system (extended system that surrounds an offering, for example Microsoft Office)
▷ Service (how you service your customers, for example FedEx)

Resource scheduling and allocation

The innovation strategy should also define, based on the total budget for innovation, the share of resources to be allocated to each type and level of innovation. The allocation of the budget will be used as a guide for project approval when it comes time to implement the strategy. As incredible as it seems, only 24 percent of companies determine their innovation budget.[17] It's best to allocate an initial total, even if it is only indicative, of the money and people that management will devote to meeting the innovation goals set. We have seen that the facilitators get resources gradually, in order to avoid wasting money on projects that may eventually fail. In innovation, resources are allocated as the process moves forward. This is why companies should not be afraid of allocating total budgets for innovation.

Similarly, the definition of the strategy includes a rough schedule of the number and types of innovation over time. Let's see the innovation strategy for the rent-a-car company that we are using as an example during this chapter:

1 Develop ten innovative projects, of which eight will be marginal and two radical.
2 Seek a strategy that is proactive in new businesses and reactive in current business areas.
3 By levels, develop the following projects:

▶ Business model innovation: radical innovation to create a new business unit. Two projects with an allocation of 300,000 dollars each. Of the two projects, the one that scores highest in assessment will be implemented.
▶ Process innovation: launch of four projects, with an allocation of 30,000 dollars each. The focuses of innovation will be:
   ▷ Savings in vehicle maintenance
   ▷ Savings through reduction in key delivery time
   ▷ Savings through increase in the number of online bookings
   ▷ Savings through upgrades in the billing system

▶ Marketing innovation through capturing new customers with the current portfolio. Two projects with an allocation of 50,000 dollars each.
▶ Innovation in products and services, portfolio extension. Two new projects with an allocation of 30,000 dollars each.

Implementing the innovation strategy

We have now defined our strategy. How do we go about implementing it? Or, to rephrase the question: How are we going to apply our strategy to our innovation processes? Or, in terms of the A-to-F model: How do we coordinate the activators' multiple initiatives with our innovation plans, goals and strategies?

All ideas and proposals received from the activators – whether the latter are company staff, the planning department, top management, external researchers, top customers or stakeholders – are reviewed and classified by the people in charge of innovation planning.

First, the ideas and proposals must be reviewed to ensure they are aligned with the corporate mission, goals and strategy, and that they reflect the innovation goals. It may be that management has stipulated a number of things – the general framework for innovation, its priorities in terms of levels and types of innovation, the innovation focus, or the guidelines (minimum expectations for a project). All these concepts are described in Chapter 3. When an idea or proposal arrives, we must ensure that is aligned with these requirements.

If a proposal is out of alignment with company goals, strategy or mission, or it does not meet the requirements specified by management, we can consider it inappropriate. However, we can further break down inappropriate ideas into two types. The first is that it is not only inappropriate, but unattractive too. In this case, we recommend dropping it, but not definitively. It's best to leave it in the "recycling bin," where it can be retrieved for possible future reconsideration or as inspiration for subsequent idea campaigns. At Shell, for example, ideas that fail this check are shelved and added to a database, where all company employees can access and improve on them.

If, however, we believe that a proposal, despite being inappropriate, has a lot of business potential, we should pass it on to top management for consideration, who can decide whether or not to invest in its development, bearing in mind that, if implemented, it will entail a revision of corporate policies.

Depending upon who your activators are, this check for alignment may make sense or not. For example, if it's senior management that activates a project, appointing a dedicated team to a specific task (top-bottom activation), we can be almost certain that it's well aligned with corporate policies. But where activation comes from employees (bottom-top activation), you do not want to give the process the go-ahead, put together the rest of the A-to-F team and start investing without first ensuring the suitability of the idea.

But let's imagine the proposal is appropriate, that is, it's aligned with our goals and strategies, both overall and innovation-related. If that's the case, all we have left to decide is when the process can proceed.

The company is likely to have other processes making their way through the pipeline. One project cannot be managed independently of our other projects, priorities, budgetary constraints and changing business conditions.[18] How do we manage the flow of proposals and projects deemed to be valid or appropriate?

We need to program the flow according to our innovation plan, which stipulates where resources go and monitors the implementation of the strategy. To do this, we use three main tools:

▷ the portfolio of projects in the pipeline
▷ the project roadmap
▷ the resource buckets

The portfolio of projects in the pipeline

The project portfolio is a list of proposals, ranked according to their difficulty, potential and risk.

The innovation project portfolio is the interface between strategy and processes, and a tool for feedback between the people in charge of innovation and the different activators. Box 10.1 provides an example for the rent-a-car company.

Box 10.1   A rent-a-car company's projects list and portfolio projects

List of projects (in upper case, the project code name)
Business models
Small plane rental with pilot (AIR)
Helicopter rental with pilot (HEL)
In-town bicycle rental (CYC)
Hourly rental of vehicles parked in the street (HOUR)
Urgent rental service: car home delivery (HOME)
Motorcycle rental for in-town trips (MOT)

Products and services
Hotel and restaurant booking service (RES)
Fuel fill-up service (GAS)
Navigation system rental service (NAV)
Vehicle pick-up anywhere (PICK)
CD rental library for use in vehicles (CD)
DVD player and movie rental service aimed at families with children (DVD)
Reduced insurance for double coverage for customers with private insurance (INS)
Vehicle breakdown insurance (BRE)

Capture of customers
Discount for new family customers brought to us by existing customers (MGM)
Professional driving lessons for new customers (DRI)
First rental free for the purchase of a 4-rental coupon for new customers (DIS)
First 100 miles free for new customers (KM)
Free car rental for new customers with minimum of 3 rentals in a year (1FOR3)
Vehicle upgrade during the first two years for new customers (UPG)

Processes

Savings vehicle maintenance

Agreement with Michelin (MIC)
Partnership with competitors for joint purchasing (PUR)
Warning system for faults detected by customers (preventive detection) (WARN)
All vehicles same model and color (ONE)
Fleet renewal system with faster turnover than at present (NEW)
Agreement with national vehicles repair chain (ALI)

Savings through reduction in key delivery time

Customer arrival notification system via SMS (SMS)
Fast vehicle exit with new parking system (PARK)
Online system with pre-filling out of rental contracts by the customer when booking (PRE)
Discount for customers who return vehicle before agreed time or date (TIM)
System for filling out contract upon delivery of vehicle (DEL)

Savings through increase in the number of online bookings

New booking system via iPhone or Blackberry (IPH)
New intranet booking system for Premium Business customers (INT)
Time-saving system for customers who book online (ONL)
Links to major hotel and travel websites (HOT)
Agreement with Google and Yahoo for preferential positioning (GOO)

Savings through upgrades in billing system

Scanning and automatic comparison of previous contracts (SCAN)
Sending of electronic bills (INV)
Automatic billing with the customer's booking information (BOO)
Billing of companies according to payment dates, to reduce collection times (PAY)

Portfolio projects for a rent-a-car company

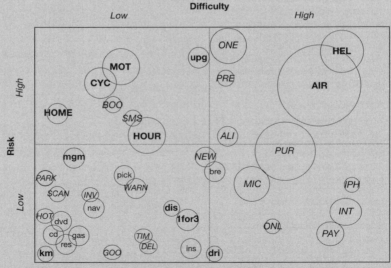

Circle size represents estimated revenues or estimated profit savings of each innovation project

The ranking of projects is a job for management. Wherever needed, you can use some of the tools described in Chapter 8 or seek the cooperation of any of the facilitators of other projects. However, the ranking of projects in portfolio is just a guide; its function is to apply the innovation strategy (number and types of innovations that are desired at any given time). Final project assessment will come as the innovation process advances, as we saw in Chapter 8.

The portfolio should reflect corporate strategy and innovation goals (it helps to balance the projects in terms of such variables as long/short term, high/low risk and radical/marginal).[19] It has been shown that companies that use this tool allocate their resources for innovation very effectively.

It's often the case that the main obstacles to innovation – the enemies of change – are within the company. Those obstacles are resource procurement, management's risk aversion and the reluctance of some executives to move certain projects forward. The portfolio is an excellent tool for overcoming these problems.

From the portfolio, projects are fed into the innovation pipeline. As the ideas, concepts and projects advance through the pipeline, the company makes decisions on what new items and projects to promote.[20] That is where the innovation roadmap comes in.

The innovation roadmap

The innovation roadmap enables you to visualize the timing of the different "processes", both those in execution and those planned for the coming years. It is used to plan resource allocation, the number of simultaneous processes and the number and types of innovations that will be launched at any given time (see Box 10.2). Using the roadmap we apply the innovation strategy (number and types of innovations) over time. For example, when Corning schedules its different innovation processes, it always seeks to strike a balance between short-term developments of existing products (improvements) and long-term projects.

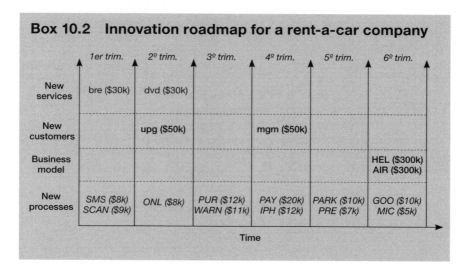

Box 10.2 Innovation roadmap for a rent-a-car company

	1er trim.	2º trim.	3º trim.	4º trim.	5º trim.	6º trim.
New services	bre ($30k)	dvd ($30k)				
New customers		upg ($50k)		mgm ($50k)		
Business model						HEL ($300k) AIR ($300k)
New processes	SMS ($8k) SCAN ($9k)	ONL ($8k)	PUR ($12k) WARN ($11k)	PAY ($20k) IPH ($12k)	PARK ($10k) PRE ($7k)	GOO ($10k) MIC ($5k)

Time

Resource buckets

Resource buckets are a means to ensure that resources are allocated according to a company's strategic priorities.

The way this works is by classifying the various projects using the same criteria that were used for resource allocation. For example, company X has decided that 50 percent of resources for innovation should go to radical innovation in new products, 25 percent to marginal innovations (that is, portfolio extensions) and 25 percent to process improvements.

The projects in the pipeline are classified in the same three groups, within each of which they are ranked according to their potential and fit for the company. After calculating the approximate budget required for each project, the top-ranking projects in each group are approved until the resources allocated to that type of innovation run out, without diverting resources from other groups. Box 10.3 shows the resource allocation for our rent-a-car company.

Box 10.3   Resource allocation for a rent-a-car company

Budget Buckets

New services ($60k)	Business models ($600k)
dvd ($30k)	HEL ($100k)
bre ($30k)	AIR ($200k)
nav ($30k)	HOME ($30k)
pick ($35k)	MOT ($70k)
ins ($25k)	HOUR ($40k)
gas ($12k)	CYC ($20k)
res ($14k)	
cd ($10k)	

New customers ($100k)	New processes ($120k each)			
	Keys delivery ($30k)	Billing system ($30k)	Online reservations increase ($30k)	Maintenance ($30k)
upg ($50k)	SMS ($8k)	SCAN ($9k)	GOO ($10k)	MIC ($5k)
mgm ($50k)	PARK ($10k)	PAY ($20k)	IPH ($12k)	PUR ($12k)
dis ($45k)	PRE ($7k)		ONL ($8k)	WARN ($11k)
km ($60k)	TIM ($12k)	INV ($10k)	HOT ($8k)	ONE ($30k)
dri ($25k)	DEL ($11k)	BOO ($12k)	INT ($9k)	NEW ($20k)
1for3 ($11k)				ALI ($10k)

Note: Projects are ranked within each category according to facilitators rating. Resources are allocated into each group until budget is fully spent. No possibility of getting resources from other categories

The process advances

Projects, once approved, will advance through innovation processes. For this to happen, if we haven't already done so, we must choose the rest of the A-to-F team, by roles: browsers, creators, developers, executors and facilitators. Then for each role we allocate the necessary resources and estimate the number of working hours, and the process is finally ready to roll. By doing so, the A-to-F model conforms to innovation planning.

All that's left to do is to select the tools for each role (see Chapters 4 to 8) and use the right collaborative formulas according to the needs of the process (see Chapter 9). These decisions can be made either by the team itself or by management (CIO or CEO).

TOTAL INNOVATION SYSTEM – Summary Chapter 10

Main person/s in charge of each role

	A Activators	B Browsers	C Creators	D Developers	E Executors	F Facilitators
activation	Top management (GM or Chief innovation officer)	Market research department	Advertising agency	R&D	Current marketing department (shared team)	Top management (GM or Chief innovation officer)
	Employees	Market research suppliers	Creativity agency	New products department	Current sales department (shared team)	Financial director
	Suppliers	Sociologists	Marketing	Operations	Dedicated marketing team	New projects committee
activation	Distributors	Marketing	Creative types	Manufacturing	New division	Chief innovation officer
	Clients	Sales	R&D	External suppliers	New company	Board
	Investors	Opinion leaders	Clients	Marketing	Third party alliances	Shareholders
activation	Universities	Watchers' panel	Suppliers	Sales		Employees
	Scientific community	R&D	Employees with creative profile	Dedicated engineers		Innovation team
activation	Inventors	Other internal departments	Other suppliers or third parties			Middle management
	Engineering companies	Other suppliers or third parties				External: experts, stakeholders or investors

Techniques employed by each role

A Activators	B Browsers	C Creators	D Developers	E Executors	F Facilitators
Scope of innovation	Innovation review	Synectics	Helping in concept definition	Marketing plan and launch plan	Subjective assessment
Innovation levels	Analysis of adjacent categories	Blue Ocean strategy	Concept test for improving design	Morphing	Purchase intention according to test levels
Focus of innovation	Internal consulting	Morphological analysis	Pictures	KPIs evolution	Delphi method
Innovation guidelines	Social trend/ social classes	Lateral marketing	Conjoint analysis for features definition	Next marginal evolution	Nominal group techniques
Innovation checklist	Market trends	Attributes listing	Drawings	Area testing	Company-wide rating
	Buying process	Scenarios analysis	Mock-up	Market testing	Phillips 66
	Innovation routes	Visits	Prototype	Product testing	Six Sigma
	Technological solutions	Co-creation	Product test	Intensity on ATRs	Cost-benefit analysis
	Design referents	Redefining customer value	Usage/home test	Experimentation	Demand estimation
	Successful strategies and tactics/learning from errors	Brainstorming	Patents		Profit and loss
	Network monitoring	Concept definition			ROI analysis
	Ethnographic				Scenario analysis
	Geolocation				Market test

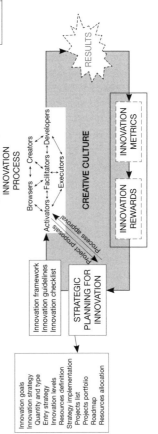

Innovation goals
Innovation strategy
Quantity and type
Entry strategy
Innovation levels
Resources definition
Strategy implementation
Projects list
Projects portfolio
Roadmap
Resources allocation

Innovation framework
Innovation guidelines
Innovation checklist

STRATEGIC PLANNING FOR INNOVATION

Project proposals
Process approval

Browsers ↔ Creators
Activators ↔ Facilitators ↔ Developers
Executors

INNOVATION PROCESS

CREATIVE CULTURE

INNOVATION REWARDS

INNOVATION METRICS

RESULTS

11 Metrics

What are innovation metrics?

Innovation metrics comprise a set of tools and systems for measuring the innovative capacity of an organization.

Innovation metrics are relatively new. The reason is that other measures, such as the overall growth in sales or profits, were previously considered sufficient to determine a company's performance.

However, as innovation has become a policy fundamental to corporate survival, companies have found they need specific tools to diagnose whether or not they are prepared to innovate, and to measure the effectiveness of their innovation strategies.

Imagine a company that is seeing rising profits or billing, but which is not innovating at all. Perhaps growth is due to an appropriate strategy, the disappearance of certain competitors or a high-performance sales team. Nonetheless, the company is not innovating. Innovation metrics clearly distinguish which part of a company's success stems from innovation.

The difference from the metrics we introduced in Chapter 8 is that the ones we deal with here are for the entire company: they measure the level of innovativeness for the entire organization, rather than the potential of a particular project or innovation process.

If we compare the list of most innovative companies today[1] with the list from two decades ago, we will see that there has been a huge turnover in names. This suggests that the problem today is not just innovation, but innovation sustained over time. Some companies had that great idea, groundbreaking business model and/or winning strategy in the past but were unable to sustain the momentum that once made them a leading innovator. Innovation metrics, aside from being an evaluation system, are also a diagnostic tool for predicting future capacity to innovate and, in the event of potential decline, understanding how to reverse the trend before it is too late.[2]

How to use them

Innovation metrics have several more functions. Since they are objective and quantifiable units of measurement they are useful for three types of comparison:

▷ To compare ourselves with other companies in our industry and rank ourselves among our competitors. However, this is not a common practice: according to McKinsey & Company, only 42 percent of companies use metrics to compare themselves with their competitors in terms of innovative capacity.[3]

▷ To compare two or more business units in the same company. The McKinsey survey didn't find a lot of companies using innovation metrics to do this either, which is surprising because interdepartmental comparison is a common practice in the business world.

▷ To measure the growth of the innovative capacity in a company or business unit over time. This comparison is essential to ascertain whether money, training and time invested in innovation is bearing fruit from year to year. It also enables a company to correct its innovation strategies over time.

Apart from these specific functions, metrics have broader strategic uses: communication (to define and inform of the strategy), control (to monitor the implementation of innovation efforts, such as investment in training, R&D, and so on) and learning (to identify new opportunities through discussion of changes in the findings from metrics).[4]

Finally, as we will see in Chapter 13, metrics also provide objective measurements in designing an incentive system for innovation.

How many companies use innovation metrics?

Despite their importance, the fact is that the use of innovation metrics is still not widespread in the business world. According to a study by McKinsey & Company[5] conducted among 722 companies, only 22 percent said they used metrics to measure the performance of their innovation policies.

Another telling statistic: 45 percent of companies do not even measure the relationship between spending on innovation and company value.[6]

It is surprising that companies do not measure their ability to innovate. First, because only with relevant data in hand can management make decisions on an issue. And second, because measuring innovation enables us to align objectives and actions.[7]

If companies were aware of the relationship between metrics and the results of innovation, they would probably grant them more importance. Robert G. Cooper conducted a study comparing companies according to their performance in innovation: poor, average and outstanding.[8] The use of metrics proved to be one of the variables that best explained performance (see Figure 11.1).

As Robert Cooper says:

A significant minority of business are now making product innovation results part of senior management's performance metrics, and in some cases tying variable pay and bonuses to the business's innovation performance. For example, at ITT Industries, new product results is now a key performance metric for business unit general managers, along with meeting profits and targets. Note that while still not widespread, this practice is seen in best performing companies almost four-times as often as in poor performers.[9]

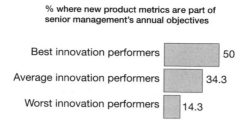

Figure 11.1 **Correlation between new product performance and use of metrics**

Source: Robert G. Cooper, *Winning at New Products: Creating Value Through Innovation*, www.stage-gate.com

The use of metrics should be part of any innovation policy. As T. Davila et al.[10] note: what cannot be measured cannot be managed. Innovation metrics and incentives are one of the four factors necessary for innovation to take place.

Types of metrics

Metrics can be grouped into four categories: those that measure the results of innovation from the economic standpoint; those that measure the intensity of innovation within a department, business unit or organization; those that measure the efficacy of innovative activity and investment; and finally those that measure how widespread the creative culture is in an organization.

Below we present a total of 25 metrics grouped according to these categories.

Economic metrics

Economic metrics measure the positive or negative results of innovation using variables from the company's economic-financial statements.

1   *Company sales from new product launches.* This is probably one of the most commonly used metrics. It is measured in percentages and is usually calculated for two time periods, for the previous year and averaging out a number of years, usually three to five. This metric is commonly used to determine medium and long-term objectives. For example, several years ago Nestlé made it an objective that new products must be above 10 percent of the company's last three years' billing.

A figure between 20 percent and 30 percent is ambitious. However, there are companies that, given the importance of innovation in their industry, attain even higher levels. For example, at Corning, a leader in the glass and fiber optics markets, 80 percent of company sales derive from products launched in the past four years.

Sometimes, rather than the weight of innovation in total sales, it is calculated based on growth; that is, what part of the sales growth can be attributed to innovation.

2   *Profits from the launch of new products.* In this case, instead of sales, we measure the profits. This metric is usually calculated based on accumulated sales over one to five years, depending on the launch. The reason is that some launches take a certain amount of time before they start generating profits.

3   *Company sales from innovations other than in new products.* This metric differs from the previous one in that here we consider innovations that do not involve a roll-out: improvements in processes, customer relations, customer experience, ideas for capturing new customers, the development of new channels, and so on. Companies should not become obsessed with launches. While it is true that the product life cycles have become shorter, that does not mean that we need a new portfolio each year. Innovations that do not involve launches can produce great results and they most likely will not require the large investments in production and marketing associated with bringing a new product onto the market. This metric seeks to measure the sales growth generated by ideas related to the management of the *current* portfolio of products and services.

4   *Profits from innovations other than in new products.* Same as the above, but measuring the final profits or contribution margin of the improvements carried out.

5   *Cost savings from innovation.* Since it is often difficult to calculate the exact profits derived from an improvement, companies use cost savings as a common alternative. This is an especially common metric in process innovation and is measured in monetary units (dollars, euros ...) or as a percentage of margin or EBITDA (earnings before interest, taxes, depreciation and amortization). For example, a company might determine that its objective is to attain a 7 percent to 9 percent rise in EBITDA through cost savings derived from process innovation.

6   *Total ROI in innovation.* This is the same metric that we saw in Chapter 8, but applied to an entire company or business unit. That is, it calculates the return on all investments in innovation over the years as the profits derived from overall innovation. In the evaluation of projects in Chapter 8, revenues were estimations for the future. In this case, the revenues are real observed data. As a metric, ROI requires a relatively long time period: five to ten years or so, but it is a good long-term indicator. Since we are dealing with a long time sequence, this metric evolves more gradually and thus correlates well with the total value of a company (in industries intensive on innovation, research and development). For example, Corning measures the results of an innovation in terms of revenue that multiplies investment in R&D (a multiplier is the inverse of ROI).

Intensity

Intensity refers to the quantity of innovation without taking into account the results derived thereof.

7 *Number of patents.* This is a typical metric in the pharmaceutical industry and in technology and R&D-intensive sectors. It may seem absurd to measure the number of patents without regard to whether they generate income. However, there are sectors where you need a lot of inventions before they will translate into value. Pharmaceutical companies need to come up with thousands of new molecules before discovering a new drug. Each of those molecules must be patented.

Some companies measure patent applications even before a patent has been awarded. This is the case at Hewlett Packard, where each patent application submitted by company technicians is rewarded with $175.

The pharmaceutical industry also keeps track of the number of expiring patents – a worrying statistic, unless their level of new patents is growing well.

8 *Number of innovations in products, services, customer experiences, processes or business models.* In this case we measure the number of innovations that we are able to implement. This metric usually separates the number of launches from the number of innovations, in the same way as we have seen in financial metrics. The advantage of computing the number is that you can set very clear objectives from year to year. For example, a company might find that 12 improvements have been implemented at the factory during one year and that 15 improvements must be implemented the next.

9 *Number of brands.* This is the marketing version of the number of patents. It makes sense in sectors where brands are short-lived, such as children's products or for distributors of products whose brands are based on licenses.

10 *Number of ideas generated per year.* This metric does not take into account the number of ideas that eventually become projects. It focuses on ideas, although many will be discarded, because ideas, as we saw in the previous chapter, are the seeds of projects. Thus the number of ideas is an indirect measure of the number of future projects and people's engagement in innovation.

11 *Number of innovation projects in the pipeline.* This metric is used to monitor the company's project pipeline. A declining number of projects in the pipeline may signal a decrease in the number of innovations within one to three years (unless the company is betting on a major project and focusing all its funds on that project). This variable is used to manage innovation in the medium term.

12 *Number of ongoing innovation projects.* This metric is used to predict the intensity of innovation in the short term, as well as the number of innovation processes that a company is capable of carrying out simultaneously.

13 *Investment in R&D.* Although this is a financial metric, it is more related to intensity. Investment in R&D is usually measured in monetary units or as a percentage of annual company billing. For example, 3M invests nearly 7 percent of annual sales in research, development and related expenditure (more than 5 billion dollars over the past five years). Investment in R&D – as a percentage of GDP – is a metric familiar to many non-business people, since it is frequently used in the media to rank regions and countries. The top six countries of the world in terms of R&D investment related to GDP are: Israel, Japan, Sweden, Finland, South Korea and the United States.

Effectiveness

These metrics seek to measure profits in relation to the use of resources with the objective of maximizing innovation outputs while minimizing inputs.

14 *Success rate in new products.* This metric is widely used to measure the results of innovation, especially in consumer products. It computes the percentage of all new product launches that prove successful. The question is: what constitutes success? The criteria depend on the company, but they are usually based on two variables: profitability and staying power in the market. Another way of measuring success is in terms of the extent to which the objectives defined at the outset of the project have been met. For example, a company may determine that an innovation is successful when it accounts for 3 percent of sales within three years of launch with the same margins as other products.

Whatever the success criteria, they are usually revised periodically. This is a common practice at Procter & Gamble, allowing the company to track the results of new products and evaluate each business unit in isolation.

15 *Time to market.* Another effectiveness metric relates to the time variable, rather than sales. This metric is more prevalent in sectors and industries where technological change is fast and competitiveness is closely related to introducing innovations within a narrow timeframe. For example, Samsung uses as a metric the speed with which innovations and upgrades reach the market. Philips offers its product development teams bonuses for meeting the specified deadlines.[11]

16 *Average investment per project.* This metric is very useful for making comparisons over time within a company. In this case, we divide the total investment in R&D by the number of innovations launched, whether they have been successful or not. By making comparisons over time we can see if the company is able to innovate with fewer and fewer resources. Of course, this comparison should differentiate between types of innovation, since radical innovations tend to consume more resources than marginal ones.

17 *Average impact of investment per successful project.* This is a variant of
    the previous metric, but in this case we divide total investment in
    innovation (for both successful and unsuccessful projects) by the
    number of projects that have met their objectives. By using total
    investment as our numerator and only successful projects as our
    denominator, we indirectly measure the company's overall effective-
    ness in carrying out valid innovations.
18 *Average expenditure on rejected ideas and projects.* Remember the impor-
    tance of error management in innovation. This metric calculates the
    average cost of rejecting an idea by adding up the costs of the ideas and
    proposals that have been discarded and dividing by the number of
    discarded ideas or projects. In this way, we can measure the company's
    ability to halt innovations before they cost too much money.
19 *Number of years as the industry leader.* Here a high score does not neces-
    sarily mean a company is innovative, especially in the case of a sector
    that is oligopolistic or slow to change. Applied to dynamic sectors,
    however, this calculation is an indicator of the ability to innovate in a
    sustainable manner.

Culture

In this case, the metrics refer to aspects related to the creative culture of the
organization. We are not interested in effectiveness, amount of innovation or
efficacy, but in measuring how widespread innovation and, in particular,
creativity are within the organization as a whole.

20 *Percentage of employees that produce ideas.* This is only possible when
    either our system for generating ideas reveals the identity of the person
    behind an idea or, in the case of an anonymous system, we can compute
    the number of individual contributors by means of some sort of anon-
    ymous ID. The ratio of employees who propose ideas over total
    company employees indicates how widespread the creative culture is.
    We may find, for example, that out of a total workforce 14 percent
    propose ideas. At Toyota, about 70 percent of the employees contribute
    improvement ideas. This might explain why their cars have been so
    near perfection.
21 *Percentage of employees that assess ideas.* This is the same idea as above
    but applied to those who assess the ideas of their peers. And the correla-
    tion with the previous metric tends to be very high. As a rule, people
    who propose also assess, since both actions derive from personal involve-
    ment in and attitude toward change.
22 *Rate of ideas per employee per year.* Here, instead of the number of
    people relative to all those who contribute ideas, we want to measure
    the intensity of our creative culture, including not only those who
    propose ideas and those who do not, but also the number of ideas

proposed; for example, our organization (or department) obtains 1.3 ideas per employee per year. What's surprising about this metric is that it tends to yield very low averages, which, on the other hand, is a helpful reminder of the inertia, complacency and aversion to change innate to human beings. There are companies that regularly record numbers lower than 1 (as low as 0.34) idea per employee per year. A variant of this metric is to compute only those individuals who produce ideas. In this case, instead of how widespread the creative culture is, we want to measure the creative intensity of our people who are committed to innovation.

23 *Percentage of time spent on innovation.* This metric computes the percentage of working hours in an organization (sometimes taking into account only those who perform tasks directly related to innovation) dedicated to generating ideas and project management. Thus it is a measure of the presence of innovation in the daily on-job routine. Some companies, as we have seen throughout the book, place great importance on this metric, such that in order to ensure that it is properly managed they simply give their employees a certain number of free hours (or days!) per week or month.

24 *Number of departments that innovate on an ongoing basis.* In large corporations, one measure of the evenness of the spread of innovation, as opposed to being confined to the marketing and R&D departments, is to identify how many departments innovate continually or repeatedly. This metric helps to develop creative culture by encouraging emulation.

25 *Propensity for risk-taking.* Although a more qualitative variable, some companies choose to measure the propensity for risk-taking due to its high correlation with the ability to innovate. Under the usual procedure, senior management, along with the human resources department, evaluates the decisions taken by upper management based on the level of risk. The annual count of all decisions by all managers allows you to calculate, although based on subjective estimates, the propensity for risk in an organization.

GE has begun evaluating its top 5,000 managers on "growth traits" that include innovation-oriented themes such as "external focus" and "imagination and courage". GE has added more flexibility into its traditional metrics, which are all about control, with its new emphasis on innovation, which is more about managing risk.[12]

There is no one universal metric, nor is one more important than another. Nevertheless, if only as a matter of interest, we include here a sample of metrics drawn up by McKinsey & Company:[13]

▷ Revenue growth due to new products and services
▷ Customer satisfaction with products and services

▷ Number of ideas or concepts in the pipeline
▷ ROI in new products or services
▷ Number of R&D projects
▷ Profit growth due to new products or services
▷ Potential of entire new product/service portfolio to meet growth targets
▷ NPV of entire new product/service portfolio

Another source offers the following ranking of metrics:[14]

1   Weight of investment in R&D over sales.
2   Number of patents per year.
3   Percentage of sales derived from launches in the last year.
4   Number of ideas submitted by employees.

In this chapter we have presented 25 important metrics. But for the reader who is interested in learning more there is plenty of literature on this subject, including entire books dedicated solely to the metrics of innovation, of processes, projects and the company as a whole. In one particular aspect of innovation, the generation of ideas alone, we find a long list of possibilities: ideas per employee, quality of ideas, time spent generating ideas, cost of creating an idea, capacity of ideas to feed the new product portfolio, total sales divided by the number of ideas, percentage of ideas used versus ideas discarded, proportion of ideas contributed by employees that are aligned with the company's strategic objectives versus those that are not, percentage distribution of ideas by type of innovation, percentage of ideas by department, and so on.

What we want to stress here is that metrics are as much science as they are art. In fact, it is relatively easy to design metrics, and doing so is something we recommend because it gives executives the measurement system that best matches their strategic priorities.

Combination of metrics

Companies tend not to use just one metric, but several. How many should we use? The 25 we have described are too numerous to consider at once. It would be both unproductive and foolish to try to apply them all to assess and manage one company's innovation activities.

But nor is it a good idea to choose too small a number, especially if they are going to be used to design our incentive system. The reason is that all metrics, like almost any means of measuring the performance of management, are a double-edged sword.

For example, a manager whose bonus depends on the percentage of sales derived from new products launched over the last 12 months, determined to collect his or her bonus, might decide to launch products one after another, with little concern for whether or not the new product is good enough to produce profitable sales.

> "Two or three metrics just don't give you the visibility to get down to root causes," says BCG's Andrew. Then there are companies that track far too many. There's one company which collects 85 different innovation metrics in one of its businesses. "That means they manage none of them," he says. "They default to a couple, but they spend an immense amount of time and effort collecting those 85." The sweet spot is somewhere between 8 and 12 metrics, says Andrew. That's about the number that Samsung Electronics Co. uses, says Chu Woosik, a senior vice-president at the South Korean company.[15]

The right combination of metrics solves this problem. In the above list, there are metrics that complement each other nicely, covering what the other does not. For example, the first metric in our list (annual turnover from new products) is complemented well by the second (profits derived from new products). In terms of coming of up with an incentive scheme, a combination of the two would avoid the problems inherent in rewarding sales alone.

The second criteria you can use to select the metrics to measure innovation performance are your objectives and strategy. In Chapter 10 we saw the different approaches to formulating an innovation strategy. Metrics should reflect the spirit of the objectives and strategy in innovation. For example, a company proposing a defensive innovation strategy with limited resources through the launch of marginal innovations to protect their market position should choose metrics such as numbers 1, 2, 14, 17 and 25.

▷ Turnover generated by new launches
▷ Profit from new launches
▷ Rate of success for new products
▷ Average investment (with the aim at reducing it) per launch
▷ Low propensity for risk-taking

The third criterion for choosing metrics relates to the key factors of success in a given industry. For example, we have seen that in the pharmaceutical industry the number of patents is a key metric; in the Internet sector, where the implementation costs are often much smaller, metrics related to the number of ideas proposed are more appropriate; in consumer goods, the number of launches and the results obtained; in industrial sectors, metrics related to the number of innovations other than launches and cost savings from innovation. And so on: each industry has its most appropriate metrics. In fact, innovation researchers have been unable to establish common metrics by industry.[16]

Ultimately, the choice of metrics can be expressed as a function:

Metrics = f (complementarity, innovation strategy, industry)

It has been shown that companies that perform well in innovation use, on average, between one and two metrics more than other companies. Moreover, the metrics they choose cover each of the stages in an innovation process, such as percentage of people involved in innovation, number of ideas, or percentage of innovations that meet deadlines.[17] The conclusion is this: You should use metrics and you should choose them according to specific criteria; your metrics should measure several aspects of innovation (and not just one) and they should be combined.

In choosing and/or designing your own metrics, you should bear in mind the following criteria:

▷ They should be understandable
▷ They should not be overly complicated to calculate
▷ They should exploit as far as possible the indicators that the company regularly uses
▷ They should be customer-related

Sophisticated combination of metrics

Once a company has acquired a certain experience in the use of metrics, and has learned to combine them efficiently, it can move on to a second, more sophisticated but higher value stage: the construction of frameworks as a diagnostic of a company's innovative capacity and its evolution over time.[18] This is a very advanced level, primarily of interest for specialists in innovation. Since this book is intended as a handy guide and compendium for executives, we will not devote a lot of space to this point, but we will outline what it consists of and how this approach to metrics can be useful.

If we examine the 25 metrics in this chapter, we will see that some of them are related to the inputs of innovation. For example, the percentage of time devoted to innovation is an input that aims to obtain results in the future. Other metrics relate to outputs. For example, the percentage of last year's sales from new products is an output of innovation policy. Still others – time to market, for instance – relate to processes.

In order to assess the relationship between inputs and outputs with regard to innovation, we can construct a scheme or framework that divides metrics into these same three categories. Thus, we can diagnose whether our innovation policies and investment are paying off and whether there is a relationship between inputs and outputs.

For example, as input a company could measure investment in creativity training for its workers and the percentage of on-job time devoted to generating new ideas. From there you can see whether the variations in training hours translate into some sort of output, for example more patents.

A company that invests more and more in innovation training and sees no improvements in output may decide that such training is no longer a priority and that the resources should be diverted to other uses: for example, instead of trainings hours, free time for generating ideas.

More input does not always equal more output. When it does not, it could be due to the processes, a question that process metrics can help us answer. For example, it might happen that, despite having invested more in training, the number of patents hasn't risen because the patent development period (this is a process metric) shows a substantial increase in time spent applying for patents.

All this may seem complicated, but it isn't really. It has the advantage that metrics are used not only to obtain objective information about our business, but also to determine whether we are investing efficiently in innovation.

To put the finishing touches to this tool, we recommend you group input, process and output metrics according to a particular issue. For example, you might have the following group of metrics for the management area "communication of the innovation strategy:"

▷ *Inputs:*
  ▷ Number of reports on innovation objectives
  ▷ Number of management presentations to other departments on the strategic priorities of innovation
▷ *Processes:*
  ▷ Percentage of reports on innovation in e-mail
  ▷ Number of pages in executive summaries to inform other departments of strategic priorities of innovation
▷ *Outputs:*
  ▷ Percentage of ideas submitted within the organization that are not aligned with innovation objectives

Other possible groupings would be: capacity of the workforce; creative culture; resources; leadership in innovation; understanding of the strategy, and so on.

The metrics and objectives

Ideally, metrics should be used to set objectives for innovation over time, as described in the previous chapter.

For example, a company could set the following objects for five years from now:

▷ Billing generated by new launches must rise from 10 percent to 30 percent of total billing
▷ Profits from new launches must rise from 5 percent to 15 percent of total profits

▷ The success rate for new products must rise from 30 percent to 50 percent
▷ The percentage of employees who contribute ideas must rise from 5 percent to 30 percent

Whatever metrics you use, the important thing is to apply the findings. It makes no sense to measure something and then not apply your findings to some purpose.

TOTAL INNOVATION SYSTEM – Summary Chapter 11

Main person/s in charge of each role

A Activators	B Browsers	C Creators	D Developers	E Executors	F Facilitators
Top management (GM or Chief innovation officer)	Market research department	Advertising agency	R&D	Current marketing department (shared team)	Top management (GM or Chief innovation officer)
Employees	Market research suppliers	Creativity agency	New products department	Current sales department (shared team)	Financial director
Suppliers	Sociologists	Marketing	Operations	Dedicated marketing team	New projects committee
Distributors	Marketing	Creative types	Manufacturing	New division	Chief innovation officer
Clients	Sales	R&D	External suppliers	New company	Board
Investors	Opinion leaders	Clients	Marketing	Third party alliances	Shareholders
Universities	Watchers' panel	Suppliers	Sales		Employees
Scientific community	R&D	Employees with creative profile	Dedicated engineers		Innovation team
Inventors	Other internal departments	Other suppliers or third parties			Middle management
Engineering companies	Other suppliers or third parties				External: experts, stakeholders or investors

Up-bottom activation
In-out activation
Bottom-up activation
Out-in activation

Techniques employed by each role

A Activators	B Browsers	C Creators	D Developers	E Executors	F Facilitators
Scope of innovation	Innovation review	Synectics	Helping in concept definition	Marketing plan and launch plan	Subjective assessment
Innovation levels	Analysis of adjacent categories	Blue Ocean strategy	Concept test for improving design	Morphing	Purchase intention according to test levels
Focus of innovation	Internal consulting	Morphological analysis	Pictures	KPIs evolution	Delphi method
Innovation guidelines	Social trend/ social classes	Lateral marketing	Conjoint analysis for features definition	Next marginal evolution	Nominal group techniques
Innovation checklist	Market trends	Attributes listing	Drawings	Area testing	Company-wide rating
	Buying process	Scenarios analysis	Mock-up	Market testing	Phillips 66
	Innovation routes	Visits	Prototype	Product testing	Six Sigma
	Technological solutions	Co-creation	Product test	Intensity on ATRs	Cost-benefit analysis
	Design referents	Redefining customer value	Usage/home test	Experimentation	Demand estimation
	Successful strategies and tactics/learning from errors	Brainstorming	Patents		Profit and loss
	Network monitoring	Concept definition			ROI analysis
	Ethnographic				Scenario analysis
	Geolocation				Market test

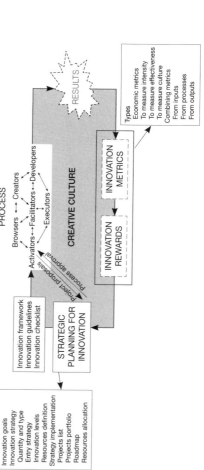

Innovation framework
Innovation guidelines
Innovation checklist

STRATEGIC PLANNING FOR INNOVATION

Innovation goals
Innovation strategy
Quantity and type
Entry strategy
Innovation levels
Resources definition
Strategy implementation
Projects list
Projects portfolio
Roadmap
Resources allocation

Project proposals
Process approval

INNOVATION PROCESS
Browsers ↔ Creators
Activators ↔ Facilitators ↔ Developers
Executors

CREATIVE CULTURE

INNOVATION REWARDS
INNOVATION METRICS
RESULTS

Types
Economic metrics
To measure intensity
To measure effectiveness
To measure culture
Combining metrics
From inputs
From processes
From outputs

12 How to Foster a Creative Culture

What is "creative culture"?

In the company, creative culture is not something tangible like a process: it is, in a sense, unseen and yet perfectly recognizable. A company with a creative culture exudes interest and proactivity in innovation. It hangs in the air – ideas arise everywhere, all across the organization and from all levels of responsibility, regardless of whether one's job has any direct relationship with new products. Wherever the staff gathers, creativity and innovation are present:

> As a leader, you don't want to ghettoize creativity; you want everyone in your organization producing novel and useful ideas, including your financial people. Over the past couple of decades, there have been innovations in financial accounting that are extremely profound and entirely ethical, such as activity-based costing.[1]

If top Management of any company were to place listening devices in the staff canteen or the staff's favourite pub, they would quickly discover…

▷ that everyone in the company has ideas about all aspects of the company
▷ that many of those ideas are well thought out
▷ that the people with ideas come from all divisions and all levels of the corporate hierarchy
▷ that many of those ideas are worth good money to the company.[2]

In a company with a well-developed creative culture, no one talks about that culture because innovation is in the company's DNA, coded into its behavior: innovation goes on continuously and in all directions.

Another trait of companies with a creative culture is that people show an interest in contributing ideas. We're talking about an interest that runs deep, sparked not just from a system of incentives, but from an inherent part of one's approach to one's job, one's area of activity and the tasks involved. A creative attitude is like joy or sadness: it's contagious. In an innovative company, the people who in other organizations wouldn't contribute ideas find themselves inventing, proposing, evaluating, always looking for ways for the company to do things better. Creativity is encouraged from above, from top management down, but so ingrained in the day-to-day routine, that eventually it is also encouraged from the bottom up, from the lower staff ranks to the boardroom. Creativity springs forth naturally and spreads from one employee to the next.

Another way to spot a creative corporate culture is that continuous innovation is an acknowledged fact; that is, everyone is aware of the changes that are implemented and the results they yield. Innovation is not restricted to certain departments or executives. Information flows and the company's achievements in innovation are brought to everyone's attention. Companies that innovate successfully tend to be leaders in their target market segments. That leadership translates into a pride of accomplishment, not a pride of vanity and complacency, but rather that of people who know they are writing the future of their industry.

All this is very appealing and easy to say, but how is it done? How do you acquire an innovative culture? There are CEOs of large corporations who believe that it is virtually impossible to transform the culture – the poor attitudes and habits of thousands of people, the inertia, the paralysis – of their companies. It is true that the larger the organization, the harder it will be to foster a creative culture, but that does not mean it's impossible. For example, hardly anyone would dispute the statement that IBM and Procter & Gamble (P&G) are both gigantic. Yet both have shown that, with effort, planning, perseverance and resources, you can evolve from a conservative culture to an innovative one. With no less than 110,000 employees all across the world, P&G changed from being a dinosaur to being a model of efficiency in innovation that no rival can match.

We have seen how creative culture is (along with planning, processes, and rewards) one of the four factors that make up the essence of an innovative company. This is a very important point because there are many executives who think all you have to do is introduce a creative culture and sooner or later innovation will happen. We have seen that this is not true. Thus, in this chapter, the reader should always bear in mind the other three factors. It is useless to follow all the rules for fostering a creative culture if you don't have, for example, strong innovation processes such as those described in the first part of this book.

That said, let's look at the key factors in establishing a creative culture in a company.

Culture builders

The CEO

The primary responsibility for creating a creative culture lies at the top, with the CEO. The freedom for workers to think creatively and independently, collaborative spirit and encouragement for everyone who has ideas to speak up and make them known to the company can only come from the upper ranks of management:

"That sort of support from the CEO is essential," says Jon R. Katzenbach, co-founder of New York-based management consultancy Katzenbach Partners LLC. "The CEO determines the culture," he says. "If the CEO is determined to [improve] the surfacing of ideas and determined to make critical choices, then the chances of an [organization's] figuring that out are much, much greater."[3]

Infosys Technologies Ltd (INFY), the Bangalore-based information technology services company that popped up at No. 10 on the Asia-Pacific list of most innovative companies, is also among the organizations that take a direct approach to making sure top management stays involved in the innovation process. Throughout this chapter, however, we will be using Procter & Gamble as a model of how to transform the culture of a large organization. In the case of the CEO:

> Only a CEO can change a business culture at top speed, and in Alan G. Lafley, P&G has its own innovator-in-chief. Lafley sits in on all "upstream" R&D review meetings, 15 a year, that showcase new products. He also spends three full days a year with the company's Design Board, a group of outside designers who offer their perspective on upcoming P&G products. "He's sort of the chief innovation officer," says P&G's Huston. "He's very, very involved."[4]

The direct relationship between CEO engagement and the results of innovation has been shown empirically. Robert G. Cooper analyzed three types of enterprises in terms of the effectiveness of their new product policies. Commitment of senior management to product development is strongly correlated with performance (Figure 12.1).

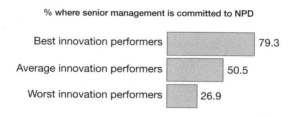

% where senior management is committed to NPD

Best innovation performers — 79.3
Average innovation performers — 50.5
Worst innovation performers — 26.9

Figure 12.1 **Correlation between new product performance and management commitment**
Source: Robert G. Cooper, Winning at New Products: Creating Value Through Innovation, www.stage-gate.com

Senior management plays a lead role in championing the innovation effort in best performing businesses, creating a positive climate and culture for innovation and entrepreneurship, much more so than in poor performing businesses.[5]

And it's not just about showing an interest. The senior management of a conservative, static company that wants to instill creativity must also act accordingly on the job. That is, managers have to contribute ideas, be creative too. Otherwise, their inferiors can hardly be expected to take their will to change the culture seriously. An example of what we mean is the president of Starbucks, who gets together with the company's 250 senior executives for monthly meetings that consist entirely of "question-and-answer sessions" focused on the company's innovation projects.

The CIO

In some large companies, where the CEO cannot dedicate him or herself fully to managing and monitoring innovation, it is advisable to create an executive position to lead innovation. This person might be called vice-president for innovation, or the CIO (chief innovation officer), or director for new products and innovation. The name doesn't matter. The important thing is that this person must have real power over other departments and executives within the organization; otherwise he or she will lack the necessary authority:

> If you don't have highly creative people in positions of real authority, you won't get innovation. Most companies in other industries ignore this lesson.[6]

> To spearhead the connect-and-develop efforts in P&G, Larry Huston took on the newly created role of vice-president for innovation and knowledge. Each business unit, from household care to family health, added a manager responsible for driving cultural change around the new model. The managers communicate directly with Huston, who also oversees the technology entrepreneurs and managers running the external innovation networks.[7]

The second reason for having such a figure in the company is that, as we saw in Chapter 10, innovation planning, innovation project portfolio management and coordination of ongoing innovation processes require someone with a 360-degree vision of everything that is going on in relation to innovative activity. These figures are the only people with a complete view of innovation and the evolution of ideas. They can see the "big picture" and thus treat each innovation as a piece that has to fit into a larger puzzle:

> "You want to have a coherent strategy across the organization. [...] The ideas tend to be bigger when you have someone sitting at the center looking at the company's growth goals."[8]

The people responsible for processes are not responsible for culture

We must distinguish between the CEO's responsibilities and those of the leaders of innovation processes, whose job is limited to a particular project, however important it may be. Some companies expect innovation will happen if you just start up innovation processes and assign someone to run them. At the end of the day, they think, we have a process with a budget, a deadline and a person in charge. That's not enough. We have seen that innovation processes, the basic units of an innovation that a company is developing at a given time, need to be framed in a portfolio of projects, which, in turn, depend on a business strategy. Innovation project leaders who don't have a figure of authority to report to, whether it's the CIO, managing director or CEO, will eventually run into serious problems. On their own, no innovation processes, much less their leaders, can bring about a creative culture in a company.

Organizational inhibitors of ideas, creativity and innovation

An inhibitor is a set of factors that prevents people from proposing ideas. Innovation needs ideas, and ideas need creativity. If the people in a company don't propose ideas it's because something is inhibiting them from doing so. This is absolutely crucial and probably one of the most important considerations in the implementation of a creative culture in a company. As long as you have inhibitors, innovation is just not going to happen. It's as simple as it is true. One of the first steps for a CEO who wants to foster an innovative spirit is to get rid of the inhibitors.

The problem is that many executives aren't aware of the inhibitors in their organizations. And not only are they unaware of them, but they'd rather not know, since the biggest inhibitors relate to management style, to informal power relations and to the company's most recent past. In Julia Janna's view:

> I believe most people aren't anywhere near to realizing their creative potential, in part because they're laboring in environments that impede intrinsic motivation. The anecdotal evidence suggests many companies still have a long way to go to remove the barriers to creativity.[9]

The main inhibitors of creativity have to do with fear in general (fear of error and of retaliation, in particular), deadlines, pressure, internal competition, crises and restructuring, and the lack of methods.

Let's examine these inhibitors one by one, providing ways to eradicate them.

Fear in general

Creativity and innovation are paths to change of unknown outcome. Innovation is probably the only business objective that we cannot specify exactly where it will lead. We could say that, rather than a goal, it establishes a direction. The uncertainty of the outcome increases the perceived risk, both real and subjective. Human beings are, as a rule, averse to risk, to the unknown.

And since innovation is a path to an unknown, it produces fear, which acts as an inhibitor of ideas and creativity. Professor Teresa Amabile, one of the world's leading experts on creativity, conducted an empirical study based on 12,000 journal entries by a sample of 238 people regarding their moods. For each date, they also wrote down their creative inputs and ideas. The study shows that the levels of anxiety, fear, sadness, happiness and love in a company are directly related to the number of ideas people generate. The respondents came up with better ideas when they were in a better mood and felt happier. Interestingly, they were more likely to come up with breakthrough ideas when they had been in a good mood the day before. It seems there is a virtuous cycle in which people who have a good day at work make cognitive associations overnight that act as incubators for ideas that show up the following day. In other words, being happy one day predicts creativity the next.[10]

It is therefore essential to eradicate the culture of fear. The best way to reduce the fear of proposing ideas is to inform personnel that the company is aware that many of their ideas and proposals will be screened out, eliminating those that are not worthwhile (remember: fail fast, early and cheap). They should be told that, while the company wants their input, it has designed and put in place methods for assessing ideas that other people in the organization will apply (see Chapter 8, Facilitators). People can make suggestions freely and without fear of risk because the company has risk-control mechanisms in place. The philosophy at Tesco is as follows: product developers are given the freedom to take risks, and other people in the company are charged with evaluating the proposals and separating out the good from the bad. Tesco discards 80–90 percent of the developments proposed, but, knowing that there is a fine-tuned mechanism for screening their ideas, its product developers generate a huge number of proposals.

Fear of error

In our culture, error is frowned upon. It is seen as a sign of incompetence. People are afraid to make mistakes and, given that creativity is associated with a high level of risk, the potential for error is high. Fear of ridicule is another major inhibitor. Many ideas, until they are improved or refined by others, seem ridiculous and, therefore, people tend to keep their ideas to themselves:

> Albert Einstein once said: "If at first the idea is not absurd, then there is no hope for it." For many people, sharing a potentially absurd idea with their company is overly risky. At best, they may be ridiculed by their colleagues.[11]

There are four ways to reduce, or even eliminate, fear of ridicule, of people snickering at our proposals. The first is by means of continuous recycling of ideas. In Chapter 10 we saw that, just as we keep a record of projects in the pipeline, we can keep a record of discarded ideas for future reconsideration, exploiting them as a secondary source of inspiration. The message is obvious: since no idea is ever actually tossed out, no idea is absurd. Even ideas that are rejected initially are filed away as possibilities for the future.

The second way is learning from mistakes. The mistakes made in the past, innovations that failed to yield the expected results, are used constructively in the company, serving as a mechanism for learning from and not repeating the same mistakes in the future. While this approach does not totally eliminate aversion to error, it does change the perception of errors and encourages a culture more inclined to risk-taking.

The third way is by ensuring ideas are anonymous. There are many formulas for doing this, and the new technologies make it even easier for people to contribute ideas anonymously (we deal with this point a bit later on), completely eliminating the fear of ridicule or of being blamed for an idea that fails in implementation.

The fourth way is to reward risk-taking in kind. For example, General Electric executives are assessed according to their imagination and boldness; they are trained in how to take risks and commit to new challenges. The assessment of their results is commensurate with this, and the company rewards the executives who have championed the boldest proposals.[12]

Fear of retaliation

Fear of retaliation is tangible and not at all subjective. Mistakes cost money, so, when a company asks its people for ideas, creativity and innovation, although they won't say so aloud, people will tend to think: "OK, we're supposed to propose ideas, innovate, be more creative, but if something goes wrong, if my ideas generate losses instead of profits, is it going to be my responsibility? What will happen to me? Will it hurt my career?"

> If the workforce does not trust the company, they will not innovate for the company. Survey after survey has shown that trust is one of the most critical factors in establishing a culture of innovation. If your workforce trusts the company, this is not an issue. If not, establishing trust must be your very first step.[13]

It is impossible to foster a creative culture if you do not make it clear who is going to take responsibility for the mistakes inherent in innovation. Because innovation means, to a large extent, managing failure. In order to obtain a few good ideas we're going to have to come up with a lot of bad ones. That's an indisputable fact.

Perhaps we already clearly separate out the responsibilities in new product innovation. But it's a different matter when we are talking about process improvements, a marginal innovation of, for instance, a procedure in the purchasing department, where the process might be developed within the department itself. If the department head has a history of being less than honest with his or her subordinates, blaming them for the department's mistakes, we can hardly expect them to produce ideas.

There are three ways around this. One, ensure that the generation and evaluation of ideas is anonymous. Two, assign innovation processes, no matter how small, to specific executives who report to other executives; this solves at least part of the problem. Three, change the behavior of department heads who don't take responsibility for their subordinates' mistakes – a task for the managing director and director of human resources.

Deadlines and pressure

There is a tendency to believe that people are more creative when they work under pressure. One way to turn up the pressure is by setting deadlines. "By such-and-such date you must have a fully developed, high-potential concept." Does an order like that make people more creative? Teresa Amabile has shown empirically that the answer is no.

> In our diary study, people often thought they were most creative when they were working under severe deadline pressure. But the 12,000 aggregate days that we studied showed just the opposite: People were the least creative when they were fighting the clock. In fact, we found a kind of time-pressure hangover – when people were working under great pressure, their creativity went down not only on that day but the next two days as well. Time pressure stifles creativity because people can't deeply engage with the problem. Creativity requires an incubation period; people need time to soak in a problem and let the ideas bubble up.[14]

We should also distinguish between the mechanisms that activate creativity and those that boost it. To activate means to awaken, to set in motion. To boost creativity means to improve creative efforts, make them more useful and effective, to ensure they yield better results. From this point of view, it is true that having deadlines, as well as processes and people in charge of them, energizes people. But pressure does not improve the quality of creative work, quite the opposite. People make more mistakes when they work with one eye on the calendar. It's distractions like that that undermine the quality of creative work. So we have to balance the need for a deadline – a given in any process, at least as a way to make people aware that there is a job to be done and it can't go on indefinitely – with the need to give people the freedom to create without being distracted by the project clock. It's better to let people concentrate on their work than to burden them with pressure that will ultimately prove counterproductive.

Overdoing internal competition

There are executives who go overboard in promoting internal competition between departments or divisions. In advertising, for instance, we find large groups that are home to a whole fleet of advertising agencies vying for the same jobs and customers, sometimes even under the same roof. This is growing trend, as former rivals merge and big fish swallow smaller ones to create more and more conglomerates housing competing teams. Internal competition has its advantages. But it also has its disadvantages, and one of them is that it inhibits creativity:

> There's a widespread belief that internal competition fosters innovation. We found that creativity takes a hit when people in a work group compete instead of collaborate.[15]

Teams are most creative when they have the confidence to share and debate ideas. But when they compete for incentives and the explicit recognition of their superiors, when their individual achievement is at stake, they stop sharing information.

Again, we must not confuse activation with the quality of innovation. Competition is a stimulus, that's true. And it serves to make people aware that we need to start innovating. But once we have awakened that need and awareness, too much internal competition will destroy the cooperation that is essential to building a culture of innovation.

Downsizing and crisis

Since 2007, the world has been immersed in a severe economic crisis. This has translated into layoffs and staffing cuts in many companies. As the economy contracts, companies are forced to downsize. Downsizing creates enormous fear and anxiety among workers, which also has an across-the-board impact on creative culture, as Teresa Amabile's study shows:

> Creativity suffers greatly during a downsizing. But it's even worse than many of us realized. We studied a 6,000-person division in a global electronics company during the entire course of a 25% downsizing, which took an incredibly agonizing 18 months. Every single one of the stimulants to creativity in the work environment went down significantly.[16]

The threat of downsizing undermines open communication, willingness to cooperate and the sense of freedom and independence, just as it sends people looking for shelter and ways to avoid risks. The impact of downsizing starts before it happens and lingers on well after: as plans to cut jobs trickle down through the organization, people worry and gossip about who is going to get the axe. Until the plans are made official, their will to innovate will be seriously damaged. And once the downsizing has been taken place, people's morale takes time to recover. That is why, at least with regard to preserving our capacity to innovate and our creative culture, it is better, where possible, to have a single round of staff cuts than to trim personnel several times over the course of a crisis.

Lack of methods and processes

Another inhibitor is the lack of methods to generate ideas. Not only is creativity rarely taught in schools, it has been almost eradicated from the Western education system, which puts much greater emphasis on the teaching of methods, logic and analytical thinking. There is a widespread misconception that you can't teach or train people to be creative. Yet if you don't show people how to generate ideas they probably won't know what to do when you ask them to be creative.

The way to eliminate this inhibitor is very simple: through training in creative techniques and systems for generating ideas – services that are available from specialized firms. In Chapter 5 of this book we discussed a number of techniques for developing the ability to come up with ideas. And there are many more.[17] For example, P&G created the Clay Street Project, an experiment in which groups of employees spent several weeks learning how to unleash their creative talents.

A lot of people who don't think of themselves as being very creative are pleasantly surprised when they try idea production techniques. Most people know about brainstorming, but that's about as far as they go. Creative games can bring creativity out of people who thought they had none. We mustn't underestimate this inhibitor. On its own it won't be sufficient (it's still a long road from creativity to innovation), but without personnel trained in creative techniques, all other efforts (planning, processes, rewards) will be in vain.

Organizational motivators of ideas, creativity and innovation

We have seen the inhibitors. Their removal is a necessary condition for a creative culture. But in addition to eliminating these barriers, we can actively promote the latent creativity among the people in our organization. Let's say that without inhibitors the ideas will start to flow, but with motivators the flow will be deeper and wider. Teresa Amabile, who heads the Entrepreneurial Management Unit at Harvard Business School, distinguishes between two kinds of motivation: intrinsic and extrinsic.

Intrinsic motivation is defined as what drives us to do something because we like doing it, because we find it interesting, enjoyable or satisfying. Intrinsic motivation is something we cannot demand of people. It comes from within them, from their own inclinations, their affinities, their likes. We cannot control a person's likes, but we can make sure our people fit their posts, tasks, responsibilities and business sector. And that's something that can be controlled, by the human resources department, both in hiring and in job mobility within the company. Obviously, in any job there are aggravations that we'd prefer not to have to deal with. But if we want our people to come up with ideas, we should ensure that they are where they want to be. In some cases, this may even include not only the job or department but the sector. Put someone who doesn't like books in a top management position at a publishing house, for example, and he or she will hardly be a wellspring of innovation. People are creative when they have reasons for enjoying and taking an interest in their jobs.

As for extrinsic motivation, which we cover thoroughly in the following chapter on rewards, here we make just one note: it's not only economic reward that's important, but recognition as well.

The misunderstood popularization of creativity

From what we have said so far in this chapter, the reader might gather that creative culture should translate into everyone in an organization being innovative. This is true, but only to a certain extent.

We must distinguish between mechanisms for everyone to contribute ideas and innovation project leadership. People come up with ideas, those ideas are screened and only a few will be developed into projects. We need to be careful about who we choose to lead our innovation projects and processes. It's not a job everyone is prepared or has the time for. It's one thing to have companies like 3M, Google or Kraft give their staff time to think about ideas and quite another to have everyone leading an innovation process.

That said, we do need all members of the organization to contribute as many proposals and ideas as possible. This can be done with an actual suggestion box, space on the company intranet for people to post their ideas or with idea management software. It is essential that such systems are simple, easy to use and not too time-consuming. The more complicated they are, the less people will use them. These sorts of systems also have the advantage that people can contribute their ideas anonymously, thereby eliminating several of the above-mentioned inhibitors, such as the fear of ridicule or blame (albeit partial) for possible mistakes in the future. Anonymity tends to favor bolder ideas, riskier and more original.

The three main potential problems with suggestion boxes and computer-based idea collection systems are overload, dispersion and repetition.

Overload occurs when there are so many ideas that the organization can't process or examine them closely enough. One way to resolve this problem is to have the workforce itself do early assessment and screening of ideas. This would be based on the same principles as participatory webs such as Wikipedia or YouTube, where the users themselves rank, assess, review and discard the contributions of their peers.

We will deal with how to avoid repetition and dispersion (where ideas are scattered rather than centered on company objectives) in the next section, but basically it entails internal communication of the company's strategic priorities in innovation. In Chapter 3, devoted to the activators, we explained how creative thinking requires a focus and how a focus does not limit creativity. One way to avoid dispersion of ideas is to provide a framework. Instead of soliciting ideas about anything and everything, the company can launch periodic campaigns asking all members of the organization for proposals on how to approach particular opportunities or solve certain problems. For example, a company in the insurance sector might make the following announcement to its workforce: "We believe there is an opportunity to exploit gas stations as outlets for car insurance. Any ideas you might have on this are welcome."

Not only do you avoid dispersion, but the ideas are also organized according to the objective, and any repeat ideas are more easily identified than if you have one platform for receiving all proposals stuffed with thousands of suggestions on a broad range of subjects.

The role of communication

Internal communication is a key instrument for changing corporate culture. The company should inform its people about: strategies, projects, heroes, innovation performance and rejected ideas. Let's take these one by one.

Communication of strategy and innovation projects

Staff should be aware of the company's overall innovation strategy, in order to center their efforts and ideas appropriately and avoid lack of focus.

Accordingly, each time we launch an innovation process for a particular project, we should explain what we are doing to the organization, answering the following questions: Why are we embarking on this project? What do we want to gain from it? What are the expected results? How can other departments assist in the process? What other departments will be involved in implementing or developing the project? How will they benefit from it? How long do we expect it will take to approve and implement?

For example, Starbucks holds what they call Open Forums, quarterly meetings by region where executives report on how their respective innovation projects are evolving. For each project, employees receive a card where they can note down their views or proposals.

Informing staff about innovation heroes

As we have said in talking about rewards, we must also let our people know about our "heroes of innovation", that is, the people who have played a key role in a successful innovation, and thus deserve public recognition. The list of heroes should include the person or people who had the original idea as well as those who developed it and those who executed it. Companies often acknowledge only the people that came up with the idea, ignoring the developers and executors. Their roles maybe lower profile, but they are just as necessary.

Communication of the results gained by innovating

And finally, communication of results. This point is crucial, especially in conservative, rigid and static companies considering a complete overhaul of their innovative culture. When management announces its intention to innovate, the workforce won't take it seriously. It's been too long since they've seen any innovation in the company and, although everyone agrees on the need, the announcement sounds more like wishful thinking than something that is actually going to happen. Converting from a conservative to an innovative culture means things must happen, changes must be made, preferably small and easy changes to start with, and they must be communicated quickly. By letting everyone in the organization know that something has changed and by communicating results, no matter how seemingly insignificant, the changes start to gain credibility: real evidence that intentions are being put into practice. That is why, in creating an innovative culture from scratch, it is best to start with small changes and to communicate achievements as they happen. We all know that credibility comes from success stories and that it takes time to build.

For example, IBM, which used to attach great importance to developing its "cash cow" businesses, has changed its culture through the internal recognition of new business divisions, however small they might be. The creation of new divisions is now a high-profile mission in the company. Today, IBM has much more will to experiment, to accept mistakes, learn from them and evolve.[18]

Communication of rejected ideas

The company should also inform its people about what ideas have been rejected. Contrary to popular belief, this does not discourage people. Rather, what discourages people from putting forward ideas is being left in the dark about what happens with their proposals. People get tired of not getting any sort of feedback and give up. However, if people who propose an idea are told that it has been turned down and why, they will be even more motivated to try to overcome the obstacles or reasons justifying the rejection. Where there are too many ideas to explain the reasons for rejecting each one, we can apply the sort of popular assessment method we've seen here, so that the person who makes a suggestion at least knows that many of his or her peers do not believe it has enough potential.

Multiculturalism and cross-functions

Creativity is based on combining existing ideas in a different way. When we travel to a different country we receive new stimuli, which, combined with our usual environment, produce new combinations and thus a tendency for a lot of new ideas to pop up in our heads. In his book *The Medici Effect:*

Breakthrough Insights at the Intersection of Ideas, Concepts, and Cultures, Frans Johansson tells of how the Medici in Renaissance Florence, through their patronage, brought together statesmen, astronomers, painters, architects, sculptors and musicians in the same environment. The intersection of methodologies and ideas favored one of the most fertile periods in Western history as far as creativity is concerned.

Based on this fact, many creativity experts advise companies seeking to boost their creative culture to promote cultural diversity, to bring in people from different backgrounds, experiences, cultures and traditions to work together. The idea is that the diversity of backgrounds will lead to a greater diversity of ideas.

This same is true of the skills or expertise of team members, where creativity can be bolstered with cross-functionality. In this book, our model of A-to-F roles promotes cross-functionality among the leaders of an innovation process. Having manifold points of view on a single project increases the probabilities of success and reduces the likelihood of errors of omission. Cross-functional teams are a common feature in innovative companies. For example, when GE embarks on an innovation project, it mobilizes experts from a range of fields, encouraging mobility among departments to foster internal relationships and link up projects. Another example: at P&G such mixed teams are vital to new product development. P&G has developed a model for structuring teams that stresses cross-functionality among its innovation process leaders from all areas of the company (marketing, engineering, R&D, and so on).[19]

The research by Robert Cooper, mentioned above, demonstrates empirically that cross-functionality is correlated with performance in new product development (NPD).[20]

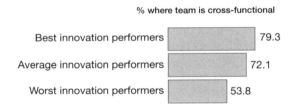

% where team is cross-functional

Best innovation performers — 79.3

Average innovation performers — 72.1

Worst innovation performers — 53.8

Figure 12.2 **Correlation between new product performance and cross-functionality**
Source: Robert G. Cooper, *Winning at New Products: Creating Value Through Innovation*, www.stage-gate.com

Customer proximity

As we explained in the first part of this book, proximity to the customer should be part of the innovation process, but a culture of innovation necessarily entails a shift in perspective: from looking only inward to looking outward too.

When he committed to creative culture, P&G president A.G. Lafley found that the company was focused on product performance to the detriment of customer sentiment. P&G had the best technical people in the business, but suffered from a lack of concern for users' experiences with the company's products. In order to correct this, Lafley radically changed the approach to the customer. This shift (from the product to the customer, from inside out) was instrumental in forging the company's creative culture.

Other no less important considerations

The newspapers and other mainstream media have given plenty of attention to creative companies like Google that offer their employees recreational spaces with pool tables, ping-pong and so on; spaces that look more like a playground than an NPD center. This has promoted a widespread belief that creative culture needs a "fun" place in which employees can let their imaginations run wild. We have left this matter until last because at this stage of the chapter it should be fairly obvious to the reader that the space for creativity is of only relative importance.

It is true that some environments encourage more creativity than others, and that a company with no spaces for creativity will find it more difficult to implement a creative culture. But we must give this issue the importance it merits. It is an important factor. But it is not decisive.

Among the features of an environment where ideas flow more freely are common spaces, atmosphere and time.

Common spaces

Lack of collaboration among departments is considered the second biggest barrier to innovation.[21] Collaboration, however, requires more than processes. The most innovative companies create physical spaces to promote collaboration and teamwork.

For example, P&G has its "Innovation Gym," a place to train department managers in the new company culture and to think about design. Other examples we have seen over the course of this book are 3M's Innovation Centers and Royal Dutch Shell's Innovation Lab.

Moreover, dedicated spaces for creativity avoid distractions, which creativity specialists, including Teresa Amabile, consider one of the main contributing factors in poor creative performance.

Atmosphere

Google is known for going to great lengths in designing an atmosphere conducive to creativity at its facilities. This includes places for employees to escape their desks and sit back and relax, free coffee, a laundry room on the premises, and so on.[22]

Another thing that affects creativity in the workplace is lighting. Natural light is more pleasant and more conducive to creativity than artificial lighting.

Time

Creativity requires a certain amount of "release time" from day-to-day business. The policies we described in Chapter 3, such as Google's "free day thinking", encourage creative culture. People can't think about new ways to do things while trying to do them well:

> Senior Managers foster creativity and innovation by allowing time off for scouting or "Friday projects" as in Kraft Foods and W.L. Gore & Associates; they are not overly risk averse and invest in the occasional high risk project; and they encourage skunk works–projects and teams working outside the official bureaucracy of the business.[23]

Steps to creating an innovative culture

We have seen all the essentials for developing a creative culture – although that is not say an *innovative* one. It must be stressed, even at the risk of repeating ourselves, that the implementation of a creative culture does not guarantee innovation. In order to complete the equation and achieve an innovative company, it is a sine qua non that a creative culture must co-exist with innovation planning, innovation processes and a reward system.

Still, there are so many factors that go into a creative culture that the executive who has read thus far in this chapter may wonder: Where do I start? What steps should I follow?

This would be the most effective way to proceed:

1   CEO informs the board and senior offices of the wish to transform the organization's culture, building a coalition backing the idea.
2   CEO signs on and commits; the rest of the organization is informed of the change in culture.
3   Eliminate inhibitors.
4   Implement motivators.
5   Draw up and implement an in-house innovation communications plan.
6   Set up a system to manage ideas.
7   Adopt an innovation process (that is, the A-to-F model or Stage-Gate).
8   Feed back stories of innovation success, and learn the causes of failure.

TOTAL INNOVATION SYSTEM – Summary Chapter 12

Main person/s in charge of each role

A Activators	B Browsers	C Creators	D Developers	E Executors	F Facilitators
Top management (GM or Chief innovation officer)	Market research department	Advertising agency	R&D	Current marketing department (shared team)	Top management (GM or Chief innovation officer)
Employees	Market research suppliers	Creativity agency	New products department	Current sales department (shared team)	Financial director
Suppliers	Sociologists	Marketing	Operations	Dedicated marketing team	New projects committee
Distributors	Marketing	Creative types	Manufacturing	New division	Chief innovation officer
Clients	Sales	R&D	External suppliers	New company	Board
Investors	Opinion leaders	Clients	Marketing	Third party alliances	Shareholders
Universities	Watchers' panel	Suppliers	Sales		Employees
Scientific community	R&D	Employees with creative profile	Dedicated engineers		Innovation team
Inventors	Other internal departments	Other suppliers or third parties			Middle management
Engineering companies	Other suppliers or third parties				External: experts, stakeholders or investors

Up-bottom activation
In-out activation
Bottom-up activation
Out-in activation

Techniques employed by each role

A Activators	B Browsers	C Creators	D Developers	E Executors	F Facilitators
Scope of innovation	Innovation review	Synectics	Helping in concept definition	Marketing plan and launch plan	Subjective assessment
Innovation levels	Analysis of adjacent categories	Blue Ocean strategy	Concept test for improving design	Morphing	Purchase intention according to test levels
Focus of innovation	Internal consulting	Morphological analysis	Pictures	KPIs evolution	Delphi method
Innovation guidelines	Social trend/ social classes	Lateral marketing	Conjoint analysis for features definition	Next marginal evolution	Nominal group techniques
Innovation checklist	Market trends	Attributes listing	Drawings	Area testing	Company-wide rating
	Buying process	Scenarios analysis	Mock-up	Market testing	Phillips 66
	Innovation routes	Visits	Prototype	Product testing	Six Sigma
	Technological solutions	Co-creation	Product test	Intensity on ATRs	Cost-benefit analysis
	Design referents	Redefining customer value	Usage/home test	Experimentation	Demand estimation
	Successful strategies and tactics/learning from errors	Brainstorming	Patents		Profit and loss
	Network monitoring	Concept definition			ROI analysis
	Ethnographic				Scenario analysis
	Geolocation				Market test

Innovation goals
Innovation strategy
Quantity and type
Entry strategy
Innovation levels
Resources definition
Strategy implementation
Projects list
Projects portfolio
Roadmap
Resources allocation

Innovation framework
Innovation guidelines
Innovation checklist

STRATEGIC PLANNING FOR INNOVATION

Project proposals
Process approval

Activators↔Facilitators↔Developers
Browsers ↔ Creators
Executors

CREATIVE CULTURE

INNOVATION PROCESS

INNOVATION REWARDS

INNOVATION METRICS

RESULTS

Culture-responsibility selection
Reduction of inhibitors
Fear in general
Fear of error
Fear of retaliation
Too strong deadlines and pressure
Excessive internal competition
Downsizing effects
Lack of methods
Motivators
Intrinsic
Extrinsic

Communication ...
... of the strategy
... of projects
... of heroes
... of results
... of rejected ideas
Multiculturalism and cross-functions
Environment
Creative spaces
Creative atmosphere
Enough time

Types
Economic metrics
To measure intensity
To measure effectiveness
To measure culture
Combining metrics
From inputs
From processes
From outputs

13 Incentive and Rewards

What are innovation incentives?

By innovation incentives we mean a set of policies intended to motivate employees to innovate (and that enable them to share the value derived from innovation).

Should we incentivize innovation?

This issue is the focus of intense debate. On one side, the proponents of incentives have no doubts:

> Several companies on the list of most innovative companies in the world have formal rewards for top innovators.[1]

> Rewarding innovative thinking is an important part of an idea management based innovation strategy. Rewards increase motivation to continue developing and sharing ideas.[2]

On the other side, critics are not dead set against incentives; they are just against rewarding innovation with money; that is, monetary rewards:

> I am always amused when people argue for or against "incentives and rewards." Incentives, by definition, must work, monetary rewards may not. [...] Effectiveness of money as a motivator depends on the relative worth of the award and how it correlates with achievements.[3]

> The experimental research that has been done on creativity suggests that money isn't everything. Quite often people say that they don't think about pay on a day-to-day basis. And the handful of people who were spending a lot of time wondering about their bonuses were doing very little creative thinking. Bonuses and pay-for-performance plans can even be problematic when people believe that every move they make is going to affect their compensation. In those situations, people tend to get risk averse.[4]

> One of the biggest mistakes companies make is tying managers' incentives too directly to specific innovation metrics. Linking pay too closely to hard innovation measures may tempt managers to game the system.[5]

A recent study by McKinsey & Company[6] indicates that three types of non-financial incentives were appreciated above all others: recognition from senior management, the sense of leadership produced by the formal recognition of being innovative, and the opportunity to lead new projects and teams as a reward for innovating.

Or, as Sheldon Laube, from the PricewaterhouseCoopers' Innovation Office, writes:

> It is popular to believe that employees are primarily motivated by money. However, in employee study after study, money is rarely the most important motivator. Recently here at my own firm, we asked the leading participants in our idea management system what type of reward or recognition they would value most. Number 1 was development opportunities with 55% of the votes, with monetary compensation as Number 3 with only 11% of the votes.[7]

Should innovation, one of the most important areas of business management, really not be encouraged with money?

To answer, we must consider the different factors that play for or against money as a motivator for innovation.

The first is the profile of the person who receives the financial incentive. A researcher isn't the same as an assembly line worker in an industrial firm. Even for a marketing professional and an engineer from R&D, the role of money as a reward for innovating is different.

As explained in Chapter 12, people who work exclusively in the field of innovation tend to like their jobs. Researchers may find it insulting to be offered extra money to innovate, because that's their job, it's what they're expected of do. They may even see "prize money" as a way to pay them less for their work, or as a sign that management doesn't trust their abilities and thus is willing to shell out only when they actually discover, patent or develop something. Technical profiles, as has been shown, appreciate other incentives, ones less directly related to money, such as professional recognition.

Marketing professionals, on the other hand, are generally paid according to a scheme of fixed and variable pay, the latter dependent on meeting objectives. Since marketing is partially responsible for innovation (the marketing part of it, at least), it makes sense to have one part of their variable compensation come from ongoing business and another from the results of new business. We can see that the incentive for innovation is not as direct as it might seem. We aren't saying "I pay you to innovate," but rather "innovation is one of the factors we calculate into your annual bonus." Some authors argue that financial incentives for innovation in marketing work best when the amount of money involved is not too large and when it is for marginal innovations; that is, line extensions and portfolio developments.

With respect to salespeople, a similar type of scheme makes sense. If you have fixed and variable portions of pay, it is logical to link the variable element to sales of new products. New product teams or divisions should even be rewarded with a percentage of sales from new products launched, since that ensures a strong post-launch.

Other evidence suggests that economic incentives work best when we're dealing with relatively unsophisticated projects. Here is where small incentives for people in lower ranks of the organization (basic administrative staff, workers, and so on) can be productive.

And, what about using incentives as a way to encourage people to come up with ideas?

> Management should not offer substantial cash rewards for ideas. This inevitably leads to greed and perceived unfairness.[8]

> Combined research from the Employee Involvement Association and Japan Human Relations Association reveals that the average number of ideas submitted per employee annually is 100 times greater in Japanese companies than in U.S. companies. Why? For one thing, we reward the wrong thing in the wrong way. The average reward in Japanese companies is 100 times less than the average U.S. reward of nearly $500. We have it backwards! In a nutshell: payment for ideas can defeat the purpose.[9]

Still, companies, as we have said, need lots of – tons of – ideas. Why shouldn't they be rewarded then? Perhaps the problem lies in rewarding only "valid" ideas, which can be seen as unfair. By doing so, the usual outcome is a low rate of participation in idea campaigns.

Monetary reward for innovation poses another issue: Who gets the money? Any innovation involves a lot of people, so it may be unfair to reward the person who had the idea and not the one who developed it or implemented it. So how about rewarding all of them? Well, it seems that this doesn't work either. Blanket incentives for groups have the disadvantage that the people who are least involved or make the smallest contributions get the same rewards as the people who really put their shoulder to the wheel to make the project a success. The best intermediate solution is to have a bonus for the team (based on an assessment, as objective as possible, of results) with each person receiving his or her share in accordance with his or her individual contribution (in this case, based on the subjective assessments of superiors or peers).

Another problem with handing out money for innovation is this: What happens if there comes a time when we have to eliminate the incentives? Will our people stop innovating?

The controversy over the desirability of monetary incentives for innovation, and the nature of creativity itself, which finds encouragement in both public and financial recognition, has spurred the development of other types of reward, of intangibles such as recognition or trophies. We examine this issue in the next point.

In any case, what we do know is that incentives encourage creativity and innovation. In our chapter on creative culture we explained how intrinsic motivation is sufficient to bring out the creativity in people. Extrinsic motivation (for example incentives) acts like a power booster for intrinsic motivation. So, there is no denying its value. The reality is that a lot of highly innovative companies use economic incentives.

In our view, to incentivize or not to incentivize, to reward or not to reward, is not the issue, but rather to ensure that the value created by innovation is shared equitably. That is why at the beginning of this chapter, we defined "incentive" as: a set of policies intended to motivate employees to innovate and that enable them to share the value derived from innovation.

If we explain the purpose of incentives in terms of the first part of our definition (as a mechanism to motivate our employees to innovate), we're likely to be met with a fair number of smirks and frowns. But if we approach incentives as a mechanism to share the value created (second part of our definition), a large majority will nod in agreement. Thus, the problem may lie less in the design of incentive than in the purpose we give it and the use we make of it.

Having addressed these issues, we go on examine the most common types of incentives.

Types of incentives

Financial incentives

Money

The main incentive is financial: money. It is usually paid in the form of:

▷ Monthly pay
▷ A raise in salary
▷ Special monthly bonuses: for example, 20 percent of monthly bonuses at General Electric in 2005 were to encourage meeting objectives measured in terms of the improvements implemented in customer relationships
▷ Success bonuses: for example, Corning offers cash rewards for innovation efforts

Cash incentives for innovation are often tied to patents: Texas Instruments pays $175,000 for a single patent; Motorola offers a bonus of $10,000 to $40,000 per patent. Adobe India goes a step further and pays $5,000 for ideas that get as far as the patent application stage.

Company shares

Here, instead of money, reward comes in the form of company stock. A study by McKinsey & Company[10] ranked the primary economic incentives thus: cash bonuses, base salary increase and stocks or stock options.

For example, Google has its annual "Founder's Awards," which reward with company stock options the most outstanding projects of the year. Starbucks also uses stock options as an incentive for its employees.

Shares are probably the most valuable incentive and the one that best reflects, in our view, the rationale behind incentives: to share value created. Shares are the embodiment of a company's value.

A portion of sales

A different and original way to reward innovation is giving employees a portion of sales, both for certain products and developments and for savings derived from implementing improvements, and so on. In the retail sector, this is sometimes applied to a given timeframe. For example, in 1999 when IKEA crossed the 53,000-employee threshold, it instituted "Employee Appreciation Day." On that day total world sales are divided equally among all employees. For some this can mean as much as their monthly salary![11]

We find yet another variation on this system at Baxter, where employees get a bonus equal to 0.33 percent of gross sales from new products, up to a maximum of $50,000.[12]

Payment in kind

In order to avoid linking incentives directly to certain sum of money, some companies prefer to reward in kind, the most common systems being seniority increases, healthcare payments, life insurance underwritten by the company, and so on. However, such incentives are rarely used to reward innovation and are most often tied to achievements in other areas.

Intangibles

Public recognition

You may think of public recognition as just an easy way out, but you would be wrong. On the contrary, public recognition is considered one of the most effective and motivating stimuli for creativity and innovation. In simple terms, recognition consists of letting people know who was behind what, making it public knowledge that certain individuals were the ones who made an innovation happen. It is interesting to see how communication, an essential element of creative culture, as was discussed in Chapter 12, becomes in itself an incentive.

Sometimes such recognition is complemented with prizes or awards:

> When I walk around our offices, I am always amazed at how people choose to decorate their offices with artifacts of their achievements. Symbols of recognition like certificates, tombstones, medals etc. are proudly displayed. This is a

picture of the office of one my firm's senior executives. Regardless of level, people want to display their accomplishments. Recognition is not a zero sum game, and it is possible to award an unlimited number of certificates, plaques etc. to as many people as needed. Additionally, the more people who are recognized the greater the marketing effect.[13]

The Spanish firm Metalquimia is a world leader in innovation in meat processing machinery. As you enter the company's head offices, one of the first things you see is a giant sword engraved with the name of the most innovative employee of the year. In a community of innovative professionals, this sort of acknowledgment is a source of pride and as powerful a motivator as money.

Recognition of the individual, team or department that has successfully innovated and thus created value for the company usually comes in one of three forms:

▷ Paper: via newsletters
▷ Digital: via intranet. For example, 3M's corporate website posts the names of technical personnel who develop groundbreaking products along with the story about how they did it
▷ In person: at meetings or special events

Access to restricted circles

Another sort of incentive is the recognition that comes with the invitation to exclusive groups, events or spaces. For example, for engineers who reach the mark of 10 patents, Nokia has its "Club 10," giving them public recognition at an annual formal ceremony attended by the CEO.

Procter & Gamble motivates its top scientists with the chance of being nominated to the Victor Mills Society, an elite group of just a dozen outstanding scientists and researchers. Being chosen as a member is considered the most prestigious award in the company.

Another option is to offer special training sessions, courses or plans inside or outside the company.

Access to key meetings is also used as an incentive. Infosys Technologies Ltd selects nine young executives (they must be under 30 years of age) who are top performers in innovation and invites them to participate in annual board meetings, as well as to present and discuss their ideas with senior management.

Some companies use access to restricted circles very intelligently to promote idea generation: they invite people whose ideas have been picked for further development, regardless of their experience in innovation processes and their place in the hierarchy of the organization, to participate actively in the process that originated with their ideas. They get to take part in the whole innovation process, from browsing information to technical development to implementation.

Time

Some companies reward people who give innovative ideas with more time to think. People who don't work directly in innovation are given time off from their regular duties to produce ideas for the company.

Research resources

Instead of giving employees time, some companies offer economic incentives to innovate in the form of resources for research. A researcher will likely be happier to get more work resources than a cash bonus. 3M has for years given its scientists an award it calls the "Genesis Grant." Each year, the company awards between 12 and 20 such grants, ranging from $50,000 to $100,000 each. Researchers can use the money to hire more researchers or to purchase new equipment.

Criteria for rewards

While all metrics should be managed, not all necessarily merit reward. There are two principal reasons for caution. First, because rewards can be counter-productive, as we explained in Chapter 11. You should be very cautious about linking incentives to a particular metric as the results can be disastrous. During the dotcom bubble many bonuses were linked to the sales of new companies to venture capital funds or large corporations, which paid out huge sums without really knowing what they were buying. The main metric was the financial valuation of the company, without taking into account any metric related to sales, profit or customer retention. This sort of incentive steered the work of executives in a direction that led to the demise of a good many companies.

A second reason for caution is that some innovation metrics can yield poor results due not only to those responsible for innovation, but also to other departments. Additionally, there are metrics that are intended simply to monitor processes, such as the number of innovation projects in the pipeline. Such metrics are used to ensure that the innovation pipeline doesn't dry up, but they aren't usually tied to incentives.

In addition to quantitative and objective criteria like metrics, we should also introduce subjective criteria evaluations (peers and/or managers evaluate innovators) to reward innovation. Subjective criteria for granting rewards work when we use a sufficiently broad base of reviewers.

Another criterion is that, generally speaking, incentives linked to processes or projects must be defined before the fact, while the rewards must be handed out later, when the process has finished and the results are known.

Subjective assessments and rewards work best for radical or disruptive innovations, where it is more difficult to define the objective. It has been found that linking bonuses to the sales generated by an innovation leads to defensive behavior, and so they are less suitable for radical innovations. In these types of innovations, the objectives tied to the bonuses need to be much more flexible and open.

And the winner is ...

Who should hand out the rewards and accolades? This is normally the job of the CEO, as a means of stressing the strategic importance of innovation. If the CEO presides over the incentive events, that means innovation is important, right?

This isn't as clear as it may seem. One of the great paradoxes in large companies is that the higher up a person is in the hierarchy the less influence they have on the lower ranks. People pay less attention to an email from the CEO than one from their immediate superior. The same goes for express recognition.

The conclusion is that public recognition should come from the highest level in the organization and economic incentives from line managers.

In sum, to conclude ...

Rewards, prizes and incentives can increase employees' commitment to the organization, boost their morale and motivate them to strive to sustain an attitude of openness and attentiveness to opportunities that a company can capture.[14] Incentives reinforce the link between strategy and results, as our Total Innovation System shows.

That's why the secret is to choose the right combination of incentives that work best for your company: the most suitable for your industry, those that best reflect the objectives you are pursuing, those that best reinforce your creative culture and those that best complement each other.

TOTAL INNOVATION SYSTEM – Summary Chapter 13

Main person/s in charge of each role

	A Activators	B Browsers	C Creators	D Developers	E Executors	F Facilitators
	Top management (GM or Chief innovation officer)	Market research department	Advertising agency	R&D	Current marketing department (shared team)	Top management (GM or Chief innovation officer)
	Employees	Market research suppliers	Creativity agency	New products department	Current sales department (shared team)	Financial director
	Suppliers	Sociologists	Marketing	Operations	Dedicated marketing team	New projects committee
	Distributors	Marketing	Creative types	Manufacturing	New division	Chief innovation officer
	Clients	Sales	R&D	External suppliers	New company	Board
	Investors	Opinion leaders	Clients	Marketing	Third party alliances	Shareholders
	Universities	Watchers' panel	Suppliers	Sales		Employees
	Scientific community	R&D	Employees with creative profile	Dedicated engineers		Innovation team
	Inventors	Other internal departments	Other suppliers or third parties			Middle management
	Engineering companies	Other suppliers or third parties				External: experts, stakeholders or investors

Up-bottom activation
In-out activation
Bottom-up activation
Out-in activation

Techniques employed by each role

A Activators	B Browsers	C Creators	D Developers	E Executors	F Facilitators
Scope of innovation	Innovation review	Synectics	Helping in concept definition	Marketing plan and launch plan	Subjective assessment
Innovation levels	Analysis of adjacent categories	Blue Ocean strategy	Concept test for improving design	Morphing	Purchase intention according to test levels
Focus of innovation	Internal consulting	Morphological analysis	Pictures	KPI's evolution	Delphi method
Innovation guidelines	Social trend/ social classes	Lateral marketing	Conjoint analysis for features definition	Next marginal evolution	Nominal group techniques
Innovation checklist	Market trends	Attributes listing	Drawings	Area testing	Company-wide rating
	Buying process	Scenarios analysis	Mock-up	Market testing	Phillips 66
	Innovation routes	Visits	Prototype	Product testing	Six Sigma
	Technological solutions	Co-creation	Product test	Intensity on ATRs	Cost-benefit analysis
	Design referents	Redefining customer value	Usage/home test	Experimentation	Demand estimation
	Successful strategies and tactics/learning from errors	Brainstorming	Patents		Profit and loss
	Network monitoring	Concept definition			ROI analysis
	Ethnographic				Scenario analysis
	Geolocation				Market test

Innovation framework
Innovation guidelines
Innovation checklist

STRATEGIC PLANNING FOR INNOVATION

Innovation goals
Innovation strategy
Quantity and type
Entry strategy
Innovation levels
Resources definition
Strategy implementation
Projects list
Projects portfolio
Roadmap
Resources allocation

INNOVATION PROCESS

Browsers → Creators → Developers
Activators ↔ Facilitators ↔ Developers
Executors

Project proposals / Process approval

CREATIVE CULTURE

INNOVATION REWARDS

INNOVATION METRICS

RESULTS

Financial
Monetary rewards
Stock options
Percentage of sales
Payment in kind
Intangibles
Public recognition
Access to restricted circles
Free or extra time
Research resources

Culture-responsibility selection
Reduction of inhibitors
Fear in general
Fear of error
Fear of retaliation
Too strong deadlines and pressure
Excessive internal competition
Downsizing effects
Lack of methods
Motivators
Intrinsic
Extrinsic

Communication ...
... of the strategy
... of projects
... of heroes
... of results
... of rejected ideas
Multiculturalism and cross-functions
Environment
Creative spaces
Creative atmosphere
Enough time

Types
Economic metrics
To measure intensity
To measure effectiveness
To measure culture
Combining metrics
From inputs
From processes
From outputs

Notes

Introduction

1   T. Davila, M.J. Epstein and R. Shelton, *Making Innovation Work: How to manage it, measure it, and profit from it.* Wharton School Publishing (2006).

Chapter 1

1   Ruth Mortimer, "Turn Creativity into Strategy for Success." *Marketing Week*, 16 July 2009.
2   Darrell K. Rigby, Kara Gruver, and James Allen, "Innovation in Turbulent Times." *Harvard Business Review*, June 2009.
3   *McKinsey Quarterly*, the online business journal of McKinsey & Company. October, 2007.
4   *The Economist*, 13–19 October 2007.
5   Infonomia, Analysis on 3M innovation policy.
6   *BusinessWeek*, 9 April 2009.
7   Philip Kotler, Robert C. Wolcott and Suj Chandrasekhar, "Masters of Value and Possibility: Optimizing the Marketing and Research & Development Relationship." *Business Insight*, http://sloanreview.mit.edu/business-insight/articles/2009/2/
8   T. Davila, M.J. Epstein and R. Shelton, *Making Innovation Work: How to Manage It, Measure It, and Profit from It.* Wharton School Publishing (2006).
9   Philip Kotler, Robert C. Wolcott and Suj Chandrasekhar (op. cit.).
10   *McKinsey Quarterly*, op. cit.
11   Philip Kotler, Dipak C. Jain and Suvit Maesincee, *Marketing Moves: A New Approach to Profits, Growth, and Renewal.* Harvard Business Press (2001).
12   McKinsey Global Survey. *McKinsey Quarterly*, October 2007.
13   Alfons Cornella, *Visionomics* (Published by Infonomia, 2010) p. 95.
14   Theodore Levitt, "Creativity is not enough." *Harvard Business Review.* Harvard Business School Publishing, 2002.
15   *Marketing Week*, 16 July 2009.
16   McKinsey Global Survey. *McKinsey Quarterly*, October 2007.
17   "Making P&G New and Improved." *Time Magazine*, 17 April 2008.
18   *BusinessWeek*, "The World's Most Innovative Companies. Special Report – Innovation." 24 April 2006.
19   Dr Robert Shaw, Honorary Professor of Marketing Metrics at Cass Business School, *Return on Ideas* (Chartered Institute of Management Accounts, the Chartered Institute of Marketing and the Direct Marketing Association). http://www.cim.co.uk/filestore/resources/agendapapers/returnonideas.pdf
20   *BusinessWeek*, "The World's Most Innovative Companies. Special Report – Innovation." 24 April 2006.

Chapter 2

1 www.fastcompany.com Aug 9, 2005.

Chapter 3

1 Philip Kotler and Fernando Trías de Bes, *Lateral Marketing. New Techniques for Finding Breakthrough Ideas.* John Wiley (2003).
2 Example extracted from www.brighthub.com/office/project-management/articles/34656.aspx
3 Infonomia.com
4 Harvard Business School, *Working Knowledge for Business Leaders.* "P&G's innovation model." 20 June 2006.

Chapter 4

1 Philip Kotler and Fernando Trías de Bes. *Lateral Marketing. New Techniques for Finding Breakthrough Ideas.* John Wiley (2003).
2 Mónica Casabayó and Borja Martín. *Fuzzy Marketing.* Deusto (2010).
3 Doug Gross, "The 10 biggest tech 'fails' of 2010." CNN, 29 December 2010.
4 Matthew E. May (*In Pursuit of Elegance*). "Customer centric design." www.openforum.com, 10 August 2009.
5 www.openforum.com (*ibid.*).

Chapter 5

1 http://www.businessweek.com/magazine/content/06_17/b3981401.htm
2 Waisburd, G. *Creatividad y transformaciones.* Mexico: Trillas (1996).
3 November 2010, *Business Life*, p. 32.
4 Alex Osborn. *Applied Imagination*, 3rd edn. New York: Scribner's (1963).
5 We include expansion and reduction in a single operation – exaggeration – since the exaggeration of a quality or attribute can be either upwards or downwards.
6 We don't include brainstorming as a technique because it is already so well known.
7 W. Chan Kim and Renée Mauborgne. *Blue Ocean Strategy: How to Create Uncontested Market Space and Make Competition Irrelevant.* Harvard Business Press (2005).
8 Example extracted from *Blue Ocean Strategy*. Kim and Renée Mauborgne (op. cit.).
9 www.innovaforum.com
10 Tony Proctor. *Creative Problem Solving for Managers: Developing skills for decision making and innovation.* Routledge, 3rd edn (2010).
11 Further information about applying this techinique can be found at www.innovateam.com
12 *BusinessWeek*, "The World's Most Innovative Companies. Special Report – Innovation." 24 April 2006.
13 Stephan Thomke and Eric von Hippel, "Customers As Innovators: A New Way to Create Value," *Harvard Business Review* (April 2002): 74–81.
14 Robert Cooper and Scott Edgett. "Ideation for product innovation: what are the best methods?" PDMA *Visions* Magazine. March, 2008.

Chapter 6

1   Philip Kotler, Robert C. Wolcott and Suj Chandrasekhar. "Masters of Value and Possibility: Optimizing the Marketing and Research & Development Relationship." http://sloanreview.mit.edu/business-insight/articles/2009/2
2   Hauser, John R. and Don Clausing (1988), "The House of Quality," *Harvard Business Review*, Vol. No. 3 (May–June): 63–73.
3   T. Davila, M.J. Epstein, R. Shelton. *Making Innovation Work: How to manage it, measure it, and profit from it.* Wharton School Publishing (2006).
4   Example provided by the market research company Salvetti & Llombart.
5   Readers interested in conjoint analysis can read: Bryan K Orme. *Getting Started with Conjoint Analysis: Strategies for Product Design and Pricing Research.* Research Publishers, LLC, 2nd edn (2009).

Chapter 7

1   Jeffrey Baumgartner. *The Corporate Innovation Machine*, www.jpb.com
2   Vijay Govindarajan and Chris Trimble. *The Other Side of Innovation: Solving the execution challenge.* Harvard Business Press (2010).
3   http://www.vijaygovindarajan.com/2010/08/the_other_side_of_innovation_s.htm
4   Theodore Levitt. "Creativity is not enough." *Harvard Business Review.* August, 2002.
5   Jeffrey Baumgartner. *The Creative Idea Implementation Plan*, http://www.jpb.com/creative/ciip.php
6   Clayton M. Christensen. *The Innovator's Dilemma.* Page xx, Introduction. Harvard Business School Press (1997).
7   Chris Zook and James Allen. *Profit from the Core: A Return to Growth in Turbulent Times.* Harvard Business Press, Updated edition (2010).
8   *Ibid.* citing Jim Collins, *Good to be Great.* Random House (2001).
9   Richard Foster and Sarah Kaplan. *Creative Destruction: Why Companies That Are Built to Last Underperform the Market – And How to Successfully Transform Them.* Crown Business (2001).
10 *BusinessWeek.* "The World's Most Innovative Companies. Special Report – Innovation." 24 April 2006.
11 Vijay Govindarajan and Chris Trimble. *10 Rules for Strategic Innovators.* Harvard Business Press (2005).
12 Jeffrey Baumgartner. *The Corporate Innovation Machine*, www.jpb.com
13 Infonomia.com
14 www.creativityandinnovation.blogspot.com, Sanjay Dalal article, based on the book *"Why some ideas survive and others die"* by Chip Heath and Dan Heath.
15 Seth Godin. *All Marketers Are Liars.* Portfolio (2005).
16 Philip Kotler. *Marketing Management.* Prentice Hall, 13th edn (2008).
17 www.infonomia.com
18 Mark Turrell and Dr Yvonne Lindow. *The Innovation Pipeline*, www.imaginatik.com
19 www.infonomia.com
20 Constantinos C. Markides and Paul A. Geroski. *Fast Second: How Smart Companies Bypass Radical Innovation to Enter and Dominate New Markets.* Jossey-Bass (2004).
21 http://innovationmarketing.wordpress.com/2007/04/08/%C2%BFcomo-llegar-a-entender-un-mercado-que-todavia-no-existe/

Chapter 8

1   James Surowiecki, *The Wisdom of Crowds: Why the Many Are Smarter Than the Few and How Collective Wisdom Shapes Business, Economies, Societies and Nations.* Doubleday (2004)

2   Shankar Basu and Roger G. Schroeder, "Incorporating Judgments in Sales Forecasts: Application of the Delphi Method at American Hoist & Derrick." *Interfaces* Vol. 7, No. 3 (May, 1977), pp. 18–27.

3   Steve Blank, "The Four Steps to the Epiphany", Cafepress.com (September 2010).

4   Edward De Bono, *Six Thinking Hats.* Back Bay Books, 2nd edn (1999).

5   http://www.brighthub.com/office/project-management/articles/2947.aspx

6   http://www.economia48.com/spa/d/analisis-coste-beneficio/analisis-coste-beneficio.htm

7   http://ec.europa.eu/regional_policy/sources/docgener/guides/cost/guide02_es.pdf

8   http://www.programaempresa.com/empresa/empresa.nsf/paginas/2E2A01A7 5B5E3BD5C125702800546C66?OpenDocument

9   Demand estimation for a new product or service is a component of the profit analysis.

10 http://www.fao.org/docrep/008/a0323s/a0323s03.htm

11 http://www.americanchoicemodeling.com/2009/demand-estimation-and-pricing/

12 Blanco Adolfo, *Formulación y Evaluación de Proyectos*, Ediciones Torán, 4th edn; ILPES, *Guía para la Presentación de Proyectos. Siglo XXI Editores.* 10th edn; John Mariotti, *Marketing.* MacGraw Hill (http://www.gestiopolis.com/recursos3/docs/mar/estmktpref.htm).

13 http://www.isixsigma.com/index.php?option=com_k2&view=item&id=1519: calculating-roi-to-realize-project-value&tmpl=component&print=1&Itemid=190

14 Patricia Pulliam Phillips and Jack J. Phillips, *Return on Investment (ROI) Basics.* ASTD Training Basics (2006).

15 http://creativityandinnovation.blogspot.com/2008/07/how-successful-is-your-new-innovation.html

16 http://www.jpb.com/creative/ciip.php

17 Jeffrey Baumgartner, *The Corporate Innovation Machine*, pp. 10–11.

18 http://creativityandinnovation.blogspot.com/2008/07/how-successful-is-your-new-innovation.html

Chapter 10

1   Robert G. Cooper. *Winning at new products: pathways to profitable innovation.* www.stage-gate.com

2   Robert Cooper and Michael S. Mills, "Succeeding at NPD the P&G way: a key element using the 'Innovation Diamond'", PDMA *Visions*, October 2005, Vol. XXIX, No. 4, p. 10.

3   Vijay Kumar, "Innovation Planning Toolkit", Paper presented at Futureground International Conference. Melbourne, November 2004.

4   Mark Turrell and Dr Yvonne Lindow, "The Innovation Pipeline". White Paper, Imaginatik Research, p. 3.

5   Bradley T. Gale, *Managing Customer Value: Creating Quality and Service That Customers Can See*. Free Press; Reprint edition (2010).
6   Michael E. Porter, *Competitive Strategy: Techniques for Analyzing Industries and Competitors*. Free Press (1998), p. 156.
7   Michael E. Porter, *On Competition*, updated and expanded edition. Harvard Business School Press (2008).
8   Thomas Egner, "McKinsey Seven S Model", Scholarly Research Paper. Grin Verlag (2009).
9   Philip Kotler, *Marketing Management*. Prentice Hall; 13th edn (2008).
10 "How companies approach innovation: A McKinsey Global Survey", *McKinsey Quarterly*, October 2007.
11 Vijay Kumar, "Innovation Planning Toolkit", Paper presented at Futureground International Conference. Melbourne, November 2004.
12 Edwin A. Locke and Gary Latham, *A Theory of Goal Setting and Task Performance*. Prentice Hall (1990).
13 Analysis of Tesco Innovation policies by www.infonomia.com
14 T. Davila, M.J. Epstein and R. Shelton. *Making Innovation Work: How to manage it, measure it, and profit from it*. Wharton School Publishing (2006).
15 Robert G. Cooper. *Winning at new products: pathways to profitable innovation*. www.stage-gate.com
16 Doblin Group, *The ten types of innovation*, http://www.doblin.com/AboutInno/innotypes.html
17 "How companies approach innovation: A McKinsey Global Survey", *McKinsey Quarterly*, October 2007.
18 Robert Cooper and Michael S. Mills, "Succeeding at NPD the P&G way: a key element using the 'Innovation Diamond'", PDMA *Visions*, October 2005, Vol. XXIX, No. 4.
19 Robert G. Cooper. *Winning at new products: pathways to profitable innovation*. www.stage-gate.com
20 Mark Turrell and Dr Yvonne Lindow, "The Innovation Pipeline". White Paper, Imaginatik Research, p. 3.

Chapter 11

1   *BusinessWeek*, "The World's Most Innovative Companies. Special Report – Innovation", 24 April 2006.
2   Amy Muller, Liisa Välikangas and Paul Merlyn, "Metrics for innovation: guidelines for developing a customized suite of innovation metrics", *Strategy & Leadership*, 2005, Vol. 33, No. 1, pp. 37–45.
3   *McKinsey Quarterly*. The Online Journal of McKinsey&Co. November, 2009.
4   T. Davila, M.J. Epstein and R. Shelton, *Making Innovation Work: How to manage it, measure it, and profit from it*. Wharton School Publishing (2006).
5   "Assessing innovation metrics: McKinsey Global Survey Results", *McKinsey Quarterly*, November 2008.
6   *McKinsey Quarterly*. The Online Journal of McKinsey&Co. November, 2009.
7   Amy Muller, Liisa Välikangas and Paul Merlyn, "Metrics for innovation: guidelines for developing a customized suite of innovation metrics" (op. cit.).
8   Robert G. Cooper, *Winning at New Products: Pathways to Profitable Innovation*, p. 12. www.stage-gate.com
9   *Ibid*.

10 T. Davila, M.J. Epstein and R. Shelton, *Making Innovation Work: How to manage it, measure it, and profit from it.* Wharton School Publishing (2006).

11 *Ibid.*

12 *BusinessWeek*, "The World's Most Innovative Companies. Special Report – Innovation", 24 April 2006.

13 *McKinsey Quarterly*. The Online Journal of McKinsey&Co. November, 2009.

14 Amy Muller, Liisa Välikangas and Paul Merlyn, "Metrics for innovation: guidelines for developing a customized suite of innovation metrics" (op. cit.).

15 *BusinessWeek*, "The World's Most Innovative Companies. Special Report – Innovation", 24 April 2006.

16 Dr Brian Glassman, *White Papers Series on Idea Generation*, "Metrics for Idea Generation". August, 2009.

17 *McKinsey Quarterly*. The Online Journal of McKinsey&Co. November, 2009.

18 Many authors stress and describe the creation of frameworks in the combination of innovation metrics. See especially Amy Muller, Liisa Välikangas, Paul Merlyn, T. Davila, M.J. Epstein and R. Shelton.

Chapter 12

1 Bill Breen, *The 6 Myths Of Creativity*, www.fastcompany.com

2 Jeffrey Baumgartner, *The Four Kinds of Corporate Innovation*, www.jpb.com

3 *BusinessWeek*, "The World's Most Innovative Companies. Special Report – Innovation", 24 April 2006.

4 *Ibid.*

5 Dr Robert G. Cooper, *Winning at New Products: Pathways to Profitable Innovation*, www.stage-gate.com

6 Darrell K. Rigby, Kara Gruver, and James Allen. "Innovation in Turbulent Times", *Harvard Business Review*, 2009 (http://hbr.org/2009/06/innovation-in-turbulent-times/ar/pr).

7 *BusinessWeek*, "The World's Most Innovative Companies. Special Report – Innovation", 24 April 2006.

8 *Ibid.*

9 Julia Hanna, "Getting Down to the Business of Creativity", Harvard Business School *Working Knowledge* (14 May 2008).

10 *Ibid.*

11 Jeffrey Baumgartner, *The Corporate Innovation Machine*, www.jpb.com

12 www.infonomia.com

13 Jeffrey Baumgartner, *The Corporate Innovation Machine*, www.jpb.com

14 Bill Breen, *The 6 Myths Of Creativity*, www.fastcompany.com

15 *Ibid.*

16 *Ibid.*

17 Michael Michalko, *Thinkertoys: A Handbook of Creative-Thinking Techniques.* Ten Speed Press, 2nd edn (2006).

18 www.infonomia.com

19 Robert Cooper and Michael S. Mills, "Succeeding at NPD the P&G way: a key element using the 'Innovation Diamond'", PDMA *Visions*, October 2005, Vol. XXIX, No. 4, p. 13.

20 Dr Robert G. Cooper, *Winning at New Products: Pathways to Profitable Innovation*, www.stage-gate.com

21 *BusinessWeek*, "The World's Most Innovative Companies. Special Report – Innovation", 24 April 2006.
22 www.infonomia.com
23 Dr Robert G. Cooper, *Winning at New Products: Pathways to Profitable Innovation*, www.stage-gate.com

Chapter 13

1 *BusinessWeek*, "The World's Most Innovative Companies. Special Report – Innovation", 24 April 2006.
2 Jeffrey Baumgartner, *The Corporate Innovation Machine*, www.jpb.com
3 Padmanabh Dabke, www.spigit.com
4 Bill Breen, *The 6 Myths Of Creativity*, www.fastcompany.com
5 *BusinessWeek*, "The World's Most Innovative Companies. Special Report – Innovation", 24 April 2006.
6 Martin Dewhurst, Matthew Guthridge, and Elizabeth Mohr, "Motivating people: Getting beyond money", *McKinsey Quarterly*, November, 2009.
7 "Rewarding Innovation", Sheldon Laube, Innovation Office, PwC Innovation Blog, February 2010.
8 Jeffrey Baumgartner, *The Corporate Innovation Machine*, www.jpb.com
9 "Do Rewards Kill Innovation and Creativity?" Matthew E. May. Blogging innovation. July, 2009. http://www.business-strategy-innovation.com/2009/07/do-rewards-kill-innovation-and.html
10 Martin Dewhurst, Matthew Guthridge, and Elizabeth Mohr, "Motivating people: Getting beyond money", *McKinsey Quarterly*, November, 2009.
11 www.infonomia.com
12 Susan Malanowski, "Innovation Incentives: How Companies Foster Innovation", September 2007, www.wilsongroup.com
13 Sheldon Laube, Innovation Office PwC.
14 Robert Brands, www.innovationcoach.com

Index

Page numbers followed by *f* and *t* indicate figures and tables, respectively.